ERRATA

Figure 7.3 page 152.

Parish of Killyman: male age of marriage.

Should read: Female age of marriage.

Figure 7.4 page 155.

Parish of Killyman: Female age of marriage.
Should read: male age of marriage.

Author W.S. MACAFEE
Should read: W. MACAFEE

RURAL IRELAND 1600-1900:
Modernisation and Change

Editors

Patrick O'Flanagan
University College Cork

Paul Ferguson
Trinity College Dublin

Kevin Whelan
National Library of Ireland

CORK UNIVERSITY PRESS 1987

First published 1987 by
Cork University Press, University College, Cork, Ireland.

British Library Cataloguing in Publication Data

Rural Ireland: modernisation and change 1600-1900

1. Ireland – Social conditions
I. O'Flanagan, T. P.
941.506   HC257.16

ISBN 0-902561-48-0

PRINTED AND TYPESET IN IRELAND BY
LEINSTER LEADER LTD., NAAS, CO. KILDARE

Contents

Figures

Tables

Acknowledgements

Ventures which involve the preparation and celebration of a conference and the subsequent production of a book, acrue a long list of individuals, committees and institutions, who individually and collectively have made our task less onerous. We would like to express our thanks to Professor J. P. Haughton, J. H. Andrews and the other staff of the Department of Geography at Trinity College Dublin, for putting an excellent lecture theatre at our disposal for the conference and for helping us in many other ways. Special thanks are also due to Stephen O'Connor in this regard. Professor L. M. Cullen, Mr. F. H. A. Aalen, both of Trinity College and Dr. W. H. Crawford of the Ulster Folk and Transport Museum, kindly acted as chairpersons and Bill Crawford also led a broad discussion which concluded the conference. To them, to the contributors at the conference and to all who participated in the many lively discussions, thanks are also due.

The Committee and Secretary, Mr. D. Counihan, Cork University Press, all have rendered critical assistance in many ways and particular acknowledgement is due here in this regard to Ms. Ann Lee. The late Dr. Michael Gilheaney supplied critical support. The Senate of the National University of Ireland through its publication fund provided generous financial assistance. So too has the Institute of Irish Studies at Queen's University Belfast and a special debt of gratitude is offered to its Director, Professor R. H. Buchanan, for giving special help at a difficult time. Secretarial assistance was provided by Ms. O. de Barra and Ms. A. Phelan of the Geography Department, and many other drafts were prepared by the Secretarial Centre at University College Cork. Connell Foley, Cartographer, Geography Department, University College, Cork, helped with many of the illustrations and Dan Murphy of the same Department provided much needed assistance often at very short notice. The encouragement and support of colleagues in our own institutions merits a special debt of gratitude.

Introduction

PATRICK O'FLANAGAN

While it is statistically correct to state that today more than fifty per cent of Ireland's population now resides in settlements defined by the census authorities as urban, it is also true to say that the dominant ethos on this island has remained overwhelmingly rural made explicit in a wide range of attitudes and behaviours ranging from recreational activities to religious observances. It would be too daunting a venture as yet to write a history of rural Ireland as there is a dearth of regional and local case-studies available. Nevertheless, congruent themes to those explored in this book have been addressed in such recent publications as L. M. Cullen's *The Emergence of Modern Ireland 1600-1900* and in the recent compendium of studies focused upon *The Irish Town* edited by David Harkness and Mary O'Dowd. What is on offer here is a selection of essays, each of which explores in depth a number of themes critical and central to any understanding of modernisation and change in rural Ireland between 1600 and 1900.

The contents of this book were originally presented as papers at a conference held at Trinity College, Dublin on 11th May 1985. Afterwards, most contributors amended their papers to respond to comments raised in short discussions which followed each pair of papers. The conference itself was the second in a series of annual gatherings organised by the editors of this work as a platform on which geographers, historians and other cognate species could exchange and share the fruits of recent research through an understanding of each others methodologies and perspectives. Contributors from different institutions from all over the island were asked to divulge the results of their most recent research so as to reach as wide an audience as possible.

Modernisation and change were selected as the filters through which critical aspects of the recent transformation of the rural Irish context could be examined in a quest to identify the generic processes which precipitated such alterations. The book does not seek to present a total explanation of change. Instead it offers a rich compendium of vital assessments of aspects of modernisation too often neglected in the past because of their perceived mundaneness – to name but one – the fate of Irish women in the nineteenth century.

For the purposes of this work modernisation is regarded, not as an inflexible sociological categorisation, but rather as a loosely defined construct within which complex social outcomes can be scrutinised and understood. In this sense modernisation is not a term with a high level of usage and a low level of meaning. Neither is it a term then which implies specifically determined outcomes, nor does it refer to a terminal state of development. Here modernisation refers to the impact of forces, of exogenous or endogenous origin, on Ireland between 1600 and 1900, ranging from changes in farming technology to colonialism. Many parts of Atlantic Europe endured these kinds of changes and their past and present economic and social structures testify to the sharing of many processes through time.

Selective analyses of change in Ireland between 1600 and 1900 have often been accomplished within the framework of invasions, plantations, exploitation and capitalistic penetration to name a few familiar themes. The examination of the emergence and metamorphosis of different kinds of commons is an innovative departure, at least, for Irish historical geography. While different types of Irish public commons can be ascribed seventeenth-century origins, subsequent events as the author, Professor Andrews argues, promoted conditions where, paradoxically, the emptiest areas became the most densely occupied. Harbouring many unsalubrious images of being outside the realms of civilization in the minds of landowners and their substantial tenants, the emergence of congested commons packed with multitudes of people anticipated arrangements of land ownership, which became more widespread in the nineteenth century. By focusing our attention on this specific, but cartographically weakly represented bounded space, Professor Andrews shows that distinctive kinds of squatting communities had emerged by the late eighteenth century and, elusive as the sources may be, it is possible to outline a causal framework to account for their development and to indicate the forces which sustained their continuity or extinction.

In a country which is supremely committed today to adapting to and innovating with technology it is surprising to note that we have paid little attention to the past contribution of technology in promoting modernisation. Indeed indigenous technology as a complex has usually been the topic of adverse comment. This may not be surprising in a state which has housed its ethnographic memorabilia in a derelict and isolated reformatory which is closed to the public. It is probably no historic accident that a revisionist assessment should come from a member of the staff of a most successful 'folk' museum at Holywood in County Down. While the thrust of his paper is directed towards an analysis of farming innovation adoption in 'high' or commercial farming areas in nineteenth-century Ireland, Jonathan Bell strongly argues that in these and other areas 'common farming' practices were much less inert and damaging activities than they were formerly believed to be even in circumstances where there was severe population pressure. By concentrating on the interface between theory and innovation, common practices and efficient farming, the author predicates that positive rather than negative outcomes resulted from the interaction between apparently opposed systems. In a further challenge, the author invites us to consider what he regards as a mistaken view, namely the fact that nineteenth-century Irish farming production systems were archaic. Drawing on a broad canvas of source material, extending from partisan literature to the assessments of contemporary observers, we are presented with a powerful revisionist appeal which should generate more detailed regional and estate based studies to match against Bell's prospectus.

Studies of social disintegration in Ireland have tended to be largely set in the nineteenth century. Dr. Seán Connolly's paper attempts to remedy this imbalance by addressing the theme in an eighteenth-century context. The authors reliance on a disparate range of highly informative and mainly primary source materials stresses how the skilful use of these documents can yield much evidence on changing social relationships. These underused sources also help to indicate how people defined themselves in relation to their perceived adversaries. He identifies certain parts of the country which remained outside the law in the early eighteenth century but he argues that these kinds of refuges along with various forms of anti-social behaviour, especially banditry and duelling, became far less common as the century drew to a close. Popular violence too did indeed make sudden and sometimes devastating appearances but, it too seems to have been far less blood thirsty than its continental parallels.

While sources which detail crime and social infringements in the eighteenth century are neither numerous nor informative, the exploitation of surrogate material can, as Connolly has demonstrated, yield fundamental insights into the successful extension of state control. Detailed regional work is also required to explain the causes and consequences of different degrees of social integration in a country in which only a few were able to derive substantial material benefit.

It is apposite that Connolly's piece is followed by a detailed local analysis of a major breakdown in public order in the last decade of the eighteenth century in County Wexford, the effective cockpit of the 1798 nationally significant turmoil. Setting the scene for this felicitous local study, Dr. Kevin Whelan uses an early census document to show that there was a high degree of spatial interpenetration in the incidence of Catholics and Protestants in Wexford. Consequently, the fall-out which ensued from the turbulent collision of the groups, both of which had become deeply politised, was considerable. The results of the violent encounter between the different religious factions was instantly dramatic, precipitating house burnings, redistributions of population, and often death. Whelan also posits that the long-term effects of the turmoil were particularly serious for the Anglican community. This kind of work emphasises the amount of ground research that remains to be completed by solid local studies before we can formulate generalizations concerning the economic, social and psychological consequences of sectarianism. It is also necessary to assess the role of religion as a contributory element prompting the disintegration of public order. Whelan argues religion was one of the chief catalytic forces in Wexford and in other parts of Ireland promoting the outbreak of the 1798 rebellion. The citation of diairies and other local source material gives this kind of analysis a pungent insider perspective of how the events unfolded.

Geographers, ethnographers and other students of Ireland's material heritage have had long standing and successful associations with the study of the Irish house and Irish settlements patterns, yet as Dr. Alan Gailey notes, even after half a century of achievement in this area little progress has been made with the pre-Ordnance Survey record. In a penetrating essay, Dr. Gailey presents a broad and incisive assessment of the canvass of pre-Ordnance Survey house-type research. His work stresses that the most valuable results have been achieved to date in Ulster. The use of estate records, however, may break this logjam and may serve as the key towards unfolding the complex story of variations in house-types especially after the middle of the eighteenth century. The rich often polychromatic record of an extensive national collection of estate maps also remains largely unexplored in this regard, and the later detailed census returns have, as yet, failed to attract many scrutineers.

Analyses and explanations of the changing character of Ireland's core urban and rural regions has had a venerable place in Irish historical geography and Professor Tom Jones Hughes's essay is a departure from this tradition. It seeks to clarify the different character of two regions distinctively defined by cultural and argicultural traits. The Cavan-Meath divide was one of the many sharp and long-standing divisions of nineteenth-century Ireland. It was a border zone which separated areas which had evolved distinctive modes of production. In this sense, the methodological framework devised by the author can serve well as a general model for an exploration of other such areas in nineteenth-century Ireland, such as the divide between the more cerealist south-east and the predominantly pastoralist south midlands. The varying fortunes of settlement and society is also profitably addressed within the bounded spaces of parish networks which act as a touchstone to measure the stark distinctions that persisted in landscape and life in both areas. The fortunes of several major social classes are examined and novel explanations are offered for their different responses to the forces promoting either change or stability in these two deeply contrasting counties.

Two papers on population conclude the book. One of them is an in depth evaluation of a specific parish register which is explored to provide a broad insight into pre-Famine population in Ulster. William Macafee examines an Anglican register from a predominantly rural area in which 46 per cent of the population were Anglican. As more and more of these registers from different parts of the country are now coming to light together with the discovery of many late eighteenth- and early nineteenth-century Catholic registers it is evident that, for this period at least, we are no longer going to be dependent on traditionally crude evaluations from generalised data. While admitting that specific problems associated with the register in question do exist, such as the under registration of child burials, the author provides a comprehensive assessment of the local conditions by evaluating such components as life expectancy, age at marriage, fertility and so on. By a careful analysis and comparison of the results with other studies, the author maintains that the results are in line with recent findings but at variance with some of the propositions made by such authorities as Connell. With the advent of sophisticated computer packages, and in the Republic, finance from short-term employment schemes and a popular awakening of interest in genealogy it is likely that many more studies of this genre will be undertaken. The formulation of a series of regional profiles will allow useful generalizations to be made concerning the relationship between the spatial characteristics of demographic change and more extensive socio-economic movements. We are still only at an initial stage of pre-census evaluation and many basic differentials, such as urban – rural distinctions and ethno-religious differences require exploration.

It is generally agreed that societies do not pass on the road to modernisation through a predetermined series of linked stages. One might also be tempted to claim that the historic demographic behaviour of females also has not been predictable. In a successful attempt to rescue the Irish female from historical oblivion and redress the balance in the historiography of the nineteenth century, David Fitzpatrick shows that the lot of most females was a constant struggle. Fitzpatrick argues that most Irish females occupied an intensely marginal situation in society especially in the early nineteenth century but as marriage, property and asset redistribution became hopelessly entangled the position of women gradually began to change. Here, for example, he is able to isolate and stress the hitherto underrated significance of female celibacy. By examining such critical indices as fertility, age at marriage, and their relationship with modes of inheritance and migration, crucial insights may be gained into understanding the activities of women in nineteenth-century Ireland. It is possible to claim that few females gained substantiallly from modernisation and emigration as virtually the only potential response by those who wished to escape to a less oppressive life world and 'modernise'! Fitzpatrick has hewn a pioneering furrow in Irish studies. His resultant picture is one of real desolation for so many and it is a timely reminder of the other kinds of famines which took root in Ireland.

An approach of this kind exposed both the challenge and constraints of such constructs as modernisation. It stresses that the outcome of these processes can as easily provoke a deterioration rather than an amelioration in the life style and living conditions. The variegated nature of Irish rural life continues to subvert simple categorisations as this collection of papers clearly demonstrates.

The struggle for Ireland's public commons

J. H. ANDREWS

All historians and geographers understand the idea of a common[1] but the distinction between public and private commons is probably less familiar. Many lawyers would reject the word 'public' in this context as either redundant, meaningless, or the embodiment of a fallacy, just as they might well deny that any one piece of land can be both private and common at the same time. However, in studying economic and social life in the heyday of the Irish landed estate between the Down Survey and the Ordnance Survey, both concepts seem to serve a useful purpose. The difference between them was certainly noted by many writers of the period;[2] and neglect of it caused serious misunderstanding when the existence and non-existence of Irish commons were simultaneously asserted in different chapters of the same eighteenth-century book.[3]

As a non-lawyer's first approximation, the words 'private common' seem permissible where rights like those of pasture, turbary and estover were granted for a limited term by a proprietor with no obligation to renew them at the end of that term.[4] In a public common such rights, once granted, were incapable of being extinguished at the will of any one party – unless perhaps he happened to be the only right-holder who remained alive.[5] Both these definitions leave ample room for disagreement among contemporaries, and uncertainty among historians, as to

1

whether any particular common should be classed as public or private. Matters may be clarified to some extent by distinguishing five varieties of Irish public common, though admittedly with many further doubts as to which public commons fell into which category at any one time and with the additional proviso that the same piece of land may move more or less imperceptibly from one category to another.

(1) On *territorial commons* the rights belonged not to any of the well-established communities of medieval or post-medieval society, such as manors or estates, but to some or all of the residents in a named territory or group of territories. The area in question probably adjoined the common, but this was not necessarily true of all its subdivisions. Thus official Cromwellian surveys often described a bog or mountain as 'common to the adjacent towns' – not to the adjacent farms. The same surveys also mention land that was common to one or more parishes, baronies, and occasionally even counties.[6] Territorial commons appear to have pre-dated the various seventeenth-century plantation settlements, perhaps by a considerable period, for in the denominations to which they were attached there are seldom any historically-authenticated organs of management that seem to have been capable of granting or regulating common rights. They resemble several other kinds of common, however, in normally occupying land unsuitable for tillage. Many territorial commons subsequently took on private status, or were believed to have done so, though perhaps retaining the name of the district they had once served, as with Ballysimon Commons (County Limerick) or Ballynatray Commons (County Waterford). Others came to be regarded as crown property or as commons of joint ownership, both to be discussed below. By *c.* 1850 the class of territorial commons was evidently obsolete: the strongest surviving candidate for membership was Bantry Commons in County Wexford, where the right-holders were identified in an official survey as 'cess payers of the barony of Bantry'.[7]

(2) The now unfamiliar term *royalty* seems applicable to all commons of which the crown was the only acknowledged proprietor, a status still occasionally commemorated in names like King's Bog, King's Meadow and King's Mountain.[8] Such lands were left out of the plantation settlements either by simple oversight or through being judged too unproductive for any grantee to accept them. Between the seventeenth and nineteenth centuries official policy was to transfer some crown land (including commons) to individual occupation while ignoring or even publicly disowning the rest.[9] So although some 'royalties' survived into Victorian times under the nominal proprietorship of the commissioners of woods and forests, there is

no modern record of such a common being created and no evidence to show how the rights in it could be acquired.[10] The most that can be said is that such rights were generally thought to be held by the occupiers of adjacent farms.

(3) *Manorial commons* each had their own proprietor, but despite his impressive title, 'lord of the soil', he was forbidden by long-established custom (or so it was believed) to disturb the rights of the manorial tenantry. Commons were by no means essential to a manor, and were generally absent from the numerous Irish manors formed in the seventeenth century;[11] most modern examples appear to be relics of the Anglo-Norman era, being chiefly confined to the region of the English Pale and often associated with residual traces of nucleated village settlement and open-field agriculture (Fig. 1:1). Typical features of such commons were their comparatively small size, their division into two or more detached parts, often on opposite sides of a village and perhaps including a village green, and their occurrence on a variety of soil types good and bad.

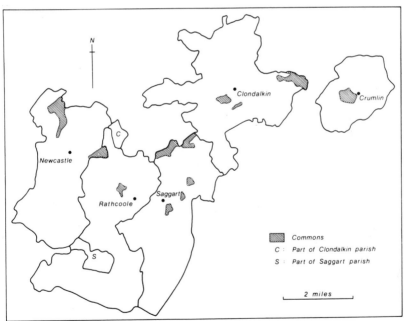

Fig. 1:1. Townland names in 'Common' in five County Dublin parishes.

(4) *Borough commons* resembled manorial commons in all these last respects, as well as in belonging to a single owner (in this case a municipal corporation) who was prevented by charter or custom from behaving like a

private landlord.[12] The main difference was that new borough commons were still appearing in the seventeenth century, notably at towns founded as part of the Ulster plantation. A few were even attached to what might otherwise be thought of as early estate towns, such as Portarlington and Lanesborough.

(5) In *commons of joint ownership,* the proprietors of contiguous estates had failed to define a precise boundary through a tract of mountain or bog of which they each had title to an unspecified proportion, and which was grazed in common by tenants from both or all estates.[13] Some of these lands had probably started life as territorial commons and might be hard to distinguish from them. Many were considerably less public, in common-sense terms, than any of the four categories previously discussed, needing only an agreement between perhaps as few as two individuals to 'privatise' them. In general the surprising rarity of jointly owned commons, and of other non-manorial and non-borough commons, among nineteenth-century Ireland's many bogs and mountains is a tribute to the vigour of the estate system and to the efficiency of the surveying profession.

To return to our original classification, the study of private commons belongs to estate history and will doubtless move at the same measured pace as the rest of that subject.[14] Public commons are at first sight more easily encompassed in a short review, but they turn out to pose their own historiographical problems, as can be quickly seen by trying to compile a list of them. This preliminary survey is based partly on a small number of well-documented individual cases, partly on the voluminous but sometimes unfashionably 'anecdotal' parliamentary inquiries of the early nineteenth century, and partly on certain standard topographical sources as far as these relate to the 290 Irish townlands that carry the name 'Common' on the Ordnance Survey maps. Such a selection is necessarily incomplete, for some public commons, like the Curragh of Kildare, have never been recognised as such in townland nomenclature. Nor is it clear how many of the Ordnance Survey's 'Commons' had remained private throughout the post-medieval period: one can only remark that many Ordnance Survey townland names were derived from local estate records and that few of the landlords who maintained these records would have been happy to see any of the land that they owned in fee described as common in an authoritative official survey.[15] With these reservations, the present sample of 290 at least has the merit of variety – locational, environmental, historical and tenurial – and of being larger than could easily be assembled by any other method (Table 1:1).

All five categories of Irish public common were involved in the conflict that forms the main subject of this paper. In England the corresponding

TABLE 1:1

'COMMON' AS A TOWNLAND NAME-ELEMENT, 1833-46

County	No. of townlands	No. of parishes	County	No. of townlands	No. of parishes
Carlow	1	1	Limerick	12	12
Dublin	33	17	Tipperary	17	12
Kildare	40	19	Waterford	9	8
Kilkenny	20	5	Antrim	1	1
Laois	1	1	Cavan	1	1
Longford	3	2	Donegal	4	3
Louth	4	4	Down	6	6
Meath	16	9	Fermanagh	1	1
Westmeath	3	3	Tyrone	3	3
Wexford	17	16	Galway	12	10
Wicklow	11	5	Leitrim	1	1
Clare	13	9	Mayo	13	10
Cork	28	22	Roscommon	2	2
Kerry	16	10	Sligo	2	2

antagonism was traditionally between commonage and enclosure, and English opinion has on the whole been remarkably favourable to the commoner, not only for reasons of doctrinaire libertarianism and historical sentimentality but also in a spirit of genuine benevolence towards the poor.[16] No doubt such feelings have their own geography. Irish lawyers have generally shared the English view of common rights as a growth that only the most heroic efforts can uproot; and it is no surprise that a modern Irish conveyance of land intended wholly for local-authority labourers' cottages should carry a solemn guarantee of all previous common rights – in these circumstances, presumably, the right to put pigs in someone else's parlour.[17] The Irish public at large has been less enthusiastic. An early example of its indifference was the erratic treatment of commons by both commissioners and jurors employed in the Civil Survey of 1654-6.[18] It took an English cartographer, William Petty, to attempt a more detailed picture, though the conductors of his Down Survey were apparently often unable to extract from local witnesses all the information that their chief considered desirable.[19]

Thenceforth it would clearly be difficult to protect the rights that Ireland's two great seventeenth-century inquisitions had done so little to make explicit, especially as the lords of Irish manors showed no more zeal for the preservation of common lands than did the representatives of the crown. The bodies with the best chance of keeping these lands intact were the corporations, for the right-holders of a borough formed a compact and easily-identifiable group (whether burgesses, freemen or inhabitants) with a legally constituted authority to represent them. And at national level there were strong precedents for opposing the alienation of municipal property as inconsistent with the quasi-charitable motives for which these estates had been originally set aside.[20] Yet the only trustees appointed specifically to manage a town common were at Drogheda (County Louth) and Killyleagh (County Down); and the only corporations known to have policed a common under threat were Duleek and Navan in County Meath, neither of them with much success.

Away from the boroughs there was little sign that either state, shire or church felt much interest in defending lands that yielded neither quit-rent, cess, nor tithe. Indeed from an 'establishment' viewpoint the main value of a common was as a reserve of land – inevitably dwindling since nothing was done to replenish it – where public buildings could be erected, troops deployed, or criminals executed; or at least where new by-roads could be laid out, many of these being evidently designed to stay on common land for as much of their course as could conveniently be managed, doubtless to avoid the need for compensating private occupiers.

Outside government circles the same apathy prevailed throughout the socio-economic literature that took its tone from Arthur Young's *Tour*. Young himself was given to understand that Ireland had hardly any public commons. Guidelines drawn up by the Dublin Society in 1801 left much the same impression, and those of the Society's statistical surveyors who went beyond their brief in this respect did little but note the neglect of common rights by many of the farmers believed to possess them.[21] Nor does the apparent absence of parliamentary enclosure in Ireland betoken any widespread solicitude for common land. It was only in a manorial context that parliamentary methods were likely to be considered appropriate, and in any case the number of parishes for which local enclosure bills did reach the statute book was larger than has sometimes been thought. The fact is that towards the end of the eighteenth century commons were becoming an object of disapproval among the agricultural intelligentsia as a combination of technical progress and rising prices made it at once easier and more remunerative to bring them under the plough; and when a bill for the enclosing of all Irish commons failed in 1805 it was more through the incompetence of the promoters than for any reason of principle.[22]

Finally, one looks in vain for the stream of polemic and invective that such a lawyer's paradise as common rights might be expected to evoke from a forensically minded nation. The one major exception unearthed so far only helps to prove this rule. On Bantry Commons in County Wexford in the 1830s the most baffling intricacies of English law were considered on all sides to be fully applicable. Yet none of the participants in this controversy aspired to become or to remain a commoner; the main purpose of the discussion was to put a notional value on common rights which everyone was anxious to submerge beneath a wholly individual title.[23]

None of this is to deny that many of Ireland's early nineteenth-century farmers still grazed their stock on common lands, or that some of them resisted the advance of enclosure.[24] The most striking feature of that resistance was its ineffectiveness. Of 44 boroughs reporting on the subject in 1833, for example, 41 admitted that since the beginning of the seventeenth century their commons had got measurably smaller. Elsewhere the Down Survey gave some indication of what was lost. Among a sample of 219 parcels expressly identified as commons on the Survey's large-scale maps, only about forty were similarly described on the first edition of the Ordnance Survey.[25] Among other signs of shrinkage on the ordnance map are the total lack of commons at numerous boroughs and supposedly medieval manors; the small size of many that did survive (Table 1:2), plainly insufficient to feed the stock of any town or village worthy of the name; the highly irregular shapes exhibited by these relics, with salients, re-entrants and sometimes enclaves all betraying a history of piecemeal encroachment (Fig. 1:2); and finally the large proportion of townland names in 'Common' which by the time of the Griffith valuation (1849-65) were denoting areas held entirely by individual tenure. Griffith recorded only forty-six 'Commons' that actually included any public commonage, and in ten of these the unenclosed area formed less than half the total surface of the townland in question.

TABLE 1:2

AREAS OF TOWNLANDS WITH 'COMMON' AS A PLACENAME ELEMENT, 1833-46

Area per parish in statute acres	Number of parishes
Less than 10	21
10–30	20
30–70	20
70–150	32
150–300	33
300–600	33
600–2000	32
More than 2000	4

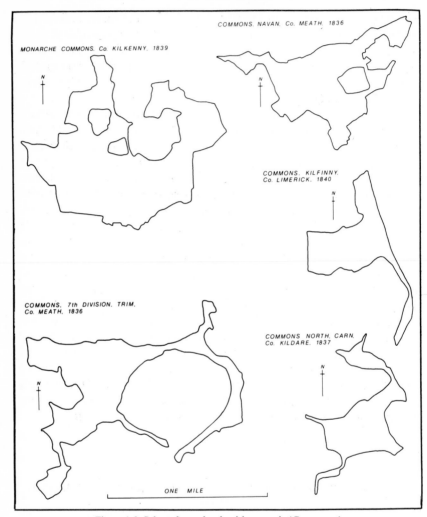

Figure 1:2. Selected townlands with names in 'Commons'.

Seen as a battle between the common and its enemies, then, Irish history can only be described as a walkover. The real opposition was between two kinds of single tenure that replaced the common: on the one hand, the conventional landed estate; on the other, the non-rent-paying freeholder or owner-occupier. If each individually-held 'Common' or part-'Common' of the Griffith valuation is characterised by the regime occupying 90 per cent or more of its surface, then the valuation included 167 landlord commons, 86 freehold commons, and 30 mixed commons.

One reason for the larger number of landlord commons was that they had been accumulating over a longer time-span. Some of them went back to the plantation grants, especially those of the restoration and Williamite settlements. In the patents of that period, common rights were occasionally reckoned in numbers of cattle and granted as a separate interest,[26] but more often they were appurtenant to a townland that was already farmed and inhabited, and took their place with water-courses, meadows, mills and various other townland amenities real or hypothetical.[27] A girdle of such grants surrounding a common might seem to have left little scope for the common itself to be conveyed as a distinct parcel, but this is what sometimes happened. Examples are the grant of the commons of Dundalk and Carlingford to Viscount Duncannon, the commons of Mullingar to Sir Arthur Forbes, and the commons of Dungarvan to the Earl of Cork. In theory it might be held that no pre-existing common right could be abolished by these transactions, but some proprietors of the new ascendancy may well have professed to read the word 'common' simply as a placename: re-establishing a common of pasture over such land, on this interpretation, would have been like giving the town of Carrickfergus back to Fergus.

A second possibility was for the owner of the soil to follow the crown's example and sell or lease 'his' common to a private client. A proprietor of historical tastes might claim the medieval English Statute of Merton as authority for appropriating as much of a common as he pleased, so long as enough remained open to meet his tenants' reasonable needs.[28] The less erudite course was to embark without ceremony on a modern-style transfer of interest: that is what the landlords who provoked the whiteboy agitation were accused of doing in the 1770s.[29] Many municipalities were taking the same course from the early seventeenth century onwards (Table 1:3), without their commoners offering much resistance even when left uncompensated for loss of rights. By c. 1850 the only commons in our sample still owned by urban local government authorities were at Carrickfergus (County Antrim), Kinsale (County Cork), Kells and Trim (County Meath), Sligo, Fethard (County Tipperary) and New Ross (County Wexford), and most of these were let to separate tenants.

Thirdly, a common with no effective owner might simply be encroached upon by farmers from the neighbouring estates. This was one of the few situations in which landlord and tenant could happily combine

TABLE 1:3

'PRIVATISATION' OF COMMON LAND: SOME EXAMPLES

Carrickfergus 1601, 1606, 1652, 1661, 1685, 1747	Wexford 1732
Dundalk 1667	Ardee 1735
Carlingford 1667	Clonmel 1741
Kinsale 1668, 1675	Lifford 1751
Athboy 1695	Kilmallock 1776
Drogheda 1699, 1719	Bangor 1792
Trim 1705	Portarlington 1802
Enniskillen 1710	Maryborough 1803

For source see note 12.

against a third party. The tenant enclosed a slice of adjacent common land and then quietly enjoyed it for the rest of his term without paying any additional rent. When the lease expired the landlord would recover a larger farm than he had originally let and could therefore draw an increased rent from the next tenant without the odium of charging more for each acre.[30] Though arguably a form of agricultural improvement, with dukes and bishops among its practitioners, this process would not necessarily be publicised by the improver. Most of the available testimony relating to it (apart from what lies buried in estate surveys)[31] comes from the parliamentary reports of the 1820s and 1830s. On the Ordnance maps of the same period a number of commons appear with scalloped or serrated edges, as if each neighbouring farmer had already taken his bite, but otherwise there was nothing unusual about the landscape of appropriation, and surveyors sent to identify an encroachment might well find the new fields to have blended indistinguishably with their surroundings.[32]

Finally, the destructive impulse sometimes arose from among the commoners themselves. Commons of joint ownership could be divided by agreement between their proprietors, either privately or by means of court proceedings, both operations usually rather difficult to track down. Parliamentary enclosure is more easily documented, at least on a superficial level. Between 1800 and 1840 this most drastic of remedies was applied to lands in twenty-eight Irish parishes, nearly all of them manorial commons in the former English Pale (Table 1:4). In principle it gave preference to neither rich nor poor, each commoner receiving an allotment of a size proportional to the value of the rights he was to sacrifice. Whatever the scale at which they were laid down, most land-

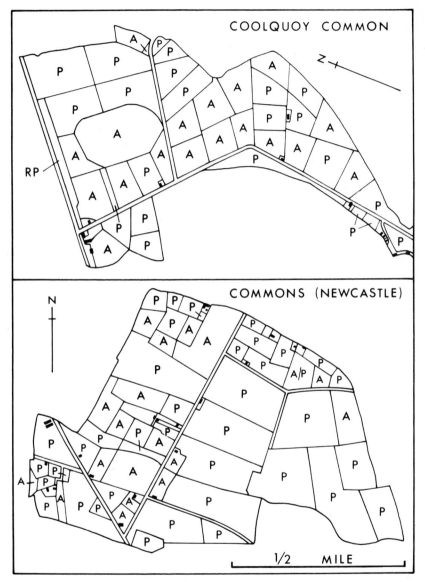

Figure 1:3. The landscape of parliamentary enclosure, two examples from County Dublin, 1871. Land use from the books of reference of the 1:2500 Ordnance Survey. A: Arable. P: Pasture. RP: Rough Pasture.

scapes of parliamentary enclosure appeared as new, rectangular, and totally individualised (Fig. 1:3). They also gave a strong impression of productivity: in a sample of nine statutory ex-commons in County Dublin less than one per cent of the surface remained under rough pasture in 1871; and for land that once nobody had wanted to plough an impressive

TABLE 1:4

LOCAL ENCLOSURE ACTS, 1800-40

1800 Dromiskin, County Louth
1803 Garristown, County Dublin
1804 Donabate and Portrane, County Dublin
1811 Rathcoole, County Dublin; Celbridge, Clonoclis,
        Donaghcumper and Kill, County Kildare
1814 Ballymore Eustace, County Kildare; Gowran, County
        Kilkenny
1816 Saggart, County Dublin
1818 Clondalkin, Kilmainham, Newcastle, Rathcoole and
        St. James's, County Dublin
1819 Clane and Mainham, County Kildare
1821 Kilsallaghan, Lusk and Tallaght, County Dublin
1824 Castleisland, County Kerry
1829 Callan, Coolagh and Knocktopher, County Kilkenny
1839 Rathkeale, County Limerick

Enclosure commissioners' maps survive for Dromiskin (N.L.I., MS 9014, photostat), Donabate and Portrane (private possession, photograph in N.L.I.) and Saggart (N.L.I., Ainsworth reports on private collections, iii, p. 872 (no. 67, Verschoyle-Campbell papers)).

TABLE 1:5

ARABLE LAND IN SELECTED TOWNLANDS, COUNTY DUBLIN, 1871

Townland	Total area (statute acres)	Percentage arable
Commons West, Swords	43	89
Racecourse Common, Lusk	163	82
Cooldown Commons, Saggart	17	63
Commons East, Swords	13	50
Commons, Newcastle	144	45
Great Common, Lusk	161	42
Coolquoy Common, Kilsallaghan	149	27
Ballisk Common, Portrane	82	25
Commons, Rathcoole	23	4

Source: Printed books of reference, 1:2500 Ordnance Survey maps, County Dublin, 1871.

proportion was now classed as arable (Table 1:5). Much the same pattern of mixed arable and pasture may be assumed for other areas of landlord appropriation.

Attention will next be turned to those commons which withstood all pressures from the estate system, and which may be claimed as a frontier of innovation to the extent that they were inhabited by owner-occupiers some half a century earlier than most other parts of Ireland. A notable feature of many commons was the inefficiency with which grazing and turf-cutting were kept in check. In the absence of effective stinting or other restrictions, a common probably supplied its poorer beneficiaries with a larger share of a family's real income than would accrue to their more affluent neighbours. It would consequently be natural for them to spend more of their time there, and it must be for this reason that commons came to be seen as haunts of an economically and morally inferior sub-culture, a complaint voiced at Enniskillen, County Fermanagh, in 1710 and subsequently repeated at various other places[33] as well as sometimes being applied to the commons of a whole county[34] and for that matter of Ireland in general. On a map the signs of such frequentation looked harmless enough – a convergence of unplanned roads and perhaps a fair green or a race course – but commons were also especially notorious in times of trouble like 1798, when the commons of Fossy, for example, became 'the resort of the principal robbers and rebels in the Queen's County'.[35]

The right simply to be on a common, in technical language the right to roam, is one that only a lawyer would ever think of doubting, and the visitations just referred to were arguably a form of 'sequent occupance' in which the use of the land could be intensified without losing its collective character. The next stage was to build permanent habitations, not on the common itself – that would be destructive of its communality – but just outside it. On John Rocque's map of County Dublin (1760) some forty houses of this kind are lined up alongside Garristown Commons like runners alert for the starting signal. Others appear in a similar posture on the early Ordnance Survey map at Carrickfergus and elsewhere, a proof of the respect accorded to at least some commons before the invisible barriers surrounding them eventually yielded to pressure of population.

When did any large number of trespassers inaugurate the quite different sequence that begins with building on the common itself? The general impression is that compared with the steady progress of landlord appropriation squatting made a slow start but later began to accelerate until by the end of the eighteenth century it could almost be seen as a national problem. Unfortunately this hypothetical curve has very few real points on it. Humble and perhaps illegitimate kinds of settlement can escape the proprietorial record with disconcerting completeness, as witness all the seventeenth-century cabin suburbs that would have gone unnoticed if Ireland's major towns had not been mapped by an exceptionally observant military cartographer in 1685.[36] Beyond the suburban fringe one can only ask whether the government would have considered settling poor people on the commons of Ireland, as is said to have been under contemplation in 1640, if the poor had already been moving in of their own accord.[37] And in that event Petty's large-scale maps would surely have shown at least one house on at least one of the two-hundred-odd Down Survey commons included in the present study; just as the census of 1659 would probably have mentioned more than just two inhabited commons in a record that extends to twenty-six counties.[38]

Such evidence can hardly be accepted as conclusive, and a hundred years later the documentation is just as bad. Eighteenth-century estate maps are understandably even less informative on squatting than on landlord encroachment; indeed the only contemporary maps that purport to show all the houses and cabins of any large rural area are Rocque's county maps. Their claim to comprehensiveness is transparently false; but in County Dublin Rocque appears to place houses on ten commons – in numbers that suggest a much lower population density than on the county's tenanted rural lowlands,[39] but still a clear enough hint of things to come.

The unsensational tenor of Rocque's evidence is in no way surprising, for it was only in the 1760s that Ireland's largest and most famous squatter colony is said to have started taking shape on the flanks of Forth Mountain in County Wexford (Fig. 1:4); and not until the 1780s that another such nucleus was first recorded on the old borough commons at Ardfert, County Kerry.[40] By that time the pace was evidently about to quicken. In 1789 the Irish parliament legislated against the overuse of commons without making any reference to trespassers.[41] Two years later it suddenly took note of 'divers encroachments . . . made on several commons of this kingdom, by which means they have become receptacles of idle and disorderly persons', and empowered sheriffs to remove the huts and cabins from any common on which they had been indicted by the grand jury as a nuisance.[42] In 1796 another act authorised the recruitment of county inspectors to supervise the larger tracts of common land.[43]

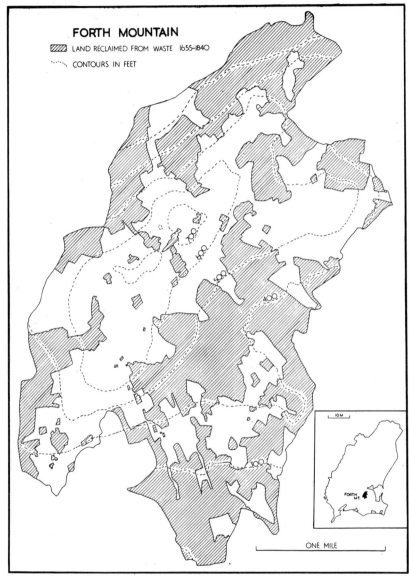

Figure 1:4. Forth Mountain, County Wexford. Boundaries of 1655 from the Down Survey boundaries of 1840 from the Ordnance Survey.

In the event there was no law strong enough to stop the squatter, any more than laws alone could cure the poverty and insecurity that spurred his action. A written lease from a rightful owner was certainly no defence against him, as tenants of the municipal commons at Navan found when they were frightened out of taking possession by the hostility of the local settlers. Parliamentary enclosure was no defence: at Broadleas Common near Ballymore Eustace, County Kildare, the official surveyors appointed under a local act of 1814 were twice driven away by a 'numerous mob' and the entire common became quickly and permanently covered by a close mesh of unparliamentary fences.[44] In practice the commons act of 1791 was no defence: it seems to have been generally ignored or forgotten, to judge from the interest aroused at Mallow, County Cork, by an unexpected attempt to enforce the act in 1843.[45] Other settlements proceeded more quietly – like the increase of houses on Swords Commons, County Dublin, from two to eighty-seven in the first four decades of the nineteenth century – and are correspondingly hard to date or quantify.[46] In general it seems that the only brake on further colonisation in the pre-Famine period was that certain commons were running out of space.

With unchecked success there came increasing confidence. On the commons of Balscadden, County Dublin, in 1836, the 'march of improvement was to be seen at every stage of its progress, from the sod hut of the new squatter, trembling for ejection, to the neat whitewashed and well plastered cottages of the old settler, who . . . thinks only of improving his property'.[47] The neat cottage might have a few inferior features, as when the Ordnance Survey distinguished the mud cabins of Duleek Common, County Meath, from the stone houses of the nearby village,[48] but they were generally rated no lower in the Griffith valuation than the five shillings that were the normal assessment for the cabins of the smallest farmers outside the commons. The house would be followed by a garden and then by one or more fields, by which time the settler, basking in his freedom from rent, tithe and tax, could hope to have risen from below to above the average level of prosperity among the cottagers and small-holders of the neighbourhood.[49]

This idyllic scenario was disrupted by the existence of other settlers. The first of these were usually bona fide commoners, or persons accepted as such. Next came migrants from further afield, each newcomer arousing resentment roughly in proportion to the distance he had travelled. Contemporaries thought it rare for a settler to migrate from one county to another and the mid-century valuation data are consistent with a hypothesis of small catchment-areas in so far as most common-dwellers' surnames can be matched from within a few miles radius of their homes. Cast away on the agrarian equivalent of a desert island, would the colonists write their own social contract, or would their interaction be nasty and brutish? A rare answer comes from Kilcullen Common, County Kildare, in 1837, where 'several heavy disputes and fights are said to have developed and where the strongest always succeeded in holding possession'.[50] How much fighting went on elsewhere is hard to say, but some commons kept their reputation for lawlessness long after being settled and it was only in the model county of Wexford that this charge appears to have been publicly contradicted.[51] Nevertheless the strongest seldom managed to seize the whole common, or even enough for the 15 acre farm that was often considered the minimum for tolerable subsistence at

TABLE 1:6

NUMBERS OF FREEHOLDS OF VARIOUS SIZE-GROUPS IN SELECTED COMMONS, c. 1850

	Statute acres				
	0-1	1-5	5-10	10-20	>20
Ardfert (Kerry)	37	14	5	5	1
Ardfield (Cork)	39	66	9	4	–
Capdoo (Kildare)	16	12	2	–	–
Kilcullen (Kildare)	9	7	1	–	–
Killinaboy (Clare)	18	28	9	4	3
Milltown (Kerry)	25	4	2	–	–
Mulrankin (Wexford)	24	16	6	2	–

Source: Griffith valuation. Separate parcels held by the same person are counted as one holding.

this period (Table 1:6). This meant that part of a settler's livelihood would probably have to come from outside his own holding. It is only at Navan, in 1821, that patterns of squatter employment can be demonstrated from contemporary census data,[52] but it seems significant that many colonies lay within three or four miles of a town or village presumably offering some chance of casual work.

Nobody was influential enough to plan a squatter settlement in advance, and the only regularities in the new landscape were those of pseudo-organic growth. One recurring feature was the alignment of houses along a lane that clung timidly to the skirts of the common as if

Figure 1:5.   The landscape of squatting in County Cork, from six-inch Ordnance Survey
               map of 1842. Heights are in feet. Dots represent townland boundaries, dashes
               and dots parish boundaries. Part of the townland of Mountain Common,
               parish of Ardfield, appears in the left of the map.

to leave as much of it as possible intact. More aggressive in style, and perhaps later in date, was a dendritic network of short branching lanes each serving one or more houses and gardens (Fig. 1:5).

The next phase began when natural increase became a major element in local population growth. Farms were now subdivided, surnames grew more repetitive, squatters held houses and lands from other squatters, sons proved themselves more law-abiding than fathers, single farmsteads burgeoned into clachans and centrality made its debut in the shape of Catholic chapels,[53] national schools and (in or near settlements of continuing ill repute) police stations. In extreme cases, as at Rathnew, County Wicklow, and Tipperkevin, County Kildare, a common could end its life as one continuous village. Thus what had once been the emptiest places in rural Ireland had now emerged among the fullest. In 1841 the 290 commons in our sample – mountains, bogs and all – returned a population density of 12 per cent above the average for rural Ireland as a whole. In the fully occupied freehold commons the density was four and a half times greater than average.

The most critical stage in the sequence of squatting has already been hinted at in a reference to 'property' at Balscadden, quoted above. One historical geographer has described the settler's claim on land as 'very slight', but this is not quite the whole truth.[54] Morally, one must admit, his position was not particularly enviable. Apart from his allegedly high crime rate, he had no right to have made a home on common land in the first place, and every day he spent there was incompatible with other people's rights. But many countries and many cultures have shown a measure of indulgence towards the squatter, and even in the supposedly 'colonial' environment of early nineteenth-century Ireland the legal balance was steadily tilting in his favour. This can best be seen in the sequence of local enclosure acts. When the commons of Saggart, County Dublin, were privatised in 1816, every squatter who had lived on them for less than thirty years became liable to ejectment. In the next batch of County Dublin statutes, passed between 1818 and 1821, this limit was reduced to twenty years, and at Callan, County Kilkenny, in 1829 to ten years. Under an act of 1839 for Rathkeale, County Limerick, it needed only five years' residence to legitimise the newcomer, and even if he had arrived more recently than that he would still be given the chance to buy his holding. This kind of latitude explains the squatter-like landscapes which sometimes (as for instance at Knocktopher, County Kilkenny) interrupt the neat handiwork of the enclosure commissioners.

Beyond the reach of parliamentary enclosure there were general statutes of limitation, dating back to James I and earlier, which gave immunity from ejectment after twenty years of undisturbed occupation, and under the real property limitation act of 1833 the original owner could in these circumstances lose his title to the land wrongfully taken from him.[55] It was through this doctrine of adverse possession that a number of Irish squatters obtained a parliamentary vote by registering themselves as freeholders.[56] Though vetoed on at least one occasion,[57] their right to do so was finally upheld on appeal in 1836 when John Doyle of Ballymore Eustace was pronounced eligible for registration after having spent more than twenty unlawful years on Broadleas Common without being challenged by either the commoners or the lord of the manor or the grand jury.[58] So much for Fair Rent (and what rent could be fairer than none?) and Fixity of Tenure. The third of Ireland's late nineteenth-century three F's was also anticipated in the 1830s when parts of Dalkey Common, County Dublin, were sold by labourers who had settled there during the construction of Dún Laoghaire Harbour – sold not to other squatters but to rich Dublin exurbanites who could afford to pay for accurate legal advice.[59]

The squatter's final triumph was to be accepted by the civil service. Many Irish commons had been validated by the Down Survey. Now after two centuries of cartographic and archival blackout they were to be invalidated by the Ordnance Survey, and by Richard Griffith's tabulation of lessors and occupants, as hundreds of erstwhile trespassers received the status of freeholder or of tenant in fee.[60] When an official directory of Irish landownership appeared in 1876 the pride of the aristocracy was to be found rubbing proprietorial shoulders with the Doyles of Broadleas Common.[61]

NOTES

1. B. Harris and G. Ryan, *An outline of the law relating to common land and public access to the countryside* (London, 1967).

2. Correspondents in all parts of Ireland were asked in 1836 for information on the 'public commons' in their parishes and hardly any of them had any difficulty in answering *(First report of commissioners for inquiring into the condition of the poorer classes in Ireland, supplement to appendix F: answers to questions circulated by the commissioners relative to the condition of the small tenantry in Ireland, H.C. 1836, xxxiii (subsequently cited as Poor inquiry).*

3. *Arthur Young's tour in Ireland in 1776-1779*, A. W. Hutton (ed.) (London, 2 vols, 1892), i, p. 82; ii, pp. 95, 99.

4. Examples of 'common' pasture belonging to individual proprietors in a non-manorial context are numerous in the Civil Survey of 1654-6, notably in County Donegal and Tyrone: see *The Civil Survey, 1654-56*, R. C. Simington (ed.) (Dublin, 1931-61) 10 vols.

5. A common with one commoner was recorded at Bannow, County Wexford, in 1833. For source see note 12 below.

6. 'The main mountains which mearest betwixt this barony [Bantry] and the county of Carlow are commons of pasture, to any of both counties by ancient custom' (*Civil Survey,* Wexford, p. 200).

7. *General valuation of rateable property in Ireland, county of Wexford . . ., unions of Enniscorthy and Shillelagh* (Dublin, 1853), p. 149.

8. King's Bog, County Kildare, was later considered to belong to the corporation of Kildare and is so described in Alexander Taylor's county map of 1783. For King's Mountain, County Sligo, see P.R.O.I., 2B.44.5.

9. In 1841 a representative of the office of woods and forests denied that the crown had any interest in Forth Mountain, County Wexford, while tacitly accepting that the area had no other proprietor (P.R.O.I., 2B.44.3).

10. An exception was the Curragh of Kildare, where common rights were redefined by act of parliament in 1870 (Walter Fitzgerald, 'The Curragh: its history and traditions' in *Kildare Arch. Soc. Jn.,* iii (1899), pp. 1-32).

11. Many new seventeenth-century manors are listed, without reference to commons, in George Hill, *An historical account of the plantation in Ulster* (Belfast, 1877), pp. 259-317.

12. Borough commons are generally well documented in *First report of the commissioners appointed to inquire into the municipal corporations in Ireland,* H.C. 1835, xxvii, xxviii, and H.C. 1836, xxiv. Subsequent references to them are based on this source unless otherwise stated.

13. For a particularly clear statement on this subject see J. L. Foster in *Report from the select committee on emigration from the United Kingdom,* p. 342, H.C. 1826-7 (237), v; also *Fourth report of the commissioners appointed to enquire into the nature and extent of the several bogs in Ireland,* p. 12, H.C. 1813-14 (131), vi.

14. It should be noted, however, that many private commons became public as a result of the post-1880 land reforms which eliminated the large proprietor and converted rent-paying tenants into owner-occupiers *(Annual report of the Irish land commissioners 1971-72,* Prl 3455 (Dublin, 1972), pp. 6-9).

15. When the agent to the Ross estate in County Down objected to the townland name 'Mountain in Common' on the ground that the mountain in question was not a true common, the government's boundary department acquiesced by changing the name (P.R.O.I., 2A.26.67: 16 October 1828). In general, however, the department's early correspondence yields hardly any evidence relating to its policy on commons.

16. For a lively treatment of English commons see the evidence of P. Birkett to the *Select committee on commons* (H.C., 1913 (85), vi). A more general survey is L. D. Stamp and W. G. Hoskins, *The common lands of England and Wales* (London, 1963). G. H. Whybrow's *The history of Berkhamsted Common* (London, n.d. [1935]) is a classic case study.

17. Sale of part of the North Commons, Ardfert, County Kerry, to the board of guardians of Tralee union, 1886, P.R.O.I., 2B.44.5.

18. The Civil Survey's only references to stinting, for example, appear to be at Lifford and Raphoe (Donegal, pp. 38, 42), Rattoo in County Kerry (Limerick, p. 499) and Forenaghts (Kildare, p. 48). The surveyors' instructions included a general reference to 'rights' belonging to the land under survey but did not explicitly mention commons.

19. Petty's surveyors were told: 'In all common land, whether profitable or unprofitable, you are to mention the names of such places or persons as have commonage in the same,

with the proportion belonging unto each of them', T. A. Larcom (ed.), *The history of the survey of Ireland, commonly called the Down Survey* (Dublin, 1851), p. 48. The last part of this order, dealing with 'proportions', seems seldom if ever to have been carried out.

20. P. Gale, *An inquiry into the ancient corporate system of Ireland* (London, 1834), ch. 3. The right of the corporation of Trim to demise its commons to individuals was the subject of *The case of John Perceval Esq.* and other pamphlets published in 1704.

21. W. Tighe, *Statistical observations relative to the county of Kilkenny, made in the years 1800 and 1801* (Dublin, 1802), p. 358; H. Townsend, *Statistical survey of the county of Cork* (Dublin, 1810), p. 264. Commons are not mentioned in the instructions printed at the beginning of these and other Dublin Society *Surveys.*

22. *Hansard* 1, 20 May 1805. Earlier proposals for general enclosure acts appear in *Commons' Jrnl Ire.*, ii, 427 (1704) and iv, 179, 198 (1735).

23. P.R.O.I., 2B.44.3. It is remarkable that no publications on commons are listed in P. O'Higgins, *A bibliography of periodical literature relating to Irish law* (Belfast, 1986).

24. For an example of the 'levelling' of fences on common land at Slieve Grine, County Waterford, see *Report from the select committee on the employment of the poor in Ireland,* p. 25, H.C. 1823 (561), vi.

25. The Down Survey maps used are the Reeves parish maps (N.L.I., MSS 715-26) and Robert Johnston's Down Survey superimpositions (N.L.I., 20.D).

26. For example, '3 acres in Kilbarry and the grazing of ten cows' (County Meath) in Royal Irish Academy, Book of postings and sales, 1700-3.

27. Irish Record Commission, *15th annual report* (Dublin, 1825), *passim.*

28. In 1704 Robert Molesworth was considering how this issue affected his estate in County Dublin, though he did not mention of Statute of Merton by name (H.M.C., *Clements*, pp. 230-1).

29. So far as can be judged from recent studies of the subject (e.g. J. S. Donnelly, 'Irish agrarian rebellion: the whiteboys of 1769-76' in *R.I.A. Proc.*, lxxxiii, 12 C (1983), pp. 293-331, and Michael Beames, *Peasants and power, the whiteboy movements and their control in pre-famine Ireland* (Brighton, 1983); whiteboy activity was directed mainly against the enclosure of private commons.

30. See, for example, *Mun. corp. Ire., rep.*, Fethard, County Tipperary.

31. For an example from County Meath, see Arnold Horner, 'New maps of County Kildare interest in the National Library of Ireland' in *Kildare Arch. Soc. Jn.*, xv (1975-6), pp. 477-8.

32. Sherrard, Brassington and Greene, surveyors, report on Forth Mountain, 1817, P.R.O.I., 2B.44.3.

33. Reports of idleness, lawlessness, vagabondage etc. come from Forth Mountain and Bantry Commons, County Wexford (P.R.O.I., 2B.44.3), from King's Mountain in County Sligo (P.R.O.I., 2B.44.5), from Duleek, County Meath *(Mun. corp. Ire., rep.),* from Navan, County Meath, and Mulrankin, County Wexford *(Poor inquiry)* and from Rathnew, County Wicklow (O.S. name-books).

34. J. Archer, *Statistical survey of the county Dublin* (Dublin, 1801), p. 217.

35. *Report from the select committee on the state of Ireland,* q. 1682, H.C. 1831-2 (677), xvi. Strictly speaking Fossy was a private common.

36. Thomas Phillips, Military survey of Ireland, 1685, N.L.I., MS 3137.

37. Gale, *Corporate system,* p. 71.

38. The census recorded nine Irish people on the commons of Santry, County Dublin, and six Irish people on the commons of Killinick, County Wexford (*Census Ire., 1659,* pp. 389, 535).

39. Only approximate limits of commons are obtainable from Rocque's map. The general county density has been obtained by random sampling.

40. T. Radcliff, *A report of the agriculture and livestock of the county of Kerry* (Dublin, 1814), p. 213.

41. 29 Geo. III, c. 30, prohibiting the 'skinning' of commons by turf-cutters and the grazing of pigs without rings or staples in their noses.

42. 31 Geo. III, c. 38. This act also empowered the grand jury of County Kildare to construct an eight-foot-wide road around the Curragh as a means of preventing encroachments.

43. 36 Geo. III, c. 1. The act applied only to commons of more than 2000 Irish acres. The inspectors were to be paid by a levy on adjacent occupiers in proportion to the length of their frontage on the common. There seems to be no evidence that this law was ever put into force.

44. S.P.O., Official papers, 574/507/7, 575/510/7 and 7A.

45. *Devon comm. evidence,* i, 790, and app. B, no. 141, H.C. 1845 (606), xix.

46. For an undated and imperfectly quantified example, see Thomas Carlyle, *Reminiscences of my Irish journey in 1849* (New York, 1882), pp. 67-8.

47. *Poor inquiry,* app. E, p. 43, H.C. 1836, xxxii.

48. Ordnance Survey Office, Dublin, fair plans, parish of Duleek, County Meath. For the instructions to ordnance surveyors on the use of different-coloured house symbols see J. H. Andrews, *A paper landscape, the ordnance survey in nineteenth-century Ireland* (Oxford, 1975), p. 319. The instructions do not appear to have been consistently followed on the plans, however.

49. *Devon comm. evidence,* i, 27 (County Cork), 57 (County Louth).

50. O.S. name-books, Kildare, parish of Kilcullen.

51. W. Harvey, Report on Forth Mountain, 1818, P.R.O.I., 2B.44.3; Mrs S. C. Hall, *Tales of Irish life and character* (Edinburgh and London, 1909), pp. 301-2.

52. Peter Connell, *Changing forces shaping a nineteenth-century Irish town: a case study of Navan* (Geography Department, St Patrick's College, Maynooth, Occasional Paper Series, no. 1, 1978), p. 21.

53. Kevin Whelan, 'The Catholic parish, the Catholic chapel and village development in Ireland' in *Ir. Geography,* xvi (1983), p. 6.

54. T. J. Hughes, 'East Leinster in the mid-nineteenth century' in *Ir. Geography,* iii (1958), p. 237.

55. J. M. Lightwood, *A treatise on possession of land* (London, 1894), chs. 9 and 10; J. C. W. Wylie, *Irish land law* (Abingdon, 1981), ch. 23.

56. *Third report from the select committee on the state of Ireland,* p. 438, H.C. 1825 (129), viii.

57. *Mun. corp. Ire., rep.,* Navan.

58. J. C. Alcock, *Registry cases reserved for consideration and decided by the twelve judges of Ireland from November 1832 to June 1837,* pt. 1 (Dublin, 1837), pp. 37-41.

59. John D'Alton, *History of the county of Dublin* (Dublin, 1838), p. 882.

60. Former squatter-holdings were also identified in the Griffith valuation by naming the immediate lessor as 'common' or 'commonage', by leaving the lessor column blank, or by classing the same person as both lessor and occupier.

61. *Return of owners of land of one acre and upwards, in the several counties in Ireland,* p. 29, H.C. 1876 (C 1492), lxxx.

The improvement of Irish farming techniques since 1750: theory and practice

J. BELL

Recent historical research has begun to question the established view that Irish agriculture during the last two centuries was backward and inefficient.[1] Levels of production from both cereal crops and livestock have been used as evidence that, by the early nineteenth century, Irish systems of agriculture could stand comparison with those of England and Scotland and certainly with those of north-western Europe. This paper will attempt to contribute to this discussion by examining some changes in cultivation techniques since the mid-eighteenth century. It will be argued that at this level also, the efficiency of Irish farming should be re-assessed. Contemporary attitudes to Irish farming practices and the approaches identified as necessary for their improvement will be outlined. Examples will then be given of both 'improved' and 'common' systems of cultivation and also of the ways in which these might be integrated. The rationality behind many practices will become evident by examining interrelations between the elements of these systems.

Contemporary attitudes to Irish agricultural practice

Almost every general account of Irish cultivation techniques emphasised their defects in the late eighteenth and nineteenth centuries.

Implements, it was claimed, were generally crude, fields weed-infested, rotations minimal and land frequently cropped to exhaustion. In their criticisms, agriculturalists tended to contrast this view of Irish tillage practices with the cultivation techniques currently advocated, and to some extent implemented on English and Scottish farms. This 'improved' farming was believed to arise from the systematic application of ideas derived from the science, or sometimes the art of agriculture. In the end, the contrast between what commentators criticised in Irish farming and the techniques of which they approved, was seen as the difference between enlightened agriculture, guided by theory, and unenlightened practice.

The early nineteenth-century agriculturalist, Martin Doyle, made a very strong claim for the central role of theory.

> It is a trite saying, that Agriculture is the mother of arts; and yet a vast portion of our farmers, even of those who are able to read without stopping to spell hard words, seldom or never take up a book on the science of husbandry . . . but rather entertain prejudices against every agricultural writer that comes through the channel of the press; satisfied to pursue the same routine which their grandfathers had followed; contemptuous alike of what they call *new schemes* and *new fangled fashions.*
>
> They do not see the connexion between the theory and practice, of Agriculture . . . and expect, because weeds spring spontaneously from the ground, . . . that their knowledge of farming is to be acquired without any culture or labour of their brains.[2]

Doyle believed that although by the 1830s progress had been made in Irish farming, 'Useful improvements have seldom, if ever, originated with the operative farmers themselves, but have been introduced by persons not practically conversant with the details of agriculture, but theoretically well informed, and therefore competent to calculate, to reason, and to apply their reasonings, so as ultimately to promote practical knowledge'.[3]

The priority given to theory was not unquestioned, however, and caution was not confined to 'operative farmers'. Doyle himself admitted 'that a great deal of nonsense has been written on points of rural economy . . . many theorists have *burned their fingers* by rash experiments'.[4] Arthur Young noted critically that 'authors seem to have disdained recording . . . practice, so much have they been employed in prescribing alterations'.[5] Hely Dutton argued that, '. . . though a rational theory should be the foundation (of farming), yet too many find, when too late, that experience gained by an extensive practice is also absolutely necessary'.[6] Some writers, certainly considered progressive, were at pains to dissociate themselves from the 'theoretically well informed' persons so respected by Doyle. Early nineteenth-century farming journals contain many statements similar to that quoted approvingly by *The Irish farmer's and gardener's magazine* in 1834: 'I am not a theorist, but a practical man'.[7] This tension between theory and practice continued throughout the nineteenth century. In 1902, the Scotsman James Wilson took the chair of agriculture at the College of Science in Dublin. Hoctor comments that Wilson was 'an excellent teacher, who always kept the practical aspects of his subject in view. In discussing conclusions in regard to any new practice or research, he invariably set himself the question: 'Does it pay?'[8]

In the following sections some Irish farming techniques will be considered as examples of the different ways in which theory and practice could be linked. These will show that, as with any successful experimentation, both theory and practice were advanced by interaction. The adoption of new techniques, especially by Irish farmers engaged in commercial production, reflected both the success of experiments in improvement, and a growing awareness among farmers of their relevance. The persistence of what agriculturalists dismissively referred to as 'common' techniques will also be discussed. It will be argued that, particularly for cultivators whose central aim was to secure a subsistence living for their families, the long-term interchange between theory and practice was largely irrelevant. Practices which were known to work were retained. When pushed to extremes by economic necessity, an immutable range of techniques could lead to a deterioration in productivity, and in a crisis such as a famine could also contribute to the scale of a disaster if the system broke down. However, when not under pressure, 'common' farming practices could work much better than many contemporaries were inclined to admit.

'Improved' practices

A very long list of farm implements can be drawn up which were introduced, or in some cases developed in Ireland during the last two centuries. The rate at which these implements were adopted varied, but by the end of the nineteenth century many were standard items on farms relying on horse-power.

Plough design in Britain underwent important changes in the later eighteenth century.[9] By the early nineteenth century, improved Scottish swing ploughs, and English wheel ploughs were being used on some Irish farms. These new ploughs required less labour and less draught than those in common use. Operating a swing plough was a very skilled task, as the ploughman had not only to drive the horses, but also control the depth and width of the furrow slice being turned. This control had, however, important advantages. On hilly or stony land the depth of the plough could be minutely adjusted to allow for unevenness in the ground. It was this sensitivity which ensured that Scottish swing ploughs remained the predominant type until well into the present century especially in hilly terrain.[10]

Wheel ploughs can be set to turn furrow slices of fixed width and depth. In 1808, the English firm, Ransomes of Ipswich, developed a 'universal body' plough, individual parts of which were standardised and replaceable. This standardisation was widely adopted, so that at the end of the era of horse-power, plough parts produced in many foundries could be used interchangeably. In 1950, for example, some of the ploughs produced by the Wexford Engineering Company could be fitted with parts made by the British firms, Ransomes, Howard, Hornsby and Sellar, and the American firm of Oliver.[11]

A large number of Irish foundries began to manufacture ploughs during the early nineteenth century. These were largely based on Scottish and English prototypes, although sometimes modified to suit local conditions. The skills required to operate the ploughs were acquired by ploughmen, and those required to repair, set and in some cases construct them acquired by blacksmiths. By the early twentieth century, the use of ploughs other than improved Scottish or English types had become very rare in Ireland.

Some implements developed in the later eighteenth and nineteenth centuries were produced as integrated sets. This can be clearly seen in the case of drill husbandry. The cultivation of crops in long straight rows or drills was argued to be advantageous in that each plant could be given a fixed growing space and also because weeding and harvesting were now much easier. Implements designed for the cultivation of potatoes in raised drills were being advertised by John Wynn Baker of Celbridge, County Kildare, in 1767.[12] Early attempts to use these implements were not always successful, but the use of drills for potatoes seems to have spread relatively quickly. In 1834, Edmund Murphy recorded: 'The drill has so completely superceded the lazy bed that in the line extending from

Dublin by Athlone to Galway, and thence to Ennis and Limerick to Dublin again, we saw but very few fields cultivated in the old way'.[13] Early implements included two-sided ploughs for making the drills and moulding up the young plants, and grubbers which could be used for weeding. In 1852, a Mr. Hanson of Doagh, County Antrim, patented a rotary action potato digger which became a prototype for many later machines. Like drill ploughs and grubbers, these implements could only be effectively used where drill husbandry had been applied as a complete system.

It is superficial and often misleading to consider the use of any farm implement without also considering the implications its adoption has for other aspects of a cultivation system. Although agriculturalists throughout the last two centuries recognised this, some new implements impressed mainly because of the increased speed with which they could perform individual operations. Threshing machines and reaping machines were two outstanding examples. Threshing machines were developed in Scotland in the eighteenth century, and were being used in parts of Ireland by 1800.[14] These machines could be worked manually, by horse-power, by water or after the middle of the nineteenth century, by steam. Large machines allowed dramatic increases in speed and savings in labour over threshing with flails. It has been estimated that a man with a horse-driven machine could thresh between five and six times as much grain as a man with a flail.[15] By the 1840s, larger Irish foundries were producing several sizes of threshing machines as standard products.[16]

There is some evidence of experimentation with reaping machines in Ireland in the early nineteenth century,[17] but it was not until the exhibition of reapers in Belfast in 1852 and Dublin in 1853,[18] that widespread attention was given to these machines by Irish agriculturalists. At tests held in several places during the 1850s it was the machine developed by the Scot, Patrick Bell, in the 1820s which was judged most efficient. After these early tests, however, Bell reapers seem to have quickly disappeared, and it was the American machines developed by McCormick, and Hussey which became the prototypes for machines manufactured in Ireland. The use of reaping machines had direct implications for several aspects of cereal cultivation. Some of these implications were of the same kind as those arising from the introduction of scythes to the grain harvest which will be discussed later.

The cited examples show technological improvement at its most effective. Although a lag between their first introduction and widespread use can be made intelligible by relating their rate of adoption to limits imposed by the availability of labour and control of capital, or other factors such as access to markets and the means by which knowledge and skills relating to their use were disseminated, their appearance in farming can be regarded fairly unequivocally as an advance. Using the adoption of these implements as a central criterion, individual Irish farmers could be categorized as either 'early adopters' or 'laggards'. In *The dynamics of agricultural change,* Grigg has listed some characteristics of early adopters which can be usefully applied in some Irish contexts.

> First, early adopters tend to have larger farms than late adopters, are often specialised producers and have easier access to credit . . . Second, they tend to have a high social status in their community and are well educated. Third, they often have more urban experience than laggards, and are thus used to an environment where change is typical. Fourth, early adopters are generally young – under 45 – while laggards tend to be older.[19]

Applying the first three of these characteristics, we would expect that, as some contemporaries claimed, new technology was first introduced to larger Irish farms, where the emphasis was clearly on commercial production.[20]

Contemporaries recognised that smaller Irish farmers were limited in the extent to which they could adopt those techniques or implements that required a long-term or a large scale investment. Even after these limits were allowed for, however, the persistence of many 'common' techniques at all levels of farming has seemed remarkable. Contemporaries tended to put this inertia down to prejudice and laziness, while some historians have discussed it in terms of peasant conservatism or a high leisure preference. It is a central argument in this paper, however, that if we consider the logic of Irish agricultural techniques, based on the knowledge current at any particular time, the need to inflate these individual attributes to the status of cultural labels largely disappears. In Ireland during the eighteenth and nineteenth centuries, caution towards new methods and implements was well justified. Practices based on theoretical principles were by no means certain to be successful, while already existing 'common' practices could be very efficient.

Only a small proportion of plough and reaper designs were ever widely applied. Large capital inputs and the use of advanced engineering were no guarantee that experiments would lead to practical advances in technique. This can be clearly seen in attempts to apply steam power to ploughing. Steam ploughing equipment was advertised in *The Irish farmer's gazette* in 1863[21] and exhibited at the Royal Dublin Society's spring show in 1864.[22] In 1863, *Purdon's practical farmer* was enthusiastic.

> Much remains to be done before steam cultivation supercedes those modes which have been in use for so long a period. It is evident, however, that such a result cannot be long delayed . . . and seeing that not only the possibility, but the actually greater utility of steam cultivation has been sufficiently proved, we have not the slightest hesitation in saying that the sooner it becomes a regular part of our agricultural system the better.[23]

However, despite the continued manufacture of steam ploughing equipment they do not appear to have won wide acceptance in Ireland. By the early twentieth century, farming texts had become much more cautious about the value of steam cultivation.

> As an adjunct to horse cultivation, steam is extremely valuable, and in many cases, it may partially displace horses. It is, however, noteworthy that after a trial of at least sixty years, it has hitherto failed to oust the horse from its position as the most generally employed power on the farm . . . The efficiency of steam cultivation does not . . . appear to be in all cases greater than that of horse tillage. Horse ploughing is quite as good as steam ploughing, and, as to ordinary harrowing, it is one of its greatest recommendations on many soils that the horses tread the ground and render it firm after sowing.[24]

Just how long, and how inconclusive, a debate between agricultural improvers could be is well illustrated by arguments about the relative efficiency of oxen and horses as draught animals. The use of oxen during the eighteenth and nineteenth centuries was especially associated with large-scale farming.[25] The level of interest in the potential of oxen for draught is suggested by the inclusion of 'Use of oxen – how harnessed', in the Royal Dublin Society's 'suggestions of enquiry' to compilers of the county statistical surveys. During the early part of the nineteenth century, 'numberless statements'[26] were made on the subject and discussion continued even into the present century.[27] At a 'theoretical' level the debate never reached a satisfactory conclusion, but at the level of practice, the use of oxen dwindled away almost entirely. The argument was seen by some agriculturalists as one which did the theoretical approach no credit. Oxen were said by one standard text to be preferred by 'gentlemen and theoretic farmers',[28] while another commented scathingly that, 'The preference has generally been given by speculative writers to the ox, and by practical farmers to the horse.'

The persistence of 'common' practices

Many agriculturalists were reluctant to admit that the 'common' practices in general use among Irish farmers had anything other than a very limited value. The term 'common', when applied to implements implied that these were 'unscientific in design, crude in construction and of a general type'.[29]

In the early nineteenth century, 'common' wooden ploughs were particularly criticised, and as pointed out in the last section improved ploughs were fairly steadily adopted by Irish farmers. However, recent research suggests that not only was there a wide variety in plough types labelled as 'common', but that at least some of these could efficiently perform the tasks for which they were designed. Watson has examined two important early nineteenth-century types, the 'old Irish long beamed plough', and the 'light Irish' plough. Long beamed ploughs were used for breaking and turning fallows, lea ground and burnt land. Light ploughs were used in conjunction with other primary tillage implements, usually for the processes of trenching or covering seed. Improved Scottish ploughs, with which Irish ploughs were most often compared, did not operate so well as the long beamed ploughs on heavy, wet, undrained land. This point was conceded by Mason in his discussion of the relative merits of Scottish and Irish ploughs.

> Some of the respectable farmers have introduced Scottish ploughs, though they are not suited to wet grounds, which are so stiff and adhesive, that the sod requires to be raised as much as possible, in order that the air may get through it, to dry and pulverize it. The Scotch plough is thought to lay the sod too flat, while the Irish plough raises it, and breaks it more; but the superiority of the Scotch plough in dry grounds is fully acknowledged, a dislike to it therefore in the former instance may have some foundation in reason. However when . . . those grounds are drained . . . pulverisation will be effected by the Scotch as well as the Irish

plough, and by its universal use, labour will be diminished, and horses spared to the farmer.[30]

Some agriculturalists also admitted that Scottish swing ploughs were not so useful as light Irish ploughs where the technique of ploughing in seed was used. The introduction of new plough types therefore implied major changes in cultivation systems. When the skills required to construct or set the new ploughs and to use them are considered, it is not surprising that many farmers did not feel any urgent need to adopt them.

An examination of hand-tools shows the efficiency of many 'common' implements even more clearly. From the late eighteenth century, there was a growing awareness that spades could be valuable tillage implements. This recognition can be closely related to the movement to reclaim marginal mountain and bog land for cultivation. Until the mid-nineteenth century, most of this reclamation was carried out by the unassisted labours of cottiers and small farmers.[31] When associated with the cultivation of potatoes, it became widely accepted that Irish spades, and the cultivation ridges constructed using them, 'supplied the most minute conceivable system of artificial drainage'.[32] Spade ridges not only prevented waterlogging, but were also argued to achieve subsoiling better than the subsoil ploughs designed by Smith of Deanston.

> Although it is the fashion to decry the Irish spade or loy, there are few implements better calculated for furrow-draining and subsoiling . . . The subsoil plough, as now in use . . . is altogether out of the reach of our peasantry; and there are few large farmers who are systematically extensive in tillage as to have the horse-power necessary for the work.[33]

The complexity of spade ridge cultivation techniques is only beginning to be understood. Recent fieldwork, however, has shown that those farmers who still make use of ridges vary their construction in response to slope, aspect, drainage, soil-type, crops grown and their place in the rotation.[34] It is no longer tenable to see spade cultivation as anything other than a refined and very efficient, albeit labour-intensive, tillage technique.

The 'common' practice least criticised by contemporary observers was the use of sickles or hooks for harvesting cereals. Where grain, especially wheat, was sown broadcast on high ridges, or late harvesting meant that crops had been flattened or twisted in bad weather, and where the crops were weedy, it was recognised that using sickles or hooks was the neatest method of reaping. The technique of grasping a handful of grain near the head while the straw was being cut, meant that weeds could be left behind, straw cut close to the ground, and grain saved which might have been shed if shaken by the cutting action of a scythe.[35] Scythes were probably introduced into Ireland by the Normans, but before the nineteenth century they were used mainly for cutting hay. The increase in speed and savings in labour possible using scythes did not outweigh the advantages gained by using the smaller tools until changes in other cultivation techniques meant that ridges were levelled, crops were less weedy, and harvesting was carried out earlier. It has been claimed that the introduction of scythes to the grain harvest in some parts of England was delayed by the availability of large numbers of Irish migratory workers, who would not, or could not, use scythes. Farmers found that cheap Irish labour meant that there was little advantage in employing quicker, but less neat, scythesmen.[36]

The integration of 'improved' and 'common' practices

'Improved' and 'common' systems of cultivation did not exist in complete separation. Despite the attempts of agriculturalists to present these techniques as mutually exclusive there are several important instances where progressive farmers integrated elements from both systems, disregarding the more rigid strictures of theorists. One clear example of this is the use of high-sided, narrow cultivation ridges. At the beginning of the nineteenth century attempts to discourage ridges were beginning in areas where cereal cultivation was well established.[37] Criticisms of ridge cultivation included claims that land taken up by the furrows between ridges went to waste[38] and that on rounded ridges, the plants growing on the sides facing away from the light were shaded and their growth curtailed. The first major impulse to level ridges, however, came with the spread of thorough drainage techniques, especially those advocated in the 1840s by Smith of Deanston.[39] Smith argued that his drainage system rendered ridge cultivation obsolete.[40] In Ireland, however, although Smith's methods were adopted enthusiastically by some land owners, this was not always accompanied by the levelling of ridges. Instead, ridge and furrow systems were integrated with thorough drainage. On the Glenfin estate in County Donegal, for example, the drains were laid down, and ridges and furrows then constructed. If the land was flat, the ridges were made to run at right angles to the drains.

If the drains ran down a slope, the ridges were made at an oblique angle.[41] This integration of drains and ridges seems to have occurred mostly where marginal land was being reclaimed for cultivation. Once reclamation had been achieved, however, there was less need for the detailed drainage possible with ridges. The spread of drill husbandry, and the use of scythes and reaping machines, could not be effective on ground which was not almost level. However, the short term integration of drains and ridges shows the readiness of some farmers to achieve their own synthesis of theory and practice, if efficiency was increased.

Changes in attitude towards common practice could be marked. The practice of paring and burning was at first condemned, but it eventually gained some acceptance. There were many variations in the technique, but the basic operations involved 'stripping off the surface sod, allowing it to dry, burning it, and then spreading the ash on the soil as a fertilizer'.[42] In the early eighteenth century, the practice was regarded as pernicious, and in 1743 the Irish parliament passed an act forbidding it. The act does not seem to have been very effective however, and by the early nineteenth century condemnations had become a lot less sweeping. This change in attitude came with the recognition that, as with ridge cultivation, controlled paring and burning could considerably speed up land reclamation. Burning some types of bog and heath could reduce tough, poor vegetation to productive ash. In 1802, Coote concluded that, 'The effects of burning land were not well understood when the legislature imposed the heavy penalty against this process'.[43] In 1807, Rawson argued that it was over-reliance on paring and burning which was detrimental, not the practice itself.

> The common practice of burning the whole surface (of upland) and then applying the entire ashes on the remnant of the soil, taking three or four exhausting crops, cannot be too much reprobated; by it the land is completely exhausted, and men say how injurious paring and burning is, not considering that the injury lies in making an improvident use of ashes.[44]

During the early nineteenth century paring and burning was fairly widely used on large-scale reclamation schemes. At Tullychar, County Tyrone, in 1835 top sods were pared using the local type of breast-ploughs known as flachters, and the sods were then burnt.[45] The practice does not seem to have been much used on large farms in established tillage areas, but like the use of ridges in conjunction with drainage, its use on marginal land shows a willingness to use common techniques if real benefits were forthcoming.

The growing acceptance of paring and burning can be contrasted with a growing caution towards the use of lime as a fertilizer. In 1780, Arthur Young gave unqualified praise to large-scale Irish liming practices. 'To do the gentlemen of that country justice, they understand this branch of husbandry very well, and practise it with uncommon spirit. Their kilns are the best I have anywhere seen, and great numbers are kept going the whole year through.'[46] Young was aware of the possibility that land could be over-limed, but claimed that he had not found this anywhere in Ireland. By the beginning of the nineteenth century, however, some agriculturalists were identifying over-liming as a growing problem. In County Armagh, for example, Coote found lime to be 'prejudicial on light soils'.[47] He alleged that tenant farmers practised liming, 'when they mean to work the soil to the utmost it can produce, or in other words, to run it out, previously to the expiration of a lease which they do not expect to be renewed'. Over-liming continued to be noted throughout the early nineteenth century. In 1863, *Purdon's practical farmer* detailed the very long-term injury which it could do to soil.

> We have sometimes met with cases where it was almost a hopeless task to undertake the improvement of over-limed land, from the state of thorough exhaustion to which it had been reduced; so much so, indeed, that after being pastured for between thirty and forty years the effects of the overdose were quite visible when the land was broken up. In a case of this kind, the soil when ploughed feels quite puffy and dead under foot; and although oats will braird freely, and seem at first to be very promising, yet in a short time the leaves become brown, and the plants rapidly die away.[48]

Starting from different positions, attitudes to paring and burning, and to liming, show a convergence arising from a growing awareness of the balance necessary if the advantages of any practice were to be maintained.

An integration of 'improved' and 'common' practices was not confined only to large-scale farming. Small farmers sometimes adapted their own implements and practices to take advantage of new methods. One clear case of this can be seen in the use of drills for potato cultivation. Swing ploughs were sometimes made temporarily into two-sided drill ploughs by having spades lashed on to their land sides.[49] In the Mourne area of County Down, this modification went even further.

Wooden swing ploughs were fitted on their land sides with large blocks or 'reests' when drills were being made. This eventually led to a curious evolution of a series of wooden drill plough types which retained some of the characteristics of the original swing ploughs.[50]

Overview

The examples given in this paper have attempted to show that changes in Irish agricultural techniques can only be understood as a movement resulting, not only from an interchange between what agriculturalists saw as theory and improved practice, but also between improved and common practice. It has also been argued that even common systems which remained relatively untouched by improvement had an internal logic which could sustain efficient farming. Accepting this view we can now re-examine some of the major defects of Irish farming practice identified by contemporaries; these include implements, minimal rotations, exhaustion of land, and weed-infested crops. The problem to be considered here is how far these defects can be said to result from deficiencies in farming at a technical level.

The claim that 'common' implements were technically inefficient is not supported by a detailed study of agricultural practice. Larger implements, such as wooden ploughs, may have been less complex in construction than improved ploughs, but ploughmen could use them effectively in the sort of work for which they were designed. Hand-tools might be simple in construction, but the techniques for which they were used were remarkable for their refinement, rather than their crudity. The limitations of all these implements arose from the amounts of labour, or draught power they required. This is the point where technical discussion changes into a discussion of broader economic and social systems.

Minimal rotations and cropping to exhaustion were not inevitable results of Irish farming practice. The large proportion of arable land under grass, the frequent breaking up of pastures, and the natural fertility of soil in much of Ireland meant that good land, which remained largely under the control of commercial farmers, did not become exhausted. Mention was made earlier of the use of long-beamed Irish ploughs for fallowing. 'Bare' or 'summer' fallowing involved repeated ploughings during the summer months. Agriculturalists criticised the practice, advocating instead 'green fallowing', where a root crop such as potatoes or turnips was used to break up and cleanse land. Criticisms of 'bare fallowing' were, however, mostly directed at the waste of land involved, rather than the ineffectiveness of the practice. In 1802, Tighe claimed that summer fallowing could only be economically practised in County Kilkenny on farms of more than fifty acres.[51] In areas of poorer land, where much of the expanding population in the late eighteenth and early nineteenth centuries was concentrated, subdivision of holdings meant that the 'common' controls on soil deterioration could not be adhered to. It was in these areas that rotations were shortened to become a 'see-saw between oats and potatoes, with occasional rests',[52] and where paring and burning might be carried on until land was ruined. Hely Dutton's comment on the use of the latter practice in County Clare, shows the alternatives facing many small farmers. 'If a total abolition of this practice was to take place, as some people totally ignorant of rural economy seem to wish, a famine would be the consequence.'[53] Here again we have moved beyond the technical level to one where wider economic and social forces must be considered.

The claim that crops in Ireland were generally weed-infested can be related to the technique of broad-cast sowing of cereals and to late harvesting. Where crops were not sown in drills, weeding became extremely difficult, and the longer a crop was left standing, the more weeds grew amongst it. Reaping grain with sickles or hooks meant that weeds could be left behind at harvesting, but how far weeds damaged crop yields remains problematic. Any discussion must be based on impressionistic evidence, since types of weeds, and their real extent, is not known. Agriculturalists differed in the emphasis which they put on this problem. In 1835, it was alleged that a traveller in Ireland would see 'weeds often growing more luxuriant and numerous than even the grass or crops'.[54] However, this must be set against Arthur Young's comparison of the carefully weeded potato crops of the Palatines, and those of surrounding farmers. [The Palatines] 'are different from the Irish in several particulars; they put their potatoes in with the plough, in drills, horse-hoe them while growing, and plough them out . . . but the crops are not so large as in the common method'.[55]

It has not been the intention in this paper to present Irish farmers as uniformly good agriculturalists. There are many practices recorded which are difficult to see as anything other than bad husbandry, since even within 'common' practice, better alternatives were available. Probably the most notorious example of bad husbandry was ploughing by the tail, where draught horses' tails were substituted for trace-ropes. Rationalizations of this practice which suggest that it shortened the overall length of the plough team, or that it made horses more sensitive to obstructions met by the plough, are not convincing.[56] Alleged instances where the horses' tails were pulled off during ploughing could mean that as harnesses, tails were not very reliable and certainly very difficult to repair. We can label ploughing by the tail as bad husbandry because an efficient system of harnessing was within the resources of even small farmers. Collars made from *súgán* (twisted straw), and traces made from straw or withies were recognised by contemporaries as easily made, cheap and effective.

The examination of the efficiency of 'common' practice has not been intended to underestimate the successes of agricultural research, which have been as impressive as those of any other applied science. In 1863, *Purdon's practical farmer* admirably described the state of agricultural research.

> We have yet much to learn and . . . in general, we are only grop-
> ing after, and have yet but faint conceptions of what are the true
> principles by which we should be guided, or the correct modes of
> reducing those principles to practice. But the knowledge of our
> deficiencies on these points ought to induce us to strain every nerve
> in order that all doubts may be cleared away, and that agriculture,
> the most important in its results of all the arts, shall be placed in its
> proper station, based upon and guided by the truths of general
> science.[57]

In any situation, however, there is a lag between the introduction of discoveries arising from this worthy project, and their widespread adoption. Even in Norfolk, identified as one of the heartlands of the English agricultural revolution, the adoption of the famous Norfolk four-course rotation was very slow.[58] Contemporaries claimed that the lag between introduction and adoption, or at another level, theory and practice, was wider in Ireland than in England and Scotland. This paper has attempted to show that at a technical level, this lag did not imply inefficiency of farming. The technical history of Irish agriculture is full of examples of the ingenuity with which farmers adopted or modified new techniques, if convinced of their value. This ingenuity manifested itself in the high yields produced by Irish commercial farming, and the skill with which the smallest subsistence farmers created a living out of previously waste land. In investigating the farming techniques of the latter category, we should set aside the question of why they did not improve, and examine instead the ingenuity of methods which allowed so many people to survive for so long. A consideration of the achievement of small farmers and cottiers also raises a related point, which is of central importance. Mokyr, discussing the evidence for high yields from Irish farming has argued that, although 'in a certain way . . . the Irish economy was well organised and [the Irish] . . . were not throwing away resources . . . [This] is not quite the same as saying they were not poor'. This statement can be applied equally well to subsistence agricultural techniques. It can be useful to grant technical systems a relative automony, as has been attempted in this paper, so that relations between elements of the systems can be explored, but this autonomy can only be temporary. In the end, the technical history of agriculture must be related to wider social and economic conditions, if its relevance to historical understanding as a whole is to be established.

NOTES

1. Peter Solar, 'Agricultural productivity and economic development in Ireland and Scotland in the early nineteenth century' in T. M. Devine and David Dickson (ed.), *Ireland and Scotland, 1600-1850* (Edinburgh, 1983).

2. Martin Doyle [Rev. William Hickey], 'Observations on Irish farming' in *The Irish farmer's and gardener's magazine* (Dublin, 1834), i, pp. 25-26.

3. Martin Doyle [Rev. William Hickey], *A cyclopaedia of practical husbandry*, rev. ed., by W. Rham (London, 1844), p. 4.

4. Martin Doyle [Rev. William Hickey], 'Observations on Irish farming', p. 26.

5. Arthur Young, *A tour in Ireland . . . in the years 1776, 1777 and 1778* (Dublin, 1780), i, p. ii.

6. Hely Dutton, *A statistical and agricultural survey of the county of Galway* (Dublin, 1824), p. 72.

7. Edmund Murphy, 'Spade husbandry' in *The Irish farmer's and gardener's magazine* (Dublin, 1834), i, p. 681.

8. D. Hoctor, *The Department's story: a history of the Department of Agriculture* (Dublin, 1971), p. 58.

9. G. E. Fussell, *The farmer's tools, 1500-1900* (London, 1952), pp. 45-67.

10. Mervyn Watson, 'North Antrim swing ploughs; their construction and use' in *Ulster Folklife*, xxviii (1982), pp. 20-21.

11. Wexford Engineering Company, *Catalogue* (Wexford (?), 1950).

12. John Wynn Baker, *A short description and list, with the prices of the instruments of husbandry, made in the factory at Loughlinstown near Celbridge, in the county of Kildare* (Dublin, 1767), p. 7.

13. Edmund Murphy, 'Agricultural report' in *The Irish farmer's and gardener's magazine* (Dublin, 1834), i, p. 556.

14. John Dubordieu, *Statistical survey of the county of Down* (Dublin, 1802), p. 52; D. A. Beaufort, 'Materials for the Dublin Society agricultural survey of county Louth', Ed. C. C. Ellison in *Louth Arch. Soc. Jn.* xxviii (1975), p. 129.

15. David Grigg, *The dynamics of agricultural change* (London, 1982), p. 132.

16. Alan Gailey, 'Introduction and spread of the horse-powered threshing machine to Ulster's farms in the nineteenth century: some aspects' in *Ulster folklife,* xxx (1984), pp. 37-54.

17. *Belfast commercial chronicle,* 1st October 1806, p. 2.

18. J. Sproule (ed.), *The Irish industrial exhibition, 1853: a detailed catalogue of its contents* (Dublin, 1854), p. 214.

19. Grigg, *The dynamics of agricultural change,* p. 155.

20. Thomas Baldwin, *Introduction to practical farming* (23rd ed., Dublin, 1893), p. 177.

21. *The Irish farmer's gazette,* December 1863 (Dublin), xii, p. 483.

22. *The Irish farmer's gazette,* April 1864 (Dublin), xxii, p. 135.

23. *Purdon's practical farmer* (Dublin, 1863), pp. 198-199.

24. R. P. Wright (ed.), *The standard cyclopaedia of modern agriculture and rural economy* (London, 1908), xi, p. 112.

25. A. T. Lucas, 'Irish ploughing practices', part 4 in *Tools and tillage,* ii, no. 4 (1975), pp. 204-208; J. Bell, 'The use of oxen on Irish farms since the eighteenth century', in *Ulster Folklife,* xxix (1983), pp. 18-28.

26. Library of useful knowledge, *British husbandry* (London, 1834), i, p. 180.

27. A. E. [George Russell] (ed.), *The Irish homestead* (Dublin, 1917), pp. 189-190.

28. *British husbandry,* i, p. 179. J. C. Loudon, *An encyclopaedia of agriculture* (London, 1831), p. 782.

29. Mervyn Watson, 'Common Irish plough types and tillage techniques', *Tools and tillage,* v, no. 2 (1985), p. 85.

30. W. S. Mason, *A statistical account or parochial survey of Ireland* (Dublin, 1819), iii, p. 633.

31. Kenneth Connell, 'The colonisation of waste land in Ireland, 1780-1854' in *Econ. Hist. Rev.,* iii, no. 1. (1950), p. 54; Peter Solar, 'Agricultural productivity and economic development in Ireland and Scotland', p. 79.

32. *Devon comm. digest* (Dublin, 1847), i, p. 79.

33. Joseph Lambert, *Agricultural suggestions to the proprietors and peasantry of Ireland* (Dublin, 1845), p. 23.

34. J. Bell, 'A contribution to the study of cultivation ridges in Ireland' in R.S.A.I. Jn., cxiv (1984), pp. 80-97.

35. J. Bell, 'Sickles, hooks and scythes in Ireland' in *Folklife* xix (1981), pp. 26-35.

36. J. A. Perkins, 'Harvest technology and labour supply in Lincolnshire and the East Riding of Yorkshire', part 2 in *Tools and tillage,* iii, no. 2 (1977), p. 129.

37. W. Tighe, *Statistical survey of County Kilkenny* (Dublin, 1802), p. 184.

38. Thomas Hale, *A complete body of husbandry* (Dublin, 1757), ii, p. 91.

39. James Smith, *Remarks on thorough draining and deep ploughing* (Stirling, 1843).

40. *The farmer's friend* (London, 1847), p. 77.

41. *Devon comm. digest,* i, p. 100.

42. A. T. Lucas, 'Paring and burning in Ireland: a preliminary survey' in R. A. Gailey and A. Fenton (ed.), *The spade in northern and Atlantic Europe* (Belfast, 1970), p. 99.

43. Charles Coote, *Statistical survey of the County of Cavan* (Dublin, 1802), p. 114.

44. T. J. Rawson, *Statistical survey of the County of Kildare* (Dublin, 1807), p. 142.

45. *Devon comm. digest,* i, pp. 610-611.

46. Arthur Young, *A tour in Ireland,* i, p. 67.

47. Charles Coote, *Statistical survey of the County of Armagh* (Dublin, 1804), p. 240.

48. *Purdon's practical farmer,* pp. 114-115.

49. E. Evans, *Irish folkways* (London, 1957), p. 127.

50. J. Bell, 'Wooden ploughs from the mountains of Mourne, Ireland' in *Tools and tillage,* iv, no. 1 (1980), pp. 46-47.

51. W. Tighe, *Statistical survey of County Kilkenny,* p. 410.

52. W. L. Micks, *An account of the constitution, administration, and dissolution of the Congested Districts Board for Ireland from 1891 to 1923* (Dublin, 1925), p. 243.

53. Hely Dutton, *Statistical survey of the County of Clare* (Dublin, 1808), p. 37.

54. Anon., 'On agricultural schools' in *The Irish farmer's and gardener's magazine* (Dublin, 1835), ii, pp. 402-403.

55. Arthur Young, *A tour in Ireland* ii, p. 138.

56. A. T. Lucas, 'Irish ploughing practices, part two' in *Tools and tillage,* no. 2 (1973), pp. 72.79.

57. *Purdon's practical farmer,* pp. 1-2.

58. Grigg, *The dynamics of agricultural change,* p. 182.

Violence and order in the eighteenth century

S. J. CONNOLLY

Violence is an evocative word but hardly a precise one. It can refer to events as different in scale, aims and level of organisation as a scuffle between drinking companions and a full-scale rebellion against the forces of the state. Historians have nevertheless found the term useful. Changes in the frequency and circumstances of violence can reveal a great deal about a society's attitudes and values, the mechanisms of social control, the relationships between individuals and groups. This paper will look at three aspects of violence in eighteenth-century Ireland, each of which casts light on wider processes of change within that society.

I

The most spectacular, if not necessarily the most lethal, form of violence is that of individuals who set themselves entirely outside the law. Ireland at the beginning of the eighteenth century still included areas in which numbers of permanent outlaws supported themselves by robbery and extortion. The activities of these outlaws, called tories up to the 1690s and either tories or rapparees thereafter, have most commonly been interpreted in political terms. Tories first appeared in Ireland in the middle decades of the seventeenth century, the period of the Cromwellian confiscations, and they have generally been seen as representing a last ditch resistance on the part of displaced Catholic proprietors and tenants to a new social and political order.[1] Some of the best known of the early tories do in fact appear to have been displaced Catholic gentry of this type. Even in the Restoration period, however, the activities of some of those whom contemporaries labelled tories are difficult to reconcile with the idea of a predominantly political or religious motivation. In 1679, for example, the Anglican archbishop of Armagh assured the Earl of Orrery that all Catholics in Ireland had been disarmed, 'but such as are particularly licenced for the security of themselves and of their houses against the tories'. Nor was it only well-to-do Catholics who required such protection. The celebrated south Ulster tory Redmond O'Hanlon, killed in 1681, was said by a contemporary to have 'kept two or three counties almost waste, making the peasants pay continual contributions'. One of O'Hanlon's men, Shane Donnelly, was still active in County Tyrone in 1706, when he issued a proclamation explicitly calling on English, Scots and Irish alike to pay him protection money.[2] Such examples suggest that an analysis of toryism should look beyond the specific religious and political conflicts of mid-seventeenth-century Ireland to the different forms of banditry which existed in most other European states at this time and later. In particular it might draw on those interpretations which highlight the link between banditry and the development of the state.[3] Banditry, in the sense of the harassment of a settled society by outlaws living within its borders, arises at the point where central government aspires to maintain a uniform rule of law throughout its territory, but has not yet developed the resources to do so effectively. It is this gap between aspiration and effective power which means that men who indulge in plunder or private vengeance, or who resist the authority of the state, are forced to assume the role of permanent outlaws, but are not then prevented from making a career as bandits. In the case of Ireland the emergence of the tories in the 1650s and 1660s may thus be seen as a reflection, not just of land confiscations and extensive social disruption, but also of the extension to the country as a whole of a new and more rigorous definition of what types of behaviour put a man outside the law.

This is not to suggest that the tories of the late seventeenth and early eighteenth centuries did not benefit from the tolerance and active support of some of the inhabitants of the territories in which they operated. The tories of Cork and Kerry, it was claimed in the 1690s, had 'above 5,000 relations and friends within their ranges', and detailed lists were supplied of Catholic gentlemen and others alleged to have given them shelter and assistance.[4] Once again, however, this was by no means unique to

Ireland. Throughout Western Europe local populations at this time and earlier showed a willingness to condone or assist the activities of outlaws living in defiance of the central government, especially when encouraged to do so by ties of kinship or regional loyalty. In some cases bandits were also patronised by local landowners and men of influence. In the case of Ireland it is difficult to know to what extent the charges of harbouring tories levelled against Catholic gentlemen were based on anything more than guilt by association. More important, however, is the fact that it was not only Catholics who were alleged to find it prudent or profitable to come to some accommodation with local outlaws. Tories in County Kerry, the government was informed in November 1694, also operated under the shelter of protections and safe conducts given them by local magistrates. 'Some of these parties impudently own that it has cost them £50 to get these safeties . . .'⁵

Toryism had been a serious problem throughout the Restoration period. Accounts from different parts of the country between the 1660s and the 1680s spoke of groups of 50, 100 or more terrorising travellers and the settled population. Similar conditions continued into the 1690s. In 1693, for example, there were complaints concerning the depredations of 'rapparees' in the counties of Sligo and Mayo, particularly in the baronies of Leyny and Costello. In County Tipperary the following year it was reported that 'the rapparees . . . are now so numerous and well mounted and armed that it is extremely dangerous travelling for they are in several parties, sometimes 10, 20, 30 or more in a company. They also surround the fairs etc. and set upon persons going to or coming from them, so that trade or commerce in this county is almost totally damped . . .' In the same way a petition from County Limerick in 1696 complained of the thieves and rapparees that infested the area, and the lack of any protection against them. By the early years of the eighteenth century, however, there appear to have been only two areas in which tories remained active on any significant scale. In the south west, the authorities continued for another decade or so to be troubled by recurrent outbreaks of tory activity in the more remote parts. A visitor to Kerry reported in 1703 that the tories 'has been in this country and Cork for some time that there was no passing the road without a guard', but that seven or eight of their number had recently been executed and 'the rest will not hold out long'.⁷ In 1707 Captain Richard Hedges reported to Dublin Castle that he was once again engaged in what he described as 'the tory war'. Armed parties had been sent out after the tories, persons suspected of harbouring them had been imprisoned, and pardons and rewards were offered to those who brought in their accomplices, dead or alive. The tory leader, Dermot Bane O'Sullivan, had responded by personally beheading the foster father of a member of one of the parties sent to track him down. In 1711 Hedges reported that he had once again suppressed groups in Cork and Kerry, the third time, he claimed, that he had cleared the country of rapparees in six years.[8] In south Armagh and adjoining areas, the problem of tory activity continued even longer. The lords justices were informed in 1714 that bands of robbers, formerly eliminated through the application of severe laws, had recently re-appeared in Ulster. When William Nicholson, late bishop of Carlisle, travelled from Dublin to his new diocese of Derry in June 1718, the army commander at Ardee in County Louth was ordered to provide an escort of ten dragoons to protect him against 'several gangs of rapparees who have lately committed two or three barbarous murders'.[9] The presentments of the grand jury of County Louth confirm that the local authorities became increasingly concerned about tory activity from around 1716, and continued to be so up to the end of the 1720s.[10]

The first two or three decades of the eighteenth century, then, saw the final disappearance of toryism even in its last strongholds of the southwest and south Ulster. It is true that the authorities continued for some time longer to issue proclamations against what they described as tories and rapparees, but these, it seems clear, referred to what elsewhere would have been described simply as robbers and highwaymen. In some cases, it is true, the distinction is far from clear cut. Some of the robbers of the mid-eighteenth century operated in substantial bands, large enough to make them a formidable challenge to the authorities. A gang active in Kilkenny and neighbouring counties in 1738-9, for example, had over thirty members, and was confident enough to respond to the formation of an association of gentlemen for the purpose of tracking them down by luring their would-be captors into an ambush and killing four of their number.[11] Some of these later outlaws may also possibly have benefited from a measure of popular support, although it is difficult to know whether figures like William Crotty and James Freney enjoyed their status as folk heroes during their active careers, or only after they were safely dead or retired. In general, however, neither individual outlaws nor larger bands appear to have exercised anything like the territorial dominance which had made the tories so formidable, and their life expectancy was considerably shorter. The Kilkenny gang, for example, had been broken up by September 1740, some of its members being captured and others killed. The most spectacular examples of outlaw activity of this kind, furthermore, appear to have come mainly from the 1750s or earlier. Robbers and highwaymen continued to operate, in Ireland as elsewhere, in the second half of the eighteenth century, but neither residents nor visitors appear to have regarded them as having constituted a particularly serious hazard.[12]

A further feature of early eighteenth-century Ireland, linked to but not identical with the problem of toryism, was the existence of certain regions which were in effect outside the normal operations of the law. In the south west, the depredations of the tories were compounded by the almost total freedom from outside control enjoyed by local landlords and other men of power. In 1714 Captain Hedges complained that some 'heads of Irish clans' 'have gained the ascendant over the civil power by their insolence and number, so that the ordinary course of the laws cannot be put in force against them, without hazard of the lives of such as go about to do it'. The main object of complaint at this period was certain O'Donoghues in Glenflesk, aided by Francis Eager, a relative by marriage. Twenty years later the 'Glenfleskers' were still regarded as cattle thieves and general troublemakers.[13] In the 1720s, meanwhile, Daniel Mahony, a Catholic middleman claiming to pay a total of £1,500 per annum in rent to different head landlords, was alleged to have 'contrived a way to make himself great and dreadful in this county', by organising his tenants and dependents into a body, known as his 'fairesses', who roamed at night 'smocked and black in their faces', 'so that none dare to execute any judicial orders against the said Mahony's fairesses or himself'.[14] Nor was it only disgruntled Catholic gentlemen who flouted the laws in this way. Francis Eager, the associate of the O'Donoghues of Glenflesk, was a Protestant whose grandfather had fought in Ireland in the 1640s and 50s. In other cases, as already mentioned, magistrates in County Kerry were alleged to have given or sold protections and safe conducts to the tories of the county. A similar absorption of a Protestant gentleman into local networks of power and influence is suggested by the complaints made during the 1690s against Captain Robert Topham, also a magistrate and for a time joint agent for the extensive Shelburne estates. Thus when tenants in 1692 applied to Topham for redress against O'Sullivan Mór, who had seized their cattle for rents claimed under the short-lived Jacobite land settlement, 'he flew into a great passion and told these deponents that he would beat them and bid them all begone to the [Devil] for a company of churls, and told them he would not for forty pounds have the ill-will of O'Sullivan Mór upon account of such rascals'. In the same year he was alleged to have illegally awarded one Roger MacMurtogh money for rents arising during the Jacobite regime.[15]

The other area notorious for its lawlessness in this period was Iar Connacht, the area of west County Galway made up of the baronies of Moycullen and Ballynahinch, and the half barony of Ross. Samuel Molyneux, visiting County Galway in 1709, maintained that 'The sheriffs of this county scarce dare appear on the west side of Galway bridge, which, though Ireland is now generally esteemed wholly civilised, may well be called the end of the English pale'. Shortly afterwards, the district was the scene of the one great outbreak of agrarian protest seen in Ireland in the first half of the eighteenth century, the hougher movement of 1711-12. This was significant, not just as prefiguring the activities of the whiteboys and other agrarian secret societies in the later eighteenth century, but also because of the willingness of some local gentlemen, Protestant as well as Catholic, to connive in the houghers' campaign and to shield them from justice.[16] Perhaps the most eloquent testimony to the state of Iar Connacht in the first half of the eighteenth century, however, lies not in its contemporary reputation but in the fact that it did not, despite its isolation and the evident lack of effective government control, figure as a centre of tory activity in the late seventeenth and early eighteenth centuries. The paradox is only apparent. Bandits existed in the south west and in parts of south Ulster because there those persons who offered a certain type of challenge to the law placed themselves in the position of outlaws, living permanently outside the bounds of civil society, even if the authorities could not then readily deal with them. In Iar Connacht in the early eighteenth century, on the other hand, there was not as yet even a formal rule of law for men to step outside. Such conditions persisted up to the 1750s, when there was a further outbreak of agrarian protest, apparently directed against new tenants recently introduced on the St. George estates. To Edward Willes, chief baron of the Irish Exchequer, writing around 1759, Iar Connacht was still a district 'inhabited by the ancient Irish, who never yet have been made amenable to the laws. No sheriff goes there to execute any process'. However he went on to note the recent erection of a barracks in the region, with the result that 'I believe [it] now will soon be reduced to live under the obedience of the laws'.[17]

How significant were these problems of banditry and of the continued existence of areas of general lawlessness? Some aspects of Irish conditions in the first half of the eighteenth century undoubtedly offered a sharp contrast to contemporary England, where bandits had long ceased to exist and where even in physically remote areas the law had become firmly established as the medium through which disputes were settled and crimes avenged.[18] However, in this it was England that was the exception. Elsewhere in Western Europe there remained well into the eighteenth century large areas in which the law was enforced intermittently if at all, and banditry presented a common hazard. Even in England, furthermore, the disorders of early eighteenth-century Ireland had their parallels. The activities of the tories were hardly much more spectacular than those of the smugglers who throughout the 1740s and 50s operated along the coast of Kent and Sussex, in some cases fighting pitched battles with soldiers and revenue officers or taking over whole towns in order to rescue impounded goods or vessels.[19] If magistrates in the south west of Ireland patronised bandit gangs, this was no more than happened in the London of the 1720s, where both professional thief-takers and officially-appointed magistrates were closely involved in a highly organised criminal underworld.[20]

From this point of view, the continued existence of banditry and of a degree of lawlessness in some parts of Ireland at the beginning of the eighteenth century is perhaps less significant than the rapid reduction of those conditions in the years immediately following. By the 1750s, it appears, bandits proper had disappeared, robbers and highwaymen were no longer the threat they had been, and the last areas of resistance to the rule of law were about to be subdued. In part these developments reflected the successful extension of government control to all parts of its territory. The construction of military barracks in the south west, in County Armagh and finally even in Iar Connacht, expressed a new determination to maintain at least a minimum level of law and order in all areas. The decline of banditry and general lawlessness can also be seen as reflecting wider social changes: improved communications, the gradual erosion of local loyalties, the creation of new economic relationships dependent on a greater degree of centralised law enforcement. Such changes were taking place in many European states in the late seventeenth and early eighteenth centuries. In Ireland, however, less than a century separated the first appearance of the tories in the 1650s and 60s from the elimination of even lesser forms of banditry. Banditry, it was suggested earlier, reflects a transitional phase in the extension of a more uniform rule of law. If so that transition was, in the case of Ireland, an exceptionally short one.

II

A different aspect of early eighteenth-century Irish society, again inviting contrast with contemporary England, was the persistence of habits of violence among sections of the social elite. Here too it is necessary to retain perspective. This was an age in which gentlemen everywhere still wore swords as a badge of rank, and were expected to be ready, where necessary, to defend their honour in a duel. Irish gentlemen of the eighteenth century, however, were regarded by contemporaries as excessively and culpably prone to duelling. In at least some cases, furthermore, these duels were not the highly stylised encounters normally associated with the term, but murderous combats fought with a minimum of restrictions. A report from County Cork in 1733 described the settlement of a dispute about a greyhound:

> They entered the lists on horseback with sword and petronel, [One] having discharged his piece and missed . . . the other rode up to his breast but missed fire, whereupon he immediately dismounted and drew, as Newell did the like, and having made some sasas at each other, both received some slight wounds, but still the combat lasted, till at length one of Raymond's spurs got hold of his stockings, whereby he fell on his face to the ground, at which the other stabbed him through the back, and [he] not long after expired.[21]

On other occasions the conventions of the duel were dispensed with altogether. When a Catholic gentleman, Robert Martin, quarrelled with a Captain Southwell in a billiard room in Galway city in 1735, the latter left to collect his sword in order to settle the matter in the usual manner. While he was away, however, a bystander, Lieutenant Jolly, made a derisive comment, at which Martin stabbed and slashed him seven times, inflicting at least four mortal wounds.[22] A similar fate befell a Lieutenant Hume who three years later became involved in a dispute with five local gentlemen in a public house in Roscrea. Evidence later collected showed that the unarmed Hume had been pursued from room to room of the house by all five attackers, sustaining a total of 16 or 17 wounds before his death. The killers then fought a pitched battle with some soldiers who had come belatedly to Hume's aid before making their escape.[23] The same disposition to resort quickly to major violence was seen in other cases. In 1737, for example, George Manly, supervising distraint of goods for rents owed him on lands in County Wicklow, levelled a gun at a tenant who resisted his bailiff. A bystander, a relative of Manly's, protested, at which Manly promptly shot

him in the chest: 'his gun being loaded with slugs, his livers came out'.[24] In
1744 a gentleman who got into a dispute with a ballad singer on a Dublin
street ran him through and wounded another man before making off.[25]

The significance of episodes like the killing of Hume and Jolly lies not just
in the disposition to violence they reveal, but also in the tolerance with which
such behaviour was regarded. Action against the five men who had killed
Hume was obstructed by the coroner and local magistrates, who delayed
sending the relevant papers to Dublin, while a key witness was spirited away
the morning of the inquest. Since Hume had been the nephew of an
influential English peer, the Dublin administration, urged on by Walpole
and Newcastle, took a special interest in the case. Despite this, however,
none of the five accused men were apprehended. In the case of Martin, the
lords justices complained that the sheriffs drew up a panel of potential
jurors 'consisting chiefly of relations of the prisoner, papists, or such protestants as were either actually confined to their houses by sickness, or
absent from the kingdom'.[26] In an attempt to undermine local solidarity,
the government transferred the location of the trial from Galway to
Dublin, but the jury nevertheless brought in a verdict of manslaughter
in self defence. A similar tolerance existed in other cases. The Rev.
Samuel Madden, writing in 1738, complained of the 'dreadful
indulgence' shown towards those who killed others in duels, so that 'in
general it is safer to kill a man than steal a sheep or a cow'.[27]

A ready and even casual resort to violence was matched by a willingness
to offer open defiance to the law. In County Waterford in 1713 a gentleman
and his servant not only rescued a horse that had been pressed to carry
soldiers' baggage, but beat up the soldier and the constable who had taken
it.[28] In 1737 Archbishop Boulter of Armagh complained of the general
disposition to insult and demand satisfaction from magistrates whose
execution of their duty caused offence.[29] When the high sheriff of County
Antrim attempted in 1729 to put the Bishop of Down and Connor in possession of lands which the latter had purchased near Portglenone, he was
resisted by relatives of the former owner, who believed that the lands had
been sold too cheaply. Aided by 'about fifty distracted country people',
they drove the sheriff and his party away with gunfire, and remained in
possession of a fortress on the estate until troops and cannon were provided
to dislodge them.[30] The most common form of lawlessness on the part of
gentlemen, however, was the practice of abduction, and here too there were
repeated examples of a general unwillingness to enforce the law against
well-born offenders. In one striking case in 1712 a Mrs. Russell was
abducted by the brother of the sheriff of County Galway, assisted by the

WARRANTY ADMINISTRATION
PO BOX 4970
CLEVELAND, TN 37320-4970

Printed in Korea

IMPORTANT POUR L'ACHETEUR

Retournez par la poste cette carte OU la version anglaise. N'envoyez **PAS** les deux.

PIÈCE NO 110844-1

IL EST IMPORTANT DE REMPLIR ET RETOURNER RAPIDEMENT CETTE CARTE AFIN DE NOUS PERMETTRE DE COMMUNIQUER AVEC VOUS DANS L'ÉVENTUALITÉ PEU PORTABLE D'UNE MODIFICATION DE SÉCURITÉ QUI SERAIT REQUISE PAR LA LOI CANADIENNE.

Assurez-vous que les numéros de modèle et de série sont identifiés ci-dessous et inscrivez la date d'installation. Les numéros de modèle et de série se trouvent à l'intérieur du compartiment des produits frais.

Modèle

Numéro de série

8 Chiffres

2 Lettres

Date d'installation

Mois   Jour   Année

☐ M.   ☐ Mme.
☐ Mlle

NUMÉRO DE
TÉLÉPHONE:

ADRESSE

VILLE _____ ÉTAT OU _____ CODE
                        PROVINCE   POSTAL

(AC)

NOM DE VOTRE VENDEUR/DISTRIBUTOR

VILLE _____ ÉTAT OU _____ CODE
                        PROVINCE   POSTAL

sheriff's clerk and by several of his dependents, and apparently with some co-operation from the sheriff himself.[31]

Habits of violence and a casual attitude to the finer points of law were not of course characteristic of all Irish gentlemen. At their upper levels, English and Irish landed society were closely intertwined, sharing the same outlook, culture and manners. It was lower down the scale of property and status that the two worlds diverged. Thus the killers of Lieutenant Hume were described by one of his fellow officers as 'men of good circumstances and reputed gentlemen (as gentlemen go in this part of the world)'.[32] The aside recalls Arthur Young's famous tirade, thirty years later, against 'the class of little country gentlemen; tenants, who drink their claret by means of profit rents; jobbers in farms; bucks; your fellows with round hats, edged with gold, who hunt in the day, get drunk in the evening, and fight the next morning . . . these are the men among whom drinking, wrangling, quarrelling, fighting, ravishing etc etc are found as in their native soil'.[33] The reasons for the persistence of a degree of violence and general lawlessness among this section of the Irish gentry are obvious enough. Even in England in the early and mid-eighteenth century, the gap between the attitudes and manners of polite society and those of the lesser country gentry – seen for example in Henry Fielding's portrayal of the coarse and drunken Squire Western in 1749 – remained a substantial one. In Ireland, economically underdeveloped, and even further removed from the centres of fashion and decorum than the most remote parts of rural England, the gap was inevitably greater still. It was widened even further by the truncated nature of the social structure over much of rural Ireland, where the permanent or recurrent absenteeism of larger proprietors left minor squires at the head of local society, unchecked by example or influence from above. Lesser Irish gentlemen were not so far removed from English ways as their counterparts in colonial Virginia, where it was only in the late eighteenth century that the formal duel replaced wrestling, punching and gouging as the normal means of settling disputes even between gentlemen.[34] They nevertheless appeared to their English contemporaries as a disorderly and sometimes dangerous group.

By the second half of the eighteenth century, however, the manners of even the lower levels of the Irish gentry showed signs of having radically altered. To some extent this may have been due to a diminishing tolerance on the part of government for excesses committed by gentlemen. In the 1730s, for example, the lords justices showed a clear determination to counteract intervention by influential persons on behalf of well-born offenders.[35] A similar toughening of attitude, although in this case taking

place only in the later eighteenth century, may be seen in the case of abduc-
tions.[36] The main reason for changing manners, however, lay in the rapid
expansion of the Irish economy in the mid and late eighteenth century,
and the resulting increase in landlord wealth. According to one estimate
rents, which has already been rising in the 1710s and 20s, doubled
between 1747 and 1770, and doubled again by 1813.[37] This growth in
landlord wealth was reflected in the construction of new town and country
houses, the growth of luxury imports, a quickening of intellectual and
cultural life and, in addition, a trend towards more refined manners. The
fifth Earl of Orrery had been intermittently resident in Ireland since the
early 1730s, and had been a bitter critic of the coarse, heavy drinking and
deeply parochial society in which he found himself. By 1747, however,
he could write in a more positive mood:

> I have known this kingdom fifteen years. More improvements than I
> have visibly observed of all kinds could not have been effected in that
> space of time. Duels are at an end. Politeness is making some progress.
> Literature is close behind her. Industry must follow. As popery
> decreases, cleanliness and honesty will find place.[38]

Orrery exaggerated. Duels were certainly not at an end, any more than
popery was in decline. Instead visitors to Ireland in the later eighteenth century continued to complain that affairs of honour were excessively common. Yet a marked change had nevertheless taken place. Young, writing in
1779, reported that duelling 'is yet far more common among people of
fashion than in England', but that the practice had declined. In the same
way Lord Charlemont, ten years later, observed that duelling, though 'still
too fashionable', was 'thanks to the increasing polish of our manners, less
practised than formerly'.[39]

III

So far we have been concerned with the violence of minorities, of permanent outlaws and of rougher elements among the gentry. What of the
remainder of the population? Analysis of popular violence in eighteenth-
century Ireland has proceeded rather unevenly, so that some areas have by
now received considerable attention, while others remain largely unex-
amined. At the same time it is possible to offer a brief overall classification of
the main forms such violence took.

Probably the most important form of popular collective action involving
violence or the threat of violence, and certainly the one which to date has

received most systematic study, was agrarian protest.[40] The first point to emerge from that study is that such protest was not, as has sometimes been imagined, a permanent feature of rural social relations. The period between 1691 and 1761 saw only one major outbreak of agrarian disorder, the hougher movement of 1711-12. Between 1761 and 1790 there were disturbances in parts of Ulster in 1763 and in 1769-72, and in parts of Munster and Leinster in 1761-76 and 1785-8. The outbreaks were linked in each case to major shifts in agricultural circumstances, most commonly a deterioration in market conditions. A total of 22 out of Ireland's 32 counties were affected to some extent by the different disturbances of the period 1761-90, but only three, Tipperary, Waterford and Kilkenny, were seriously affected in each of the three decades. Protest, furthermore, was in all cases defensive in character, arising in response to changes in existing patterns of land use or economic relationships, and seeking to preserve what were seen as existing rights within the agrarian system. The methods used to pursue these limited aims were correspondingly restrained. The houghers of 1711-12 destroyed large numbers of cattle and sheep, but did not systematically attack either persons or other forms of property. The agrarian campaigns of the 1760s, 1770s and 1780s involved more serious violence: individuals who had offended against the code of behaviour laid down by agrarian societies were beaten, mutilated or otherwise maltreated. In many cases, however, these punishments were conducted with a degree of ceremonial which suggests that the aim was as much to dramatise public rejection of the offender as to instil terror. In most cases, moreover, violence stopped well short of homicide. No one was killed by the Whiteboys of the 1760s. In the much more widespread protests of 1765-8 there were six deaths, of which three were unpremeditated and a fourth appears to have been in pursuit of a private quarrel. Altogether, it has been suggested, the total number of deaths attributable to agrarian protest in the period 1761-90 was probably no more than fifty.[41]

Urban protest has so far attracted far less attention than its rural equivalent. At the same time it seems safe to suggest that the pattern was in most cases broadly similar: a defence of what were seen as existing rights, backed by a controlled and discriminating use of violence. Thus a characteristic form of urban protest, in Ireland as in England and elsewhere, was the food riot, in which consumers reacted to shortages and high prices by disciplined collective action against what were seen as unacceptable practices: overcharging, the creation of artificial shortages as dealers held back stocks in expectation of higher prices, and the transport of provisions out of the area while local demand remained unsatified. Crowds who broke into corn warehouses in Cork and Limerick in the famine year of 1729, for example, did not simply loot, but sold the contents at what was regarded as a fair price. In Dublin, similarly, a crowd took over potato barges moored at Aston Quay 'and sold the roots there for 3d per peck, which was half price'. In Kilkenny, in 1766, the inhabitants went to the houses of farmers and mealmen and carried any oatmeal they found there to the weighing house for immediate sale.[42] Other types of collective action reflected a similar consciousness of enforcing generally accepted rules of behaviour. In Dublin in the 1720s, for example, parties of apprentices went at intervals to workshops connected with their trade, taking up employees from outside the city 'and colting them out of town, that is making them ride on a long pole carried on men's shoulders through the city, having often music going before them'.[43] The element of public ceremonial did not mean that the custom was not a violent one. The apprentices responsible went about their business armed with clubs, and the custom came to public notice in 1728 when a perukemaker's servant died of the effects of having been colted. At the same time it seems clear that what was involved here, as in many of the proceedings of the Whiteboys and other agrarian societies, was not random violence, but a ritual of popular justice.

To the violence of explicit popular protest may be added the violence arising from resistance to unpopular laws, or to what was regarded as the illegitimate intrusion of the authorities into private concerns. This was the case, for example, with the many violent clashes which occurred when revenue officers seized smuggled goods, or the apparatus and output of unlicensed distillers. In the same way, violent confrontations between the authorities and persons engaged in taking away goods from wrecked vessels may have represented, not simple disregard for law, but the continuance of a long standing belief that such goods were common property.[44] Not all examples of popular resistance to law, however, can be explained in these simple terms. In some cases urban populations showed an apparent disposition to come together in resistance to all laws, or at least to the agencies which enforced them. In 1733, for example, soldiers conveying John Shuite, a local butcher with a criminal reputation, to jail on a charge of assault, were attacked by a crowd of several hundred, who continued to obstruct them until two of their number were shot. In Dublin the following year a city constable named Paul Farrell was seized while conveying prisoners to jail and his mangled body hung from a tree in the Liberties of the city, where it remained for several hours before the authorities could remove it. The motive for this demonstration of popular hatred remains unclear, but Farrell's nickname, 'Gallows Paul', suggests that his performance of his duties must in some way have marked him out as a target for vengeance.[45]

The need to understand popular disorders as forms of social protest, governed by their own conventions, is by now a familiar theme in studies of eighteenth-century European societies. Almost equally familiar is the theme of licensed aggression, and of what might be termed the recreational uses of violence. The faction fights which were a common feature of rural Irish life in the eighteenth and early nineteenth centuries have been the subject of much puzzled comment. Yet they were little different from the regular violent encounters between the young men of adjacent villages seen in rural France at the same period, or the almost equally violent football matches and similar contests which enlivened holidays and festivals in rural England.[46] In each case, it seems clear, such encounters met a social need. Tensions, frustrations and surplus energies were given a recognised outlet in forms of violence which could be tolerated so long as they remained within their clearly defined limits. The faction fights of the countryside had their urban equivalents in longstanding feuds between rival groups. In Dublin in the later eighteenth century, for example, there was regular fighting between the butchers of the Ormonde market and the weavers of the Liberties.[47] The less predictable but still frequent brawling which took place at social gatherings may be seen in the same light, not as an aberration but as an integral part of such occasions. In a poor society, fair days, patterns, holy days, weddings, funerals and other festivals offered intermittent relief from a daily routine that provided little scope for entertainment or sociability. It was this role as the occasional outlet for long pent-up energies which gave them their unrestrained and often violent character.

Recreational violence did not always take the form of simple brawling. In some cases, as in other European societies, aggression was directed towards animals rather than human beings. Bull-baiting, cock-fighting and other blood sports were well established, at least in the towns. In other cases, displays of aggression were given ritual form. In 1735, for example, Lord Orrery complained of the long-standing custom whereby the lower orders of Cork city, on the day a new Mayor was elected, claimed the right to pelt passers-by with a mixture of meal and flour, 'which they throw into harmless people's eyes as plentifully as beggars at Paris bestow holy water in churches'. In this case, what was involved was not generalised aggression, but a more specific claim to harrass social superiors with impunity. 'The higher your rank', Orrery noted, 'the greater the quantity of meal, so that if his sacred Majesty was to walk on this day from North-Gate to South-Gate in his black velvet coat, his black cravat and his black feather, he would only fulfil the Merlinian prophecy of the White King'.[48]

Institutionalised displays of aggression of this kind were tolerated by those at whom they were directed as part of the price which the privileged classes of eighteenth-century Europe were prepared to pay for the acceptance on all other occasions of a deeply unequal social order. In other cases, popular violence was actively encouraged by social superiors. The Dublin crowds who smashed the windows of houses not illuminated to celebrate the Peace of Utrecht in June 1713 did so in the knowledge that their action would be condoned and even applauded by the ruling Tory party. In the same way the crowd which invaded the parliament house in 1759 to protest against proposals for an Anglo-Irish union presumably knew that they could count on at least the passive sympathy of many of their betters.[49] (To what extent those involved in either case really cared about the issues involved, and to what extent they merely seized the opportunity to rough up their betters with relative impunity, is another matter.) Contested elections provided numerous further instances of popular violence sanctioned by social superiors. Other forms of urban riot – for example, against the importers of foreign goods, or against forestallers or bakers of bad bread – may also have been encouraged by the knowledge that they would be viewed with a degree of sympathy.

Popular violence in eighteenth-century Ireland, then, shared many characteristics with what took place in other parts of Europe. Thus, the frequent appearance of violence at social gatherings was closely tied up with the character of popular festivals and holidays as brief, intense periods of release from a frugal and demanding routine. In other cases, popular violence had the sanction of social superiors, either implicitly, as in the case of occasions of licensed aggression, or explicitly, as in political riots. Even where violence formed part of open social conflict, it was in general employed with discrimination, within a framework of clearly understood conventions. It was only in the 1790s, as an international crisis radiating outwards from revolutionary France reacted fatally on the deep divisions within Irish society itself, that this traditional restraint was abandoned, both by those involved in movements of social protest and by the forces engaged in their suppression.[50]

All of these points relate only to one form of popular violence, that arising out of different types of collective action. Clearly it would be dangerous to move directly to conclusions concerning the overall level of violence within eighteenth-century Irish society. For that one would also need to take account, for example, of the use of violence in association with crime, in the settlement of personal disputes, in relationships within the family. Ideally one would look at statistical evidence on the incidence of different types of violent action, which could then be set against similar material from other societies of the same period, an exercise which the virtually complete destruction of central and local records of legal administration in eighteenth-century Ireland makes impossible. At the same time, two points may be made. First the relatively restrained use of violence in connection with popular protest, even in cases where major conflicts of interest were involved, does not suggest a society in which men resorted casually to homicide or the infliction of serious injury. Secondly, there is the limited statistical evidence provided by the Crown book at the Cork assizes of 1789, apparently the only record of its kind to have survived from this period. Of 82 cases heard at the spring assizes in 1789, for example, 5 were Whiteboy offences, 22 involved assault and a further 9 robbery with assault. Not all of this last group necessarily involved serious violence: one case, for example, concerned a man attacked and robbed by three women. The remaining 46 cases, mostly of either pickpocketing or theft from houses, involved no violence at all. The assaults, furthermore, included only three cases of homicide, one of them a man convicted of manslaughter after striking his wife on the face with his hand and accidentally killing her.[51] Nor does 1789 appear to have been an unusual year in this respect. Statistics printed by Thomas Newenham in 1807 showed that over the preceding forty years a total of 32 persons had been executed for murder in County Cork and a further three transported.[52] Even if only a proportion of crimes of violence came before the courts, such figures once again hardly suggest a chronically violent society.

IV

What, finally, does all this have to do with the wider issue of modernisation? Charles Tilly, in a well-known essay, has classified the main forms of collective violence in Western Europe between the seventeenth and the twentieth centuries into three broad categories. The first of these, 'primitive violence', was communally based and in most cases small-scale and localised. More important, it was not linked to shifts in the balance of power and advantage within a society, but instead was the product of stable social and political relationships. 'Reactionary' violence, by contrast, was also communally based, but arose out of the pressures of social change, in particular out of opposition to the growing demands of the national economy and the national state. 'Modern' collective violence, finally, is based on specialist as opposed to communal associations, and seeks to promote rather than to resist change. The teleological nature of the terminology is unfortunate, but the categories nevertheless highlight important changes in the nature of collective violence. Primitive violence, for example feuds between families, neighbourhoods or occupational groups, declined from the seventeenth century onwards, and had disappeared almost entirely by the early twentieth century. Reactionary violence – food riots, protests against taxation and conscription, machine breaking, forcible occupations of land – was the dominant form of social protest up to the early nineteenth century, but then gave way to what Tilly has classified as 'modern' forms, the timing of the transition varying from state to state. In England it was largely completed by the 1830s, in France by the 1860s, in southern Italy not until the early twentieth century.[53]

Such an outline, however schematic, permits conditions in Ireland during the eighteenth century and after to be put into a wider perspective. All three of the forms of collective violence described by Tilly existed in eighteenth-century Ireland, and it is also possible to detect a clear pattern of change over time. Thus one major development was the decline of what Tilly would categorise as 'primitive' violence: that is, violence as a way of life, unconnected with major social changes. Banditry was eliminated during the first decades of the eighteenth century, and lawless behaviour among sections of the gentry declined over the same period. Popular primitive violence, in the form of faction fighting, continued longer, but by the 1830s it too had gone into rapid decline and feuds between rival urban groups also disappeared at the same time or earlier. 'Reactionary' violence, localised, communally based, defensive in its aims, also remained common throughout the eighteenth century and intensified, in the countryside at least, as the pace of economic change quickened from mid-century onwards. Collective action of this kind was to disappear only very gradually, dying out in some areas only in the early twentieth century.[54] At the same time the appearance in the 1790s of the Defenders and the United Irishmen seems to mark the clear beginnings of a 'modern' pattern of collective violence, going beyond merely defensive aims and associational rather than communal in its organisational basis.[55] A similar development may be seen in the case of urban protest, with the emergence by the early nineteenth century of more sophisticated forms of trade union organisation.[56]

If the changing forms of violence in Ireland in the eighteenth century and after fall easily into a European pattern, the same may be said of the scale of that violence. For most of the eighteenth century Ireland does not appear to have been by contemporary standards a particularly violent society. In the 1790s, it is true, social, political and religious conflict became increasingly unrestrained, culminating in localised but bloody civil war. This, however, was part of a crisis affecting the whole of Europe. Outside that single decade, the violent element in Irish social and political conflict proves strangely elusive. Between 1881 and 1889, the period of the 'Land War', for example, a total of 43 agrarian murders were recorded, 17 of them in one year 1881.[57] Instances of armed rebellion, in 1848 and 1867, owe their prominence in the historical record less to their scale than to the later endorsement of a victorious nationalism. The years 1916-22, of course, saw more real violence, but even then Ireland's experience hardly appears exceptional in comparison with, for example, Germany or Italy during the 1920s and 30s. Violence, as Tilly has emphasised, is an integral part of the political history of modern Europe. The stress commonly placed on its supposedly exceptional role in Ireland can be attributed partly to Ireland's proximity to an unusually peaceful polity, Great Britain, and partly, perhaps, to the anxieties created by current events in Northern Ireland. Irish historians can still learn a great deal from the study of violence. For most of the time, however, and certainly where the eighteenth century is concerned, their subject is likely to prove less important in itself than for the way in which wider processes of social development may be traced through its changing forms.

NOTES

1. For example, R. Quinn Duffy, 'Redmond O'Hanlon and the outlaws of Ulster', *History Today,* xxxii (1982). The only modern discussion of tories in the early eighteenth century is some tantalisingly brief remarks by L. M. Cullen, 'The social and cultural modernisation of rural Ireland, 1600-1900' in L. M. Cullen and F. Furet (eds), *Ireland and France* (Paris, 1980), pp. 205-6.

2. Michael Boyle to Orrery, 18 March 1679 (P.R.O.I. Wyche Papers 1/1/30); T. W. Moody, 'Redmond O'Hanlon', *Proceedings of the Belfast Natural, Historical and Philosophical Society,* I (1937); W. R. Hutchinson, *Tyrone precinct* (Belfast, 1951), p. 79.

3. For an enlightening recent discussion see B. D. Shaw, 'Bandits in the Roman empire', *Past & Present,* 105 (1984).

4. 'Proposals for reducing the tories' (P.R.O.I. Wyche Papers, 2/120); Charles Monck to ——, 16 June 1694 (Ibid. 2/124).

5. 'Mr. Barton', 3 Nov. 1694 (Ibid. 2/125).

6. Percy Gethin to Kean O'Hara, 27 Aug. 1693 (P.R.O.N.I. T2812/4/82A); Richard Aldworth to O'Hara, 5 Sept. 1693, 7 Oct. 1693 (T2812/4/84, 89); *C.S.P.D. 1696,* p. 10.

7. Sir John Peyton to O'Hara, 20 March 1703 (P.R.O.N.I. T2812/5/76).

8. Hedges to Joshua Dawson, 15 July 1707 (P.R.O.I. M757); Hedges to Thomas Browne, 26 Feb. 1711 (Ibid.); Hedges to ——, 22 April 1711 (Ibid.).

9. William King, archbp. of Dublin, to Sunderland, 31 Dec. 1714 (T.C.D. Ms 750/4/2, p. 27); Nicholson to William Wake, 17 June 1718 (Dublin City Library, Pearse St., Gilbert Mss, no. 27, pp. 176-7).

10. N.L.I. Ms 11, 949.

11. *Dublin Gazette,* 16-19 Dec. 1738, 13-16 Jan. 1739. (For these and other references to contemporary newspapers I am indebted to Mr Graeme Kirkham.) See also *Puleston Mss* (H.M.C. 1898), pp. 321-2.

12. For a brief account of eighteenth-century robbers and highwaymen see Constantia Maxwell, *Country and town in Ireland under the Georges* (Dundalk, 1949), pp. 286-91.

13. M. A. Hickson, *Selections from old Kerry records* (series 2, London, 1874), pp. 143-4; Edward McLysaght (ed.), *The Kenmare Manuscripts* (I.M.C. 1942), pp. 45, 48.

14. Hickson, *Kerry records,* pp. 157-63.

15. Ibid., pp. 119-22.

16. A. Smith (ed.), 'Journey to Connaught – April 1709', *Miscellany of the Irish Society,* I (1846), 171. S. J. Connolly, 'The houghers: agrarian protest in early eighteenth-century Connacht', in T. H. Aston and C. H. E. Philpin (eds), *Nationalism and popular protest in Ireland* (forthcoming).

17. Edward Willes to Earl of Warwick, c. 1759 (P.R.O.N.I. Mic 148, pp. 16-17).

18. Alan MacFarlane, *The justice and the mare's ale: law and disorder in seventeenth-century England* (Oxford, 1981).

19. Cal Winslow, 'Sussex smugglers', in Douglas Hay et al. *Albion's fatal tree* (London, 1975).

20. Gerald Howson, *Thief-taker general: the rise and fall of Jonathan Wilde* (London, 1970).

21. *H. M. C. Puleston Mss,* p. 314. In this case, admittedly, one of the participants was the son of a gamekeeper. For another duel, involving Henry St. Laurence and Hamilton Georges, brother to Lord Howth, which was in reality an impromptu shoot-out, see Ibid., p. 312. The letter, however, should be dated 1737 – see *Dublin Gazette,* 4-8 Jan. 1737.

22. Lords Justices to Duke of Dorset, 12 May 1735 (P.R.O.N.I. D2707/A/1/7, pp. 28-9); *Dublin Gazette,* 6-10 May 1735.

23. *H. M. C. Polwarth Mss,* V (1961), pp. 152-8.

24. *Dublin Newsletter,* 25-28 June 1737.

25. *Faulkner's Dublin Journal,* 6-9 Oct. 1744.

26. Lords Justices to Dorset, 12 May 1735 (P.R.O.N.I. D2707/A/1/7, pp. 28-9).

27. [Samuel Madden], *Reflections and resolutions proper for the gentlemen of Ireland* (Dublin, 1738), pp. 151-2.

28. Dawson to Mr. Bagg, 2 April 1713 (Bodl. Ms Eng. Hist. b 125 (31, 758), f. 63v).

29. Boulter to Devonshire, 7 June 1737 *(Letters written by his excellency Hugh Boulter . . . to several ministers of state and some others* (2 vols., Oxford, 1769-70), II, 228). The case to which Boulter referred, involving a recent convert from Catholicism, had strong sectarian overtones. But he noted specifically that such behaviour was too common among Catholics and Protestants alike.

30. *Dublin Intelligence,* 4, 11 Oct. 1729; 'Calendar of Church Miscellaneous Papers, 1652-1795', in P.R.O.I. *58th Report of the Deputy Keeper* (1951), 83.

31. Dawson to sheriff of Galway, 26 Jan. 1711[12] (Bodl. Ms Eng. Hist. b 125 (31, 758), f. 16v).

32. *H. M. C. Polwarth Mss,* V, 153.

33. Arthur Young, *A tour in Ireland* (2 vols., London, 1892), ii, 154-5.

34. Rhys Isaac, *The transformation of Virginia* (Chapel Hill, 1982), pp. 94-8, 319, 322.

35. Boulter to Carteret, 11 June 1730 (*Letters,* II, 19); Lords Justices to Dorset, 25 April 1735 (P.R.O.N.I. D2707/A/1/7, p. 26); Lords Justices to Devonshire, 23 May 1736 (D2707/A/1/8, pp. 8-9).

36. L. M. Cullen, *The emergence of modern Ireland, 1600-1900* (London, 1981), pp. 245-8.

37. Ibid., pp. 43-4.

38. *The Orrery papers,* Countess of Cork and Orrery ed. (2 vols., London, 1903), I, 320-1.

39. Young, *Tour,* II, 152-3; *H.M.C.* Report 12, App. X, *Charlemont Mss* (1891), 108fn.

40. See Connolly, 'The houghers'; J. S. Donnelly, 'The Whiteboy movement 1761-5', *Irish Historical Studies,* xxi, 81 (1978); Idem., 'Irish agrarian rebellion: the Whiteboys of 1769-76', *R.I.A. Proc.* lxxxiii, C, 12 (1983); Idem., 'Hearts of Oak, Hearts of Steel', *Studia Hib.,* 21 (1981); Idem., 'The Rightboy Movement, 1785-8', *Studia Hib.,* 17/18 (1977-8).

41. T. Bartlett, 'An end to moral economy: the Irish militia disturbances of 1793', *Past & Present,* 99 (1983).

42. Boulter, *Letters,* I, 285, 287-8; *Dublin Intelligence,* 18 March 1728/9; William Colles to Barry Colles, 14 June 1766 (P.R.O.I. Prim Mss, no. 87, pp. 71-5).

43. *American Weekly Mercury,* 21-28 Nov. 1728.

44. J. G. Rule, 'Wrecking and coastal plunder' in Hay *et al. Albion's fatal tree.*

45. *Faulkner's Dublin Journal,* 1-5 Jan. 1733/4; *Dublin Gazette,* 20-24 Aug. 1734.

46. Olwen Hufton, *The poor of eighteenth-century France* (Oxford, 1974), pp. 360-4; R. W. Malcolmson, *Popular recreation in English society, 1700-1850* (Cambridge, 1973).

47. W. J. Fitzpatrick, *The sham squire and the informers of 1798* (3rd ed. London, 1866), pp. 70-71.

48. *Orrery Papers,* I, 137-8.

49. Margaret Dean to Henry Boyle, 23 Jan. 1713 (P.R.O.N.I. D2707/A/1/2/1B); F. G. James, *Ireland in the empire, 1688-1770* (Cambridge, Mass., 1973), pp. 260-1.

50. Bartlett, 'An end to moral economy'.

51. P.R.O.I. Crown and Peace Records, Co. Cork. A more complete analysis of this document is at present in progress.

52. Edward Newenham, *A view of the natural, political and commercial circumstances of Ireland* (London, 1809), appendix, pp. 43-8.

53. Charles Tilly, 'Collective violence in European perspective', in H. D. Graham and T. R. Gurr (eds), *Violence in America: historical and comparative perspectives* (rev. ed., London, 1979).

54. For early twentieth-century agrarian conflict see Samuel Clark and J. S. Donnelly (eds), *Irish peasants: Violence and political unrest 1780-1914* (Manchester, 1983), 281-3, 374-417.

55. Marianne Elliott, 'The origins and transformation of early Irish republicanism', *International Review of Social History,* xxiii (1978); Tom Garvin, 'Defenders, Ribbonmen and others', *Past & Present,* 96 (1982).

56. F. A. D'Arcy, 'The trade unions of Dublin and the attempted revival of the guilds', *J.R.S.A.I., ci (1971).*

57. Charles Townshend, *Political violence in Ireland: Government and resistance since 1848* (Oxford, 1983), p. 195.

The religious factor in the 1798 rebellion in county Wexford

KEVIN WHELAN

The 1798 rebellion in County Wexford remains a fascinating but elusive enigma. One of the central elements in the tangled web of circumstances which forced the county into a bloody civil war was that of religion. Modern commentators have tended to shun this factor, although contemporary commentators stressed it above all others in their efforts to explain the causes of the rebellion. An assessment of the local religious context in the light of more recent research re-establishes the importance of the religious argument.

The density of the eighteenth-century Protestant presence in the north of the county is central to the Wexford experience, especially in the baronies of Scarawalsh and Gorey, the storm centres of the rebellion, focusing on a quadrangle between Enniscorthy, Bunclody, Arklow and Kilmuckridge.[1] This colony owed its initial existence to the north Wexford plantation of the 1620s and subsequent immigration and internal migration. We still await a detailed socio-economic study of this plantation and its effects. Unlike their precarious position in many other southern communities, the Protestants of Wexford were strongly established in the countryside in both the farming and labouring classes. The towns of Enniscorthy and Gorey had sizeable concentrations. The smaller villages (Camolin, Clogh, Ballycanew) had almost exclusively Protestant populations. In the countryside, the strong farmers formed a

vigorous endogamous community. A 1776 census of the parishes of
Ferns, Clone and Kilbride allows us to look in some detail at the structure of this community.[2] In all, there were 1,113 Protestants in the three
parishes, comprising a total of 216 families. These were strongly concentrated in the villages of Ferns and Ballycarney and there were also dense
nodes of Protestant settlement in adjacent townlands (Fig. 4:1). Embedded
in this matrix were 'Catholic' townlands, for example, Effernogue and
Corah. This pattern of alternating townlands appears to have been
typical of all north Wexford, to judge from surviving eighteenth-century
records. The immediate vicinity of the Gorey-Enniscorthy axis had the
strongest Protestant presence: Catholics appear to have retained a
footing in the hill country along the Wicklow border to the north and to
the south in the confused morainic country in the Kilmuckridge/
Blackwater area.

A survey for the Portsmouth estate (centred on Enniscorthy) reveals
the socio-economic structure of this Protestant core area in more detail.[3]
In 1785, Protestant families enjoyed a marked advantage over their
Catholic neighbours. In the town, the large, high-value slated houses of
the Market Square/Church Street area were occupied almost exclusively
by Protestants. John Devereux and Patrick Sutton were the exceptions.
In 1798, Patrick Sutton and his son Mathew were to play a leading role
in the Enniscorthy area. The Catholics of Enniscorthy were still huddled
in Irish Street in small thatched cabins, or lined up in the cabin suburbs
of Templeshannon which fringed Vinegar Hill, or in the straggling lanes
leading down to the Slaney from the town centre. A decrepit thatched
chapel at the foot of Irish Street symbolised their lowly status. In the
rural areas of the estate, Protestant middlemen leased townland units on
advantageous long leases and derived substantial profit rents from sub-
letting. They lived in large, imposing houses, set in orchards and trees
and obviously aspired to gentry status. Such were the Reverend Philip
Heyden of the Moyne, Richard Newton King of Ballynahallen, Richard
Bennett of Blackstoops, John Hawkins of Ballycoursey and Wheeler
Sparrow of Killabeg. In turn, these men let primarily but not exclusively
to medium-sized Protestant tenants, holding 30-50 acres as, for example,
in the townlands of Monageer, Corbally, Clovass, Clone, Tomsallagh
and Ballynabarney. Holding beneath them, these farmers had 2-3 cottiers,
normally but not exclusively Catholic; some families also supplemented
their income from the woollen trade of the area. Typical of these families
were the Barbers of Clovass who farmed 20 acres and kept a woollen
workshop. Jane Barber comments 'Although all our neighbours of the

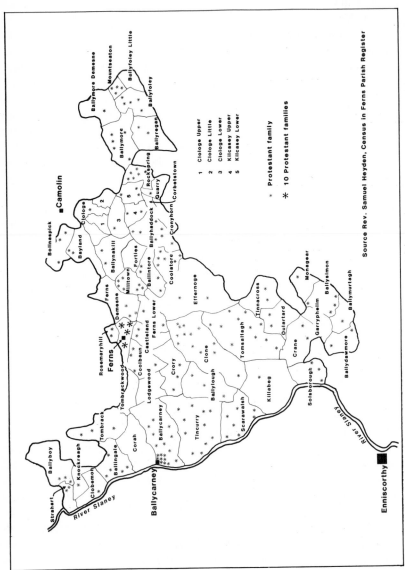

Figure 4:1. Distribution of Protestant families in Ferns, Clone and Kilbride, 1776.

better class were Protestant (for we lived in the midst of twenty-two families of our own persuasion), yet, all those we employed were Roman Catholics'.[4]

Interspersed with these almost totally 'Protestant' townlands were other 'Catholic' ones. Oulartard and Effernogue fitted into this category. Luke Byrne was the largest Catholic farmer, with a 100-acre dairy farm in Oulartard. In 1796-7 he moved into malting in Enniscorthy. Here, like the Suttons, he was to play a prominent part in the events of 1798, as were other members of his family, Peter (of Kilnamanagh) and Morgan (of Castlesow). This dualistic structure was replicated elsewhere in north Wexford.[5] By contrast, west of the Slaney, the principal tenants were never uniformly Protestant, and Catholics were an important component of middleman society. Thus, on the Carew estate of Castleboro, Nicholas Fitzhenry of Gobbinstown, William Fitzhenry of Ballymackessy and James Downes of Adamstown were Catholic, while Justin Doran of Wheelagower was a recent convert from Catholicism to Protestantism.[6] They shared equal status in the 1780s with the Quaker Goffs and Cullimores and the Protestant Greenes and Robinsons. This type of mix, with Catholics to the forefront, seems to have been typical of the baronies of Bantry, Shelburne and Shelmaliere. On the Leigh estate of Rosegarland, the two most important tenants (the Sweetmans and Rossitters of Newbawn) were both Catholic.[7]

Superimposed on this religious profile was an interesting political profile. There was a specific group of Wexford landlords who had developed a strong political base, in which anti-Catholicism was a very prominent element. This grouping was controlled by the Marquis of Ely (Loftus family) with the support of the Rams, Tottenhams and Ogles. George Ogle of Bellvue was the great champion of the Protestant ascendancy in the county which was defining itself more sharply as the century drew to a close.[8] In the 1780s, Ogle had been instrumental in ensuring that Catholics were not admitted to the Volunteers. In 1792 and 1793, he strenuously resisted the Catholic Relief Acts. To counterbalance this, there was also a strong liberal party in the county, based on the Grogan, Colclough and Harvey families. Their main base was in the south of the county, as opposed to the northern base of the ascendancy party. These liberals supported and tended to be supported by the Catholics and as a result, a sectarian dimension was built into Wexford politics.[9]

Elections in Wexford became increasingly bitter affairs, with the balance switching in the 1790s to the ascendancy party, culminating in their success in the critical election of 1797, which involved electioneering on a scale seldom seen in the eighteenth century. The Liberal party claimed that only the intervention of the sheriff, James Boyd in refusing to allow suspected Roman Catholic freeholders to vote, tilted the balance away from them. This election brought many of the key figures of 1798 into the public arena, for example, Edward Hay and Thomas Cloney. The bitterness of the fight, its sectarian edge, the politicisation of a vast electorate, the hint of United Irish involvement – all these contributed to a tense situation in the county in the winter of 1797 and the spring of 1798.[10] The victorious ascendancy party was in no mood to be generous in its victory and the yeomanry groups under their control became increasingly a party force. As Reverend James Gordon commented 'These yeomen, being Protestant, were prejudiced against the romanists by traditionary and other accounts of the former cruelties of that sect in Ireland and acted with a spirit ill-fitted to allay religious hatred'.[11]

In the late eighteenth century, the Catholics of Wexford were also well organised politically. In the Catholic Committee of the 1780s, the Wexford gentry Catholics had played a prominent role, especially the Talbots, Esmondes and Hays but also the Devereuxs of Carrigmenan, Suttons of Clonard and Mastersons of Monaseed.[12] However, when the Catholic Committee moved to a more radical stance in the 1790s, the older generation of these gentry families withdrew and a younger, more aggressive Wexford membership became involved. These included Edward Hay of Ballinkeele, James Devereux of Carrigmenan and Edward Sweetman of Newbawn. The 1792 and 1793 Catholic Relief Acts were tangible if incomplete evidence of the growing power of Catholics.[13] Yet, the older generation did not like the truculent tone adopted by the younger men. Harvey Hay disinherited Edward, as a mark of disapproval of his aggressive political stance. John Colclough of Tintern's sneering comment on old Harvey is indicative of the rift: 'he wishes to be a man of great consequence, to which he thinks nothing contributes so much as being on the Grand Jury or being taken under the arm by Lord Ely'.[14]

The growing political awareness of Wexford Catholic society was expanded by the work of James Edward Devereux, Edward Hay and other Catholic activists in the mid-1790s. At the recall of the pro-Catholic Earl Fitzwilliam as viceroy, a massive campaign was launched in the county, spearheaded by Hay, to demand his retention. The Liberals of Wexford were also disturbed by Fitzwilliam's departure. The list of fifty-four names of freeholders who requested a meeting to discuss this issue is especially interesting.[15] Among them were the leading Liberals (Grogans, Carew, Harvey, Colclough) and the leading Catholics

(Talbot, Hay, Esmonde, Fitzhenry, Masterson, Sutton, Meyler). Also present were many of the later leaders of the rebellion (B. B. Harvey, Mathew Keugh, John Henry Colclough, William Hatton, William Barker). The seeds of the future conflict were already being set in these campaigns and battle lines drawn. Thomas Handcock commented in 1798 that the Hays were 'a family long suspected of disaffection'.[16]

The initial spread of the United Irishmen in Wexford was also linked to this group of Liberals. It was primarily a gentry and middle-class phenomenon, concentrated in the town of Wexford and the barony of Forth. This was the open United Irishmen Society, prior to its suppression, after which it became an oath-bound secret society with revolutionary aims. A Gorey Society of United Irishmen existed in 1792, one of the very few units outside Belfast or Dublin at this stage. It is likely that Anthony Perry was the mainspring of this society. The later proscribed organisation was to develop primarily in north Wexford and we have concrete evidence of at least three early cells (Coolgreaney/Inch, Clonegal, Killan).[17] However, we must also try to come to terms with another shadowy organisation, who may have added appreciably to the emerging sense of imminent strife in the county – the Defenders.

Originally an Ulster borderland phenomenon, the Defenders had spread south into Meath, Kildare, Laois, Wicklow and Carlow in the 1790s, utilising a cellular structure which was remarkably impervious to outside penetration. Feeding off hereditary fears of Protestants, vaguely millenarian, populist, with a strong working class base, the Defenders were ideally suited to the troubled conditions of north Wexford Catholics. Although some observers felt that they had played a part in the 1793 militia disturbance in the county, it is very unlikely that they were present in Wexford until late in 1797. The loose use of the term 'Defender' by contemporaries to refer to any form of political dissident renders it difficult to be precise about the presence of this ultra secretive society in County Wexford in the 1790s.[18] Musgrave comments on the presence in the lead mines of Ballymurtagh (just across the border in Wicklow) of a very active Defender cell, based on a group of displaced Louth Defenders.[19]

These had brought the northern practice of spreading rumours of impending massacres in order to whip up support, a practice which was also subsequently adopted by the United Irishmen of north Wexford.[20] In a mixed religious area, such rumours were to play an important role in igniting the fuse which lit up the area in 1798. By 1797, the Earl of Mountnorris had received a letter from Lt. Smith of the Camolin cavalry informing him that 'the bulk of the people in the area have been corrupted by Defenderism'. Mountnorris replied, 'I do really believe the baneful spirit of Defenderism has made some progress but not to the extent you suppose'.[21] He did make efforts to quell the spreading alarm especially when his political rivals made moves to have a large part of north Wexford (his political base) proclaimed. He forced the Catholic priests of the threatened parishes to get their flocks to take an oath of allegiance dictated by him. Some of the priests demurred: 'We have been unwarrantably pointed out as proselytes to Defenderism'.[22]

By the spring of that year, Mountnorris was reporting that 'The Defenders are present in an area stretching from Newtownbarry to Slieveboy, to Slievegower, to Little Limerick, to Arklow, and down to Lord Courtown's'.[23] This was the Wicklow/Wexford borderland, where sectarian tensions were most in evidence, both prior to and during 1798. Another shadowy figure in this area was the priest Mogue Kearns of Kiltealy. He had been curate at Clonard on the Meath/Kildare border, but had been sacked by Bishop Delany for being actively involved with the Defenders.[24] The Killan area, to which Kearns returned, was soon reported by the local magistrate, Dudley Colclough, to be involved in treasonable swearing practices. Kearns was one of the first in open rebellion in 1798.

Certainly, the presence of the Defenders in the county, if proved, would help to explain the bitter sectarian tinge which coloured many of the rebels' activities in the rebellion. It would also help explain why prophecies of various types circulated freely in the spring of 1798, of a millenarian and anti-Protestant kind, a curious mix of Pastorini and Colmcille. Jane Barber of Clovass reported the tradition that 'King James in his flight stopped to take breath on Coolnaheorna hill and a prophesy said that before another hundred years had elapsed, the Irish would again muster on that hill, strong and victorious'. Poignantly, she adds 'the truth of that prophesy I myself saw but too clearly confirmed'.[25] Robert Whitney of Moneytucker and Jane Adams of Summerseat both report another very common prophesy; 'There would be but one religion and it would be theirs. . . '[26]

Alongside the still tenuous figure of the Defender, we must line up the equally vague figure of the Orangeman. Contemporaries were agreed that the first public appearance of Orangeism in the county was made by the North Cork Militia under Lord Kingsborough.[27] There may have been earlier aristocratic members in Dublin lodges, for example, Lord Ely. It is also possible that two official lodges existed in the county prior to this, at Camolin and Clonegal. The Gowan family may also have initated three private lodges on the Wickow/Wexford border in early 1798. The other militias present in Wexford had lodges attached – three in the Armagh, two in the Cavan, one in the Tyrone, Donegal, Downshire, Dublin County and Sligo.[28] Perhaps because of the flamboyant loyalism of Kingsborough himself, the North Corks openly displayed the symbol of Orangeism, and made efforts (successfully) to gain recruits in the Enniscorthy area. Although Capt. Snowe put a stop to the determined recruiting efforts of one of his sergeants, when the rebels came to storm Enniscorthy, all the ladies wore orange cockades.[29] Even more persuasively, a contemporary account of the Lett family of Rathsilla, (Kilgibbon) tells us that William Lett and his three sons, Nicholas, Benjamin and John used 'to mount their horses at their own half-door, attired in Orange insignalia, and their horses bridles decked with orange and blue ribbons, and ride a distance of four miles in the face of the whole country to the meetings of the Orange Lodge in Enniscorthy'. The Letts were well aware that this provocative gesture 'made them more obnoxious than many others of their name or religion to the ferocious and bloodthirsty papists'.[30]

These developments led to a great fear in the spring of 1798 in County Wexford, a fear of a bloody sectarian massacre. This fear was expertly played upon by manipulators on both sides, heightening the general tension. In the last week of May, these rumours were to assume a terrible reality for many people when word spread of the summary executions at Dunlavin and Carnew. The Carnew incident, in particular, seems to have had a galvanising effect on the Wicklow/Wexford border area. The activities of the hard-line Hunter Gowan had added immeasurably to these fears. Miles Byrne, even at the lapse of nearly half a century, describes with great emotion the horrific scene in Monaseed chapel a few days prior to the rebellion breaking out, when two of his United Irish colleagues (Garrett Fennell and James D'Arcy) were waked there, having been brutally shot by Gowan's 'black mob'. Additional fuel was added to Catholic fears when a series of disarmings of suspected Catholic 'United' men in several yeomanry corps in north Wexford took place in the late spring of 1798, at Coolgreaney, Castletown and Ballyellis.[31]

Tensions ran just as deep in the Protestant community. At Ballycanew and Wingfield, stories circulated amongst the Protestants of the red tape placed around the necks of the Catholic children to distinguish them when a general massacre of Protestants took place.[32] In the Kilanerin/Arklow/Castletown areas, a reward was offered for the apprehension of those responsible for a rumour that all Protestants were to be killed on a given night by the Catholics.[33] The Letts of Kilgibbon were fully convinced that 'Romanists everywhere armed and drilled and only waited for the arrival of the promised succours from France to fall upon and kill every Protestant man, woman and child'. No wonder then, that Protestant as well as Catholic should sleep out in the ditches in that tension-filled spring as Samuel Wheatley of Dranagh and George Williams of Ballyadams testified.[34]

In these conditions, the Boolavogue incidents ignited the spectacular jacquerie of May 1798. We can piece together with some confidence the train of local circumstances involved, based on stitching together the surviving published, manuscript and traditional accounts of the events involved. John Donovan of Tobergal played a critical role. A Protestant and a yeoman, he had a Catholic wife, a sensitive issue in the prevailing climate. In the week prior to the flashpoint, Donovan had been insulted on this score while drinking in the Harrow, and had vowed revenge, invoking Cromwell's name. There are hints that the local United Irishmen orchestrated the response to inflame local feeling. Problems in the supposedly peaceful handing in of arms in the area may also have been utilised in this fashion. At Coolatore near Ferns, the Boolavogue men returning defenceless from Ferns were humiliated by neighbourhood yeomanry. By Saturday evening, decisive counter action had taken place. John Donovan's yeomanry scouting party, involved in a house-burning raid in the Boolavogue area, was attacked and he himself slain, being killed by his Catholic cousin Tom Donovan of Boolavogue. The most surprising aspect of the attack was that John Murphy, the local Catholic curate, was amongst those involved. John Murphy was very friendly with Tom Donovan who was almost certainly a United Irishman. He may have been sucked in through his friendship with him and other prominent United men in the area. His brothers in Tincurry also fought throughout the campaign.[35] The United Irishmen in the county reacted quickly to mobilise support after this incident had occurred. Immediately after the affray in the Harrow, it was Tom Donovan's son Jerry who was deputed to bring news of the event to another group of United Irishmen in the Castlebridge area. Here, his contact man was his uncle Morgan Byrne, whose family connections were primarily in the disturbed north Wexford region and whose brother Luke, was heavily involved in orchestrating the activities of the United Irishmen in the Enniscorthy area in the preceding weeks. Thus, a web of

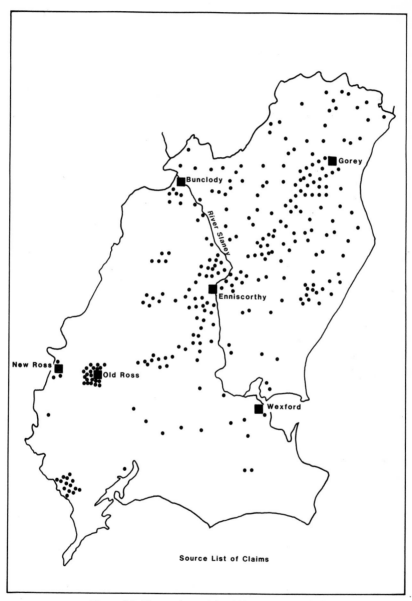

Figure 4:2. Houses burned in 1798 (towns excluded).

organisational and familial ties helped to rapidly spread the growing rebellion from its Boolavogue core.

In its initial phases, the campaign became one of reprisals and paying off old scores. As Hay phrases it, an 'emulation of house-burning' took place.[36] Jane Barber of Clovass looked out on Whit Saturday night in the Ferns direction and saw 'eleven distinct blazes in the distance, every one, from its situation, marking out to us where the house and property of a neighbour, friend or relative was consuming'.[37] By the end of the week, the same sight met many a Protestant eye, from Tomgaddy to Garrybritt. Often the burnings were reprisals. Thus, George Grimes of Clone, a yeoman, killed Carton of Ballycarney, a blacksmith suspected of making pikes. As a witness reports it, 'the cry in Ferns was that Grimes had killed Carton, and if he was not taken, he would ruin the country'. Laurence Butler, the rebel captain in the Ferns area, sent his men immediately 'to take Grimes and also to burn all the houses in Clone'.[38]

A map of the house burning in the county in '98 is illuminating (Fig. 4:2).[39] One can note a number of specific targets – Clogh, Camolin, Gorey and Duncannon – villages and towns with a strong Protestant composition. Some exclusively Protestant rural townlands also were decimated – Tomgaddy, Clone, Garrybritt – especially if these abutted onto primarily Catholic townlands. A fierce animosity to newcomers fired the campaign against the Palatines of Old Ross and their kinsmen in Killan. As late as 1956, local opinion considered that the Palatines were 'more Jew than Gentile'.[40] Of one hundred houses in Old Ross, only four were left standing in '98, which marked a deep crisis for the colony with the strange-sounding names – Hess, Hartrick, Horneck, Jekyll, Whitney, Frizell . . . An intimate perspective on the rebellion in the Old Ross area is provided in the detailed series of letters which passed between the Elmes family of Old Ross and their cousin Robert Morris in London in the years between 1792 and 1798.[41] The Palatines, following on visits from John Wesley, had also become Methodists (or 'Swaddlers' to use the local derogatory term) which made them even more ostentatious. In this situation, it is understandable that the only Protestant church burned in Wexford was at Old Ross. Thomas Cloney was involved in this episode: his cousin, Martin Cloney, the miller, was the only propertied Catholic living in the Old Ross area.[42]

Looking at the map of house burning as a whole, one is surprised at the sharpness of some of the boundaries. Thus, the ancient frontier line marking off Rochesland emerges clearly in the Skreen/Blackwater region (this line had marked the southern limit of the plantation of the 1620s). Quiescent estates also emerge with some clarity: for instance, the Earl of Courtown's and the Shapland-Carew estate at Castleboro. The stability of the whole south Wexford region, in comparison with the turbulent north, is striking. The Protestant presence in this area was minimal and sectarian animosities of the North Wexford type were never as highly developed here. This southern zone (south of a line linking New Ross and Wexford town) could be traced across into the adjacent parts of counties Waterford and Kilkenny, which also avoided major involvement in '98. On a more local level, some family groupings took a severe hammering – the Earles of Ballinahown, the Gills and Gainfords of Monglass, the Peppers of Tincurry, the Sparks and Swaynes of Scarawalsh, the Copelands of Aughnagally, the Thackaberrys of Tomgaddy – reflecting local hostilities to entrenched families. For example, it was their poor Catholic neighbours, Boulger and Fitzharris, who burned out the Peppers at Tincurry.[42] The Murphy family were the only Catholics to hold a large farm (70 acres) in this townland, being surrounded by Protestant farmers. This was the environment in which the young John Murphy was reared; it may have informed his decision to rebel in Boolavogue.[43]

Similarly, if one looks at those Protestants killed in '98, some striking patterns emerge (Fig. 4:3).[44] Old Ross does not figure because the inhabitants fled *en masse* to New Ross, to the protection of Charles Tottenham. The role of the various rebel camps is immediately apparent, for example, in the vicinity of Vinegar Hill, Gorey and the Three Rocks. The central camp of Vinegar Hill accounts for the carnage in Enniscorthy as well as the fact that two major battles were fought here. There is an unusually large cluster in the small southern village of Tintern, because twenty-seven of its inhabitants were despatched to Scullabogue, there to perish when the prison-barn was deliberately incinerated. The Tintern dead were typical of the poor Protestant population of a small landlord-induced village – a shoemaker, a slater, two weavers, a mason, a butcher, a labourer.

Similarly, the Killan concentration arose from local antagonism to a sponsored Protestant settlement on the Monksgrange and Woodbrook estates, which also acted as a receptacle for the spillover from the Old Ross colony. This area had inherited sectarian tensions from an incident in the 1770s Whiteboy disturbances, which led to hostility against the Hornick family of Gurrawn and their numerous relations in the Killan area.[45] In July 1775, George Hornick had made a successful defence of his home from a Whiteboy attack. He subsequently formed a Whiteboy

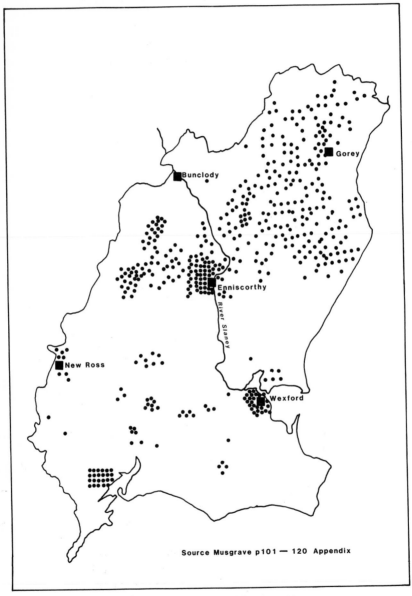

Figure 4:3. Protestants killed in 1798.

Defence League . . . 'On Sunday, 23 July, they paraded to Killan Church, in regular order, under arms, by beat of drums, and headed by Mr Hornick. Even the women were armed'.[46] The first target that Fr Philip Roche made for in 1798 was Hornick's house: as George was being piked to death, he was asked sarcastically 'Do you remember 9 July 1775 now?'[47] Eventually seven of the Hornick clan in Killan were to be killed by the rebels. The same clarity of intention, tenacity of memory and grimness of purpose underlay other almost ceremonial killings – that of John Boyd (of Wexford), and Edward Turner (of Newfort), for example. People with unpopular occupations were another common target; Daniels, Robinson and Prior (gaugers), Mathewson (toll-gatherer), Hamilton (bailiff), Kavanagh (recruiting officer), Atkins (tide-waiter). Inevitably, private spites were also indulged. Francis Turner was killed by his own servant, Thomas Cleary, who alleged that he had abused him. Mary Redmond helped her husband to kill Henry Kinch in Gorey, because Kinch had reported them for furze-stealing.[48] All yeomen and all informers were considered legitimate targets. Thus, Francis Murphy, who had informed the authorities of Fr Thomas Dixon's efforts to get him to join the United Irishmen at confession in Blackwater, was executed, and in a highly formalised manner, on the bridge of Wexford; this was orchestrated for maximum public impact by Thomas Dixon, the priest's cousin.[49]

The rebels tried, or claimed to try, to distinguish between 'Orangemen' and 'Protestants' in general but a purely sectarian motive was evident in many of the killings. Yet, some targets were exempt. Quakers were universally respected as non-partisans[50] and women were also considered as non-combatants. Protestants with a good popular image were allowed to remain free – thus, the Alcock family of Wilton were spared because of their reputation as liberal landlords.[51] Reverend John Elgee and Reverend Joshua Nunn were cherished by the rebels because of their universal reputation as charitable men. This contrasts with the treatment of Reverend Roger Owens, who was considered an enemy of the people, and was consequently exposed to abuse and degradation. He may also have been an Orangeman, and his activities as a magistrate had inflamed opinion in the Gorey area, not least through his use of the pitchcap.[52]

Caught in this maelstrom of violence, many Protestants temporised and became converts to Catholicism. This strategy was especially prevalent in Wexford town and the barony of Forth generally, where amicable relations existed between the two denominations and where Catholic neighbours encouraged their Protestant friends to save themselves in this way. Hay comments: 'Great numbers [of Protestants] flocked in the most public and conspicuous manner to the Catholic chapel, where they affected the greatest piety and devotion. The epithet of crawthumpers, opprobriously applied to Catholics for contritely striking their breasts at their devotions, was never more strongly exemplified than by these converts'.[53] The Catholic priests were very willing in the south of the county to maintain the fiction that these conversions were genuine and to be respected. Fr Corish (Mulrankin), Fr Murphy (Bannow), Fr Stafford (Lady's Island), Fr Whitty (Kilmore), Fr Doyle (Suttons parish) Fr Shalloe (Adamstown), Fr O'Connor (Oylegate), and the Franciscan friars of Wexford town (Broe, Corrin, Lambert, Scallan) all participated in this exercise. Among the most prominent converts were Colonel and Mrs le Hunte of Artramont and Mrs Thomas Richards of Rathaspeck. A packed gallery in the Franciscan chapel in the town was a tribute to the large numbers involved.

Many other Protestants fled to the towns initially, or Duncannon Fort, thence to Dublin, or to Wales, where a large *émigré* colony was temporarily established. This type of siege mentality was also reflected in the falling-back on the local 'Big House' for refuge, as at Monksgrange. Some few Protestants choose voluntarily to fight with the rebels - George Sparks of Crosshue, Jack Bennett of Crossabeg, William Hackett of Coolatuarn, amongst them.[54] The United Irishmen's non-sectarian ideals had apparently been internalised only among the liberal Protestants of Forth and Bargy, and of these, a surprising number sided with the rebels in the fight – Harvey, Grogan, Grey, Boxwell, Hughes, Keugh, to name but some.

What of the Catholics involved? Some of the more prominent were obviously sucked in by their involvement in Catholic politics prior to '98. These included the Hays, John Henry Colclough and Robert Carthy. Intriguingly, many of the 288 names from Wexford on the Catholic Qualification Rolls between 1793 and 1796 also figure prominently in 1798, indicating the often neglected point that Wexford Catholics were in many respects highly politicised prior to 1798. Among those who signed these Rolls were Robert Carthy of Birchgrove, Michael Clinch of Knockanure, Edward Hay of Ballinkeele, William Kearney of Wexford, John Kelly [of Killan?], Richard Monaghan of Wexford, James Edward Devereux of Carrigmenan and Walter Devereux of Enniscorthy [and the Leap]. All of these were involved in the build up to the rebellion.[55] To take an example, twenty-seven Catholics from two townlands, Drumderry and Ballyshonogue (near Clonegal) signed these rolls in 1796. In 1797, prior to the actual outbreak of rebellion, an active United Irishmen cell was uncovered in this area, with a significant overlap of members with those signing the rolls.[56] So, even in a relatively remote rural community like this, and at a low level in the social hierarchy, Catholic politics were deeply entrenched in the few years before 1798. Significantly many of the more prominent Catholic families in Wexford avoided involvement in 1798. Most noticeable of these were the Talbots of Castle Talbot and the Esmondes of Ballynestraw. Other prominent families to remain practically invisible were the Tooles of Fairfield, Rossiters of Newbawn, Houghtons of Ballyanne and Boulgers of St Austin.

Lower down the social scale, the successful trading families of rural communities uneasily straddled the two sides, reflecting a deeply ambiguous attitude to the rebellion. Younger members, like Nicholas Dixon of Castlebridge, Michael Downes of Adamstown or Nicholas Sweetman of Newbawn were all United Irishmen: older members took no part, or were opposed to the rebellion.[57] For some other families, it provided an opportunity to pay off old scores, in some cases, very old scores. Thus, the Roches of Garrylough were the representatives of the Roches of Artramont, who had been displaced by the Cromwellian le Huntes. Edward Roche's involvement in 1798, his early adherence to the United Irishmen, the willingness of his followers to back him through thick and thin – all these may have reflected that simple fact. As late as 1898, the title deeds of Artramont were still in the possession of the Roche family of Garrylough, and in 1924, Mark D. Roche (Edward's great-grandson) took a case to the new Irish High Court, attempting to re-establish the Roches' right to Artramont.[58]

Some of the more prominent families in the county (who were in an analogous position of representing displaced seventeenth- century landowners) may also have been pushed into involvement because of this ancestral burden. The Furlongs of Templescoby, the Meylers of Gurteenminogue, the Rossiters of Garrywilliam, the Devereuxs of Tomhaggard, the Byrnes of Monaseed, the Brownes of Mulrankin and the Fitzhenrys of Ballymackessy may all have fallen into this category. Thus the Furlongs of Templescoby were the representatives of the Furlongs of Horetown. Michael Furlong (and his brother Mathew of Raheen) were early United Irishmen in the Bantry area. The Devereuxs of Tomhaggard were in direct line from, and on the same farm as, Colonel John Devereux of Mount Pill, who was dispossessed in the Cromwellian period. Richard Devereux fought alongside John Boxwell of Sarshill in 1798. The Meylers of Gurteenminogue were the representatives of the Meylers of Duncormuck. Both Robert and John Meyler were active in the Forth area in 1798. The Brownes of Fardystown had survived adjacent to their ancestral seat of Mulrankin and Richard Browne fought in the rebel army in 1798.[59]

Miles Byrne provides a vivid insight into the ethnic anguish felt by such families: 'how often had my father told me of the persecutions and robberies that both his family and my mother's had endured under the invaders - how often had he shown me the lands that belonged to our ancestors now in the hands of the sanguinary followers of Cromwell'.[60] This racial sense of opposition to the seventeenth-century settlers is equally evident in Cloney's sneering comments about the 'knot of descendants of Cromwellian settlers in the Enniscorthy area who were ever tenacious about the tenure by which they held their possessions and ever ready to crush the slightest ebullition of popular feeling'.[61] A contemporary song caught the mood very well:

> 'Hell's so full of Orangemen, the croppies can't get in,
> and we'll make the Devil a begging cap from Lowcay's yellow
> skin'.[62]

Similar sentiments are expressed in a street ballad of 1806 referring to the bitterly contested election of that year:

> 'Ye honest men of Wexford, draw round me in a ring,
> And list as to the Holy Mass, unto the song I sing,
> In praise of our brave candidates, so firm stout and true,
> Bold Colclough of the open hand and kindhearted Carew.
> Send Orange Loftus to the North and Satan's rampant Ram
> To eat sourkraut with Billy's goat in dirty Rotterdam.
> In spite of Ogles bloody blues and Gowans pitch-cap crew,
> We'll send our men to Parliament, brave Colclough and Carew'.[63]

As late as 1938, a Courtown schoolboy was writing in his copybook: 'The ancestor of the Earl of Courtown was a drummer in Cromwell's army, who was given the land between Tara Hill and Courtown for his services'.[64] Peter Foley of Oulart, a 1798 veteran, told Luke Cullen that 'Hawtry White was a descendant of Cromwell's soldiers and he was forged in the same terrible mould of reckless devastation as his ancestors'.[65] The Protestants were equally aware of their origins: Jane Barber tells us that: 'Our farm . . . had been in our family since the Battle of the Boyne, for I am descended from a Williamite.'[66] In this climate of opinion, it is not surprising that mixed families had a particularly difficult time. The evidence of the Ferns parish register is that 8 per cent of marriages in the period from 1770 to 1804 were mixed.[67] We have already commented on the strains which this imposed on at least one of these families – the Donovans. In a similar fashion, Valentine Mowles of Ballymurlough, the yeoman who set fire to Boolavogue chapel, had a Catholic wife. John Beaumans decision to disarm the Catholics of his yeomanry unit may have been partially precipitated by the fact that his three sisters were all Catholic, and he may consequently have felt that his own loyalty was suspected. Other mixed families may have had equally difficult choices to make, including the Colcloughs and the Letts. The Letts of Newcastle, for example, were active United Irishmen, while the Letts of Rathsilla (Kilgibbon) were amongst the earliest Orangemen in the county. These families shared the same grandfather.

The aftermath of 1798 was almost equally painful. For many Wexford Protestant communities, it marked a turning point. By 1810, for example, the Ram estate at Old Ross had still not recovered from the devastation which it received in 1798 and Catholic tenants were beginning to move into what had been a monolithically Protestant area. The evidence of the Tithe Applotment book in the 1830s and of the Griffith Valuation in 1850s, shows the almost total collapse of the Palatine colony. By 1928, a local newspaper was recording the death of the very last member of this group – George Hartrick, a plumber in New Ross.[68] The Protestant gentry seem also to have suffered a great loss of confidence. The old moral economy had been irretrievably sundered, and reading the gentry women's accounts of their experiences in the rebellion, it is their sense of this breakdown which is most striking. This psychological shift was symbolised in the 'Big Houses' which were temporarily abandoned at this time – Camolin Park, Ramsfort, Woodbrook and Newfort.

Many families of Protestants emigrated after 1798, for example, the Ellison family of Killan, who left their shop in the village and went to Dublin.[69] Jane Barber comments on the effects of 1798 on the Clovass area: 'besides my father, I lost 14 uncles, cousins and near relations'. She also comments: 'The yeomanry ruined young boys, who continued in the same careless, easy life, till they were quite unable to pay their rents. They then emigrated to America, and on the very ground which thirty years ago, was in the possession of old Protestant families, there now lives the descendants of those rebels who may be said to be the origin of all this evil'.[70] In the pre-Famine period, there was a sizeable out-migration of north Wexford Protestants, for example, to Ontario,

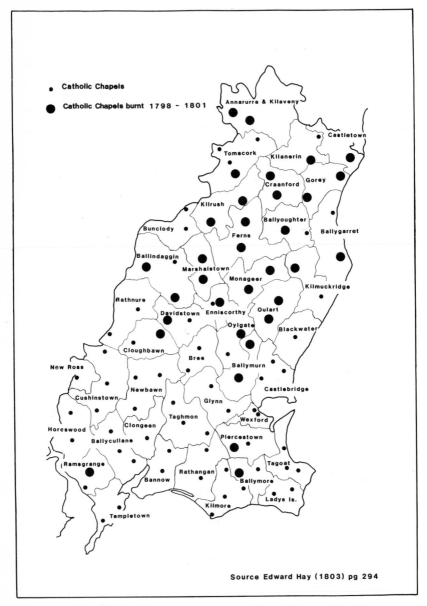

Figure 4:4. Burning of Catholic chapels: Diocese of Ferns, 1798-1801.

reflecting again the loss of self-confidence in these communities. Amongst those who left was the illegitimate son of Hunter Gowan, who subsequently founded the Orange Order in Canada.

In the decade after 1798, Protestant society in Wexford became defensive, introspective and suspicious. The Orange Order spread with great rapidity in the north of the county. Protestant secret societies attempted to intimidate Catholics out of bidding for leases, as at Court in Oulart parish, in a replica of what happened in Armagh a few years previously.[71] Even more revealingly, an epidemic of chapel-burning took place, especially in north Wexford, between 1798 and 1801. In all, thirty-three chapels were consumed, in an episode which was almost entirely confined to the planted area of north Wexford (Fig. 4:4).[72] James Caulfield, the Catholic bishop, commented: 'I could hardly get a priest to venture to the Mackamores, to the neighbourhood of Gorey or Camolin, so much afraid are they of the Yeomanry of them [sic] parts'.[73] The brutal murder of Rev'd William Ryan on the Wicklow/Wexford border in 1799 would have confirmed them in their prejudice.[74] In a typical incident, the body of James Redmond (executed for the murder of the Protestant clergyman at Kyle, Revd James Burrowes) was exhumed from its grave on 3rd August 1801 and propped up on the scalán (or temporary shelter) on the site of the burned-down chapel of Monamolin, so that Catholics attending Mass the following morning were presented with this gruesome spectacle.[75]

Catholics also suffered in the immediate aftermath of 1798. In particular, concerted pressure was brought to bear on the prominent Catholics who had become involved in the rebellion, and a witch-hunt took place, highly reminiscent of a similar episode after the Whiteboy disturbances in Tipperary in the 1760s. The body of a man dead for fifteen months was dug up so that a fourteen-year-old boy could identify it, in an effort to prosecute Robert Carthy of Birchgrove.[76] In a vindictive move, Sir Thomas Esmonde and his cousin, Laurence Doyle of Springhill were arrested, although both had fought with the yeomanry in '98. Sir Thomas's son, William, was sentenced to transportation on the flimsiest of evidence. The Kildare involvement of another son, John (who was executed as a rebel), targeted him as a suspect.[77]

In a similar vein, an effort was made to target prominent liberal politicians, and Cornelius Grogan was executed as a result. A vigorous effort was also made to implicate the head of the other leading liberal family, John Colclough, led by his local rival Charles Tottenham of New Ross and his satellites, Lowcay, Kennedy and Glasscott.[78] Catholics too paid a price in terms of depressed living standards. The 1800 valuations of Wexford parishes are amongst the lowest in the whole country, indicating a severe fall in Catholic income in the years after '98. Families like the Hays of Ballinkeele, the Staffords of Ballymore, the Fitzgeralds of Newpark and the Cloneys of Moneyhore disappeared in the generation after '98.[79] The Cloneys experienced great difficulty in renewing the advantageous long leases they had held from various Carlow and Wexford landlords.[80]

Beyond these local realities, polemicists on both sides made constant use of '98. The mythologising began instantaneously, and even contemporary accounts have to be treated with the utmost caution, as both sides attempted to play down their own culpability for what had occurred and to affix all blame on their enemies. The mythologies of '98 are a fascinating and important theme: popular perception and actuality (in so far as we can now determine it), are often remarkably at variance. It is to be hoped that the historiography of the 1798 rebellion will receive detailed treatment in the future, in a way which will help us further to understand this critical event in the history of eighteenth-century Ireland.

NOTES

1. L. M. Cullen, *The emergence of modern Ireland, 1600-1900* (London, 1981), pp. 210-33.

2. Rev. Samuel Heyden. 'A census of the Protestant inhabitants of Ferns, Clone and Kilbride in 1776.' Original manuscript in the possession of Dean David Earle, Ferns.

3. 'Survey of the Earl of Portsmouth's estates, manors of Enniscorthy and Kilhubbock' 1785, Wallop papers, Hampshire Public Record Office, Portsmouth.

4. Jane Barber, 'Recollection of the Summer of 1798'. Transcript copy in N.L.I., p. 1.

5. T. Jones Hughes, 'A traverse of the coastlands of County Wicklow and east County Wexford' in *Baile* (1983), pp. 5-10.

6. E. O'Byrne (ed.), *The convert rolls* (Dublin, 1981), p. 82.

7. A. K. Longfield, *The Shapland-Carew papers* (Dublin, 1946).

8. E. Hay, *History of the insurrection of the County of Wexford* (Dublin, 1803).

9. T. J. Powell, The background to the Wexford rebellion 1790-98. (Unpub. M.A. thesis, N.U.I. 1970).

10. L. M. Cullen, 'The 1798 rebellion in its eighteenth-century context' in P. Corish (ed.), *Radicals, rebels and establishments* (Belfast, 1985).

11. James Gordon, *History of the rebellion in Ireland in the year,1798* (Dublin,1801), pp. 86-7.

12. R. D. Edwards (ed.), 'The minute book of the Catholic Committee 1773-92', in *Archiv. Hib.*, ix (1942), pp. 3-172.

13. E. O'Flaherty, 'The Catholic convention and Anglo Irish politics 1791-3', in *Archiv. Hib.*, xi (1985), pp. 14-34; T. Bartlett, 'A end to moral economy: the Irish militia disturbances of 1793' in *Past and Present*, 99 (1983), pp. 41-64.

14. Letter of John Colclough (Tintern) to Caesar Colcough, 15 Sept. 1796. P.R.O.N.I. McPeake papers, T./3048/c/8.

15. Hay, *History,* Appendix VI, p. xviii.

16. Thomas Handcock, 'Narrative of the battle of Enniscorthy, with a detail of circumstances antecedant and subsequent thereto . . .' N.L.I. Ms. 16, 232, p. 32.

17. Powell, 'Background to the Wexford Rebellion', p. 43.

18. For comments on Wexford Defenders, see George Taylor, *A history of the rise, progress, cruelties and suppression of the rebellion in the County of Wexford in the year 1798* (London, 1864), pp. 14-15; John Jones, *Impartial narrative of the most important engagements which took place during 1798* (Dublin, 1798), pp. 31-3.

19. Richard Musgrave, *Memoirs of the different rebellions in Ireland . . .* (Dublin, 1801), pp. 301-2.

20. *Miles Byrne Memoirs,* (ed.) S. Gwynn (Dublin, 1907), pp. 8-9.

21. A. F. Wheeler and A. M. Broadley, *The war in Wexford* (London, 1910), p. 36.

22. See the addresses signed by Catholic clergy (including Fr. John Murphy), in Musgrave, *Memoirs,* Appendix, pp. 79-82.

23. Wheeler and Broadley, *War in Wexford,* p. 37.

24. Jones, *Impartial narrative,* pp. 31-33.

25. Barber, *Recollections of the summer of 1798,* p. 1.

26. Robert Whitney's, deposition, in Musgrave, *Memoirs,* Appendix, p. 118; Jane Adams, Narrative of her experiences in 1798 in, T. C. Croker, *Researches in the south of Ireland* (London, 1824), p. 38; John Alexander, *A succinct narrative of the rise and progress of the rebellion in the County of Wexford, especially in the vicinity of Ross* (Dublin, 1800), p. 22; Elizabeth Richards, Diary 26 May-26 June 1798 (N.L.I. Microfilm pos. 6486).

27. Hay, *History of the insurrection,* p. 54; Francis Plowden, *An historical review of the state of Ireland from the invasion of that county under Henry II to its union with Great Britain . . .* (2 vols. London, 1803), ii, p. 712.

28. P. Ó Snodaigh, 'Notes on the volunteers, militia, yeomanry and Orangemen of Co. Wexford' in *The Past,* 14 (1983), p. 40.

29. Handcock, Narrative, p. 95; Musgrave, *Memoirs,* p. 373.

30. A transcript of this family account (the original of which has been destroyed) is in the possession of Mrs. Margaret Miller of Shortalstown House, Killinick, County Wexford.

31. Byrne, *Memoirs,* pp. 22-7, 33.

32. Taylor, *Rise, progress and cruelties,* pp. 31-2; Musgrave, *Memoirs,* p. 443.

33. Musgrave, *Memoirs,* Appendix, p. 82.

34. Testimony of Samuel Wheatley, Musgrave, *Memoirs,* appendix, pp. 83-4; Testimony of George Williams, ibid., pp. 97-100.

35. It is not proposed in this essay to discuss in detail the role of the Catholic clergy in the 1798 rebellion in Wexford.

36. Hay, *History of the insurrection,* p. 90.

37. Barber, *Recollections of the summer of 1798,* p. 3.

38. Trial of Lawrence Butler, rebel captain, N.L.I.Ms. 17, 795(4).

39. The source of this map is the detailed list produced by the Commissioners for enquiring into the losses sustained by such of His Majesty's loyal subjects as have suffered by the rebellion. There is a separate listing for County Wexford available at the N.L.I. See also J.I.H.C. (1800) appendix, vol. 19 (ii).

40. The reminiscences of Edward Fitzgerald of Kilscanlan. Dept. of Irish Folklore, U.C.D. Ms. 577, pp. 19-20.

41. These letters are in the possession of King Milne, Ballymorgan, Ferns. A microfilm copy (pos. 8361) is available at N.L.I.

42. Observations on the Old Ross estate c. 1810. Ram papers, N.L.I. Ms. 8238/10.

43. Handcock, Narrative, pp. 24-5, 130; Musgrave, Memoirs, p. 328. Appendix, p. 108.

44. This list is compiled primarily from Appendix 19 in Musgrave, Memoirs, pp. 101-16, supplemented and corrected where feasible.

45. 'A contemporary account of the 1798 rebellion in the Enniscorthy area'. N.L.I. Ms. 25,004, pp. 4-5; Musgrave, Memoirs, pp. 374-5.

46. James Donnelly, 'Irish agrarian rebellions: the Whiteboys of 1769-76' in R.I.A. Proc., 83, (1983), C, no. 12, pp. 324-29.

47. N.L.I. Ms. 25,004, p. 7.

48. Trial of Mary Redmond, S.P.O., Rebellion papers, 620/3/26.

49. Hay, History, p. 145.

50. Joseph Haughton, 'Narrative of events during the Irish Rebellion of 1798', N.L.I. Ms. 1, 576; Dinah Goff, Divine protection through extraordinary dangers experienced by Jacob and Elizabeth Goff and their family, during the Irish rebellion in 1798 (London, 1857); Barbara Newtown Lett, 'Diary of my experiences in 1798' in The Past (5) 1949, p. 123.

51. Thomas Cloney, A personal narrative of those transactions in the County Wexford in which the author was engaged during 1798 (Dublin, 1832), pp. 7-8; Handcock, Narrative, p. 71.

52. Byrne, Memoirs, pp. 149-50; Taylor, Rise, progress and cruelties, pp. 219-220.

53. Jackson, Sufferings and escape, pp. 57-8; Richards, 'Diary', p. 11; Hay, History, pp. 143-5.

54. For Sparks see Luke Cullen, Personal recollections of Wexford and Wicklow insurgents of 1798 (Enniscorthy, 1959), p. 10. For Hackett, see 'Deposition of William Hackett and Catherine Hackett', Colclough papers, N.L.I. Ms. 24,555 (36).

55. Catholic Qualification Rolls. P.R.O.I.

56. For the United Irishmen in Clonegal, see 'Examination of Nicholas Thomkin of Drumderry', S.P.O. Rebellion papers, 629/34/20.

57. For Nicholas Dixon, see D. Goodall, 'The Dixon family of Castlebridge' in Irish Genealogist (6), (1984). See also Nicholas's evidence at the courtmartial of James Murphy, N.L.I. Ms. 17, 795 (2). For Nicholas Sweetman and Michael Downes, see K. Whelan, 'The Sweetman families of County Wexford' in The Past (forthcoming).

58. Wexford People, 23 April 1898 and information from Nicholas Furlong, Drinagh Lodge, Wexford.

59. W. H. Jeffreys, 'The Furlongs of Co. Wexford' in Old Wexford Soc. Jnl. (6) (1976-77), pp. 74-9. Manuscript history of the Devereux family in Tomhaggard, in the possession of James Devereux (Thanks are due to Thomas Kehoe (Tenacre) for alerting me to this source). Meyler family tree, G.O. Ms. 170, pp. 141-2. G.O. Ms. 179, pp. 141-4. Browne family papers in possession of Bernard Browne, Millquarter.

60. Byrne, Memoirs, p. 7.

61. Cloney, Personal Narrative, p. 7.

62. Schools Ms. 874, p. 50, Department of Irish Folklore, U.C.D.

63. T. A. Ogle, The Irish militia officer (Dublin, 1893), p. 143.

64. Schools Ms. 889, p. 63, Department of Irish Folklore, U.C.D.

65. Luke Cullen, Wicklow and Wexford insurgents, p. 20.

66. Barber, *Recollections of the summer of 1798*, p. 1.

67. Church of Ireland Parish Register, Ferns, in the possession of Dean Earle.

68. *New Ross Standard*, 18 April 1928.

69. Henry Ellisson, *In search of my family* (Dublin, 1971), pp. 6-23.

70. Barber, *Recollections of the summer of 1798*, p. 19.

71. Hay, *History*, p. 295.

72. *Cox's Irish Magazine*, 1808, pp. 214-25, 'List of Catholic chapels burned in 1798
. . .'

73. Letter of James Caulfield to James Troy, 1 June 1799, in P. F. Moran (ed.) *Spiciligium Ossoriense Third Series* (Dublin, 1884), p. 572.

74. J. Brady, *Catholics and Catholicism in the eighteenth-century press* (Maynooth, 1965), p. 307.

75. Hay, *History*, p. 301.

76. Courtmartial of Robert Carthy of Birchgrove, N.L.I. Ms. 17, 795 (4).

77. Byrne, *Memoirs*, p. 21; Hay, *History*, p. 189. Courtmartial of William Esmonde, S.P.O. Rebellion papers, 620/3/26/6.

78. Letter of John Colclough (Tintern) to Caesar Colclough, 22 August 1798. McPeake papers, P.R.O.N.I. T.3048/c/18.

79. C. Vane (ed.), *Memoirs and correspondence of Viscount Castlereagh*. 12 vols. (London, 1850-53), IV, pp. 156-9.

80. Cloney, *Personal narrative*, pp. 101-3. Some of the other prominent Wexford families may have declined or disappeared, irrespective of their participation in the rebellion. Thus, Edward Fitzgerald of Newpark was unmarried, Edward Roche of Garrylough had only a daughter, and the Kyans of Mount Howard had largely withdrawn from County Wexford by 1798.

Changes in Irish rural housing, 1600-1900

ALAN GAILEY

Discussion of vernacular or 'traditional' rural housing before 1900 excludes only a tiny minority of buildings, the dwellings of the landed and professional classes. Their houses were usually the products of professional design frequently inspired from external sources. The building enterprises of this social minority have been well studied,[1] whereas the social history of the more modest housing of the mass of the Irish population is less well known.[2] Detailed investigation of the domestic buildings of the Irish population for any part of the historic period has hardly begun. Archaeologists know little of housing in medieval Ireland, apart from what has been discovered in the excavations in Dublin. Post-medieval urban archaeology remains in its infancy, though a start is evident in Derry City and Coleraine. Detailed analysis of the known cartographic sources of the late sixteenth and early seventeenth centuries in the proper context of the related contemporary documentation has only been carried out for the Ulster Plantation records of rural housing. Folklorists, ethnologists and geographers have, during the last ten years, concentrated study on survivals of single-storey thatched houses which formed the majority of rural dwellings in all areas until the nineteenth century. Minority house types of earlier periods and larger sized houses have tended to be ignored. Important evidence for social changes in the elaborated vernacular dwellings of the nineteenth century has also been disregarded. Two needs in Northern Ireland have forced a more comprehensive approach to the study of all rural housing during the past fourteen years: authentication of the merit of buildings for statutory listing ultimately leading to grant-aiding their restoration and conservation; and selection of representative, mostly vernacular buildings for inclusion in the Ulster Folk Museum. Northern emphasis in this paper is therefore explicit, but recent work in the north has been evaluated in a wider geographical context, where this is possible.

Documentation of rural housing before the 1770s has generally been regarded as so fragmentary as to discourage the search for it; nevertheless those records relating to northern housing have proved valuable, even if difficult to interpret, when considered in an interdisciplinary way. Archaeological excavation and ethnological field work have an important role to play. Tribute must be paid to the outstandingly successful dendrochronological work at Queen's University, Belfast; tree-ring datings provided for a number of houses in Ulster have greatly clarified the chronology of vernacular architecture in Ulster and indeed in Ireland generally.

Later documentation presents different problems. For example, a number of studies of rural housing have centred on two elements each characteristic of fundamentally different house types. In most traditional houses of eastern and central Ireland the 'jamb wall' screens the kitchen hearth from the main entrance to the dwelling, forming a lobby inside the doorway. Three documentary references relating to this feature in Ulster are available. They are the maps of c. 1620 by Thomas Raven of the Londonderry Plantation towns,[4] a unique plan of 1615 for a house to be built on Drapers' Company property at Moneymore,[5] and drawings by William Greig of the 'common cottage or cabin' he had discovered on the Gosford and Drumbanagher estates in County Armagh which he surveyed about 1820.[6] For the rest of Ireland only Tighe's description in his Kilkenny survey of 1802 is to hand, and that is far from unambiguous unless there is prior experience of the house type involved:

> Most houses have a porch to the door, which ought to be indispensible; the chimney is often rightly placed in the centre, which warms the whole house; the kitchen being on one side of the entrance, and the parlour on the other, separated by a little passage, the breadth of the chimney, into which the outward door opens. Such are the best farm houses; . . .[7]

Secondly, many houses in north and west Ireland (with three known outliers on the Armagh/Louth border), were characterised by a bed accommodated in a corner of the kitchen, beside the hearth and usually diagonally opposite the principal entrance. This kitchen-corner bed was often accommodated in an 'outshot' projecting at the back of the house especially in County Donegal. Where the outshot was known, literary references to occupants of houses sleeping in their kitchens do not therefore necessarily betray cramped domestic circumstances or poverty: it could equally well be a matter of tradition. Six possible literary or documentary references to the outshot in Ulster counties in the nineteenth century are summarised elsewhere.[8] For the rest of Ireland only M'Parlan's Mayo survey of 1802 presently provides a description, referring to:

> . . . a little recess called a *hag,* which is made into the side wall,
> opposite the family fire, for one bed; this is divided from the fire and
> the body of the house by straw mats, which hang parallel with the
> wall from the roof, by way of curtain.[9]

Further localised references from Connacht, Munster and Leinster to both jamb wall and outshot will undoubtedly come to light, but if the Ulster experience is representative, few new ones can be expected. The significance of this illustration of the exigencies of the formal documentation is in the case of the outshot, the probability that a medieval or earlier origin can be plausibly argued from early manuscript sources.[10] The jamb wall is a defining element of a house type known to have been spreading broadly westwards in Ireland until about 1800, which in Ulster can be proved to have been an introduction from southern England in the early 1600s.[11] In both cases, therefore, interpretation of origins and of social and cultural significance rests necessarily on interdisciplinary approaches.

Rural housing about 1600

Two types of housing may be interpreted from the documentation of the early seventeenth century.[12] The well-known 'creats' (flimsily built and invariably temporary structures), so took the fancy of contemporary English observers that assumptions of nomadism were put forward, especially given the practice of moving to and from one pasture and another. Circular or curvilinear in plan, with post-and-wattle walls, thatch roof, and chimneyless, they differed little from simple timber-framed dwellings which might also be rectangular in plan, to judge from Boullaye Le Gouz's description.[13] These houses lacked load-bearing walls and argument as to how their roofs were supported and constructed remains unresolved.

Sturdily built broadly rectangular houses represented a more permanent class of dwelling. A thatch-covered hip-ended roof was supported on 'couples', probably implying a double-skin roof-carpentry tradition. These houses were normally without a chimney and they were built over a hearth placed somewhere between their ends and there were no internal partitions. Walls were thick, perhaps of earth or turf strengthened with posts and sometimes had a wattle skin. Solid earth walls may have been a medieval introduction from the European mainland or from Britain; the earliest known documentary reference in Ireland and Britain to earth walling is to 'one hall of forks constructed with earth walls and straw thatch' in an extent of the lands of Thomas Fitz Maurice in Kerry in 1298.[14] It now seems likely that many of these sturdier houses had couples which were forms of cruck truss (fork in the reference above has the same connotation), that is, timbers not sunk in post holes and rising from near ground level to support roof framing.[15] It is possible, however, that by 1600 the spread of load-bearing walling of solid earth (or of stone in some localities) was permitting abandonment of crucks, or their degeneration towards principal rafters (also called 'couples' in the later historical documentation) supported on the wall heads.

Interpretation of these houses in the north has come from close scrutiny of the well-known cartographic sources of Bartlett and Raven in the context of other contemporary documents. It finds support from recent excavation of sites in County Antrim, where sub-rectangular houses with thick walls of stone footings, probably carrying sod upper walls, were without post-holes. Sod is not a load-bearing material, posing the problem of roof support, and the likelihood of crucks has been advanced. Hearths in these houses were sited between their ends, offset from the entrance. This suggests that instances on some maps of c. 1600 of dwellings apparently with entrance and a chimney in line betraying the internal hearth position, may be cartographic stylisation rather than actual detail.[16] Relevant excavated sites of rural houses elsewhere in Ireland are the late medieval ones at Caherguillamore, County Limerick,[17] and the seventeenth-century dwellings at Liathmore-Mochoemóg in Tipperary.[18] At both sites, entrance/hearth relationships, similar to those in the recent Antrim excavations, were found. The latter reveal the existence of essentially the same house plan in differing circumstances; at Tildarg in a large permanent dwelling within a small fortification;[19] in Glen-makeeran in a smaller, seasonally occupied house associated with summer pasturing, a broadening in one end of the plan has been interpreted as allowing accommodation of a bed in the corner of the house akin to the function of the outshot in later houses.[20] Evidence from all sources therefore, points towards a widespread house type, not confined to Ulster.

Improvement of rural housing after 1600

Two kinds of innovation were introduced to the Irish rural built environment in the seventeenth century, constructional changes and a new internal arrangement or plan type. Their dissemination socially and geographically continued through the eighteenth century and as a consequence the physical appearance and internal comfort of rural housing in many areas underwent major change. Had these changes been able to evolve in a stable social environment in the seventeenth century once they were introduced, perhaps there might have been an Irish 'great rebuilding',[21] the beginnings of which have been inferred in the north from consideration of the tree-ring datings of a number of houses, mainly from the 1650s onwards.[22] However, it is fairly clear that although there was development in the formal domestic architecture patronised by the wealthy, vernacular housing in general experienced degeneration, especially after the middle of the eighteenth century. In particular there was an enormous proliferation of sub-standard one-room housing attributable to the demographic pressure of the later eighteenth and early nineteenth centuries.[23]

In Ulster new house types were introduced mainly in the early 1600s, but it is possible that rather earlier introduction of timber-framed dwellings on English models occurred in southern Ireland; such houses certainly appeared in a number of towns.[24] Box-framed houses were built in the Ulster Plantation, in the Londonderry towns for which explicit carto-graphic illustrations and detailed building records survive, and in rural situations as well. The internal planning of these houses was to be more significant than their mode of construction. They were of the hearth-lobby type, providing the source from which developed the jamb wall as it survived in later dwellings still available for field study. This plan type is incapable of accommodating people and their cattle in the same space and contrasts with the earlier Irish housing which had been, and was later, adaptable to pastoral practices. Nineteenth-century byre-dwellings studied in the field in western districts of Connacht and particularly in Ulster, were the Irish representatives of a wider Atlantic-

European tradition.[25] In Ulster the distribution of lobby-entry houses was established in areas of English settlement, consistent with derivation of the type from areas in southern England where it had evolved about the middle of the sixteenth century, whence it also spread to other parts of England contemporaneously with its arrival in Ireland. It was also appearing in the American Tidewater settlements. Not all planters' houses were of this plan. Two-storey stone-wall houses were also constructed, having a plan difficult to distinguish from the later development of Irish houses, with hearths placed at the gable ends.

Changes of building materials accompanied the new house types. Later depletion of timber resources and the ease with which they could be set alight, undoubtedly were significant factors in the gradual disappearance of timber-framed houses on the English model, but a few survived into the nineteenth century, for example in County Antrim.[26] Yet even a few years after the commencement of building at Coleraine, the Irish Society was prohibiting timber construction in the town, because what had served adequately in an English climate was rotting too quickly due to damp in the north of Ireland. Stone houses were replacing timber ones in Coleraine by the 1670s; they were always the norm in the west of the county around Derry city.[27] Documentation suggests that wherever English settlers built in stone they constructed houses with gable hearths and chimneys, at least sometimes with brick-lined ovens, in contrast to the hearth-lobby configuration of their timber-framed dwellings. It is also interesting that no specifically Scottish features can be detected amongst building innovations at vernacular level at this period, although there were Scottish influences in the contemporary or slightly earlier castles of the wealthy. From what is known of Scottish vernacular housing it is clear that it shared constructional and plan elements with Irish rural housing at the end of the medieval period.[28] However, there has been too little study of vernacular architecture in the west lowlands and the southwest of Scotland, the principal source areas of Scottish emigration to Ulster in the seventeenth century, to be certain that this is the whole explanation.

Two elements mentioned here were of prime importance: gables and chimneys. The apparent pre-1600 ubiquity in Ireland of the rural house with hip-ended roof was now gone. The density of gabled houses was most marked in the north, hipped roofs persisted in Leinster, east Munster and east Connacht. Later colonisation of more marginal land at higher altitudes almost everywhere in Ireland was represented by gabled dwellings. Dwellings with hipped roofs, often also associated with hearth-lobby plans, characterised many more prosperous districts where houses were better maintained. In poorer districts, especially in the north and along the western seaboard, houses were less substantially constructed, requiring more frequent replacement and so the gabled form was more readily able to displace the hipped. It is by no means a truism that the most archaic architectural features persist longest in the most remote districts: there is the paradox that modest prosperity may breed conservatism, and poverty, innovation, the reverse of architectural innovation in the 'great tradition' patronised by the wealthy.

Walls built of mass materials also became common after 1600, although as we have seen, earth walling had been present in Irish building much earlier, and use of wattle and sod was to persist well into the nineteenth century. Use of stone seems to have commenced initially in more settled, prosperous areas, reflecting a requirement of stable social circumstances to accommodate the slower pace of building it entailed. Mass walling materials also gradually permitted abandonment of older constructional techniques, so that crucks for example, could be replaced by principal-rafter trusses. Yet it has been instructive to discover brick houses in north Londonderry[29] and west Fermanagh,[30] regarded in local oral tradition as the earliest attempts to use brick, in which crucks continued to support the roofs, relieving the walls of much of the burden. In both cases the principles of brick bonding were obviously not understood and in this way an archaic but tested technique therefore persisted.

Depletion of suitable timber resources must have contributed to the dissemination of building in mass-walling materials. Native oak has not been discovered in any Ulster house dating after 1720, and use of fossil timber from peat bogs although attested from very much earlier, became widespread thereafter and into the nineteenth century until it too became difficult to locate or retrieve. From 1850 imported sawn softwood was being widely used, even by poorer levels of society for roof timbering and for doors and windows, and slightly later for flooring. Its use commenced much earlier, higher up the social scale, and the earliest newspaper advertisements for its importation from northern Europe and North America relate well to the dating of the last houses using native oak.[31]

At the technical level of roof timbering systems, British influence also introduced a system of principal-rafter roof trusses connected by means of butt purlins allowing 'single skin' roofs in which the backs of the principals served also as common rafters, since both lay in the same plane.[32] There can be little doubt that Irish roof-carpentry practice about 1600 was a 'double skin' roof in which roof trusses were overlain by longitudinal purlins. These in turn were overlain by common rafters stretching from wall head to roof ridge, either continuous common rafters on small roofs, or rafter sections overlapping on purlins in larger ones.[33] Butt-purlin roof systems were introduced to both urban and rural housing in the north in the seventeenth century, but thereafter had remarkably little influence on vernacular carpentry, whereas at upper social levels, their use persisted so long as native oak was available.

The study of roof timbering systems in Ireland is in its infancy, but already in the north a working hypothesis has been partly outlined.[34] In the eighteenth century, butt-purlin principal-rafter roofs persisted, the oak of their seventeenth-century predecessors being replaced with softwood. From about the middle of the eighteenth century they were being influenced by ideas taken from architectural pattern books, and king-posts begin to appear. This evolution was increasingly associated with the housing of the wealthy, and by the latter part of the century it was associated with rural institutional buildings such as churches and schools. Institutional use of the same system was evidenced earlier in the towns. Two oak butt-purlin roofs from seventeenth-century institutional buildings on the site were brought together on a rebuilt gaol in 1746 in Downpatrick, later taken over as the Down Hunt Rooms. In addition softwood was used in reworking the two original roofs into one. By contrast, at vernacular level, a house in south Antrim illustrates the fate of imported carpentry practices. A small two-room house built with hearth-lobby plan by English settlers and covered by a butt-purlin oak roof was later altered when the house was reworked and enlarged to achieve a tripartite plan, with central hall and formalised façade. In lengthening the roof, the new timbering was arranged as though purlins overlaid the roof truss. Another house, of about 1717 and the last recognised so far to be built with oak, from near Toome Bridge, illustrates a fusion of the two systems in its roof rather than replacement of one by the other.[35]

Such evidence from study of roofs has implications in regard to the organisation of carpentry in Irish house building. Obviously by the early part of the eighteenth century there were co-existing traditions. Rural craftsmen were building vernacular houses using through-purlin roofing; many of them may not have been specialists earning a living exclusively from their craft, and construction of rural houses by their residents must have been fairly common in the eighteenth century as it was also in the nineteenth. By contrast, specialist house carpenters who derived their skills and practices from imported traditions were patronised by the wealthy in building their rural mansions in the seventeenth century and later in both urban and rural contexts their work depended also on public and institutional support.

Storeyed houses were introduced in the early 1600s to Ulster by British settlers and they were only possible because they came with chimneys which, confining and leading the smoke from hearths at ground-floor level, thereby made the upper part of houses habitable. Chimneys were being introduced into urban situations elsewhere in Ireland in the latter part of the preceding century.[36] In rural areas chimneys seem not to have become widely used in the seventeenth century, and so lofts and upper storeys likewise were uncommon, as they were to remain in many rural areas until late into the nineteenth century. This delay was perhaps attributable to the general cultural impoverishment experienced during the time when population levels were rapidly rising after the middle of the eighteenth century. Other areas of Ireland's material culture became similarly impoverished at the same period: witness the disappearance of cheese-making from most, if not all districts.

The extent of improvement 1800-1850

Changes identified in rural housing between 1600 and 1800 are mainly qualitative, established from a synthesis of evidence from formal documentation and from field study. In the absence of statistics illustrating the nature of rural housing before the 1841 census data, the extent to which building innovations leading to improved living conditions had progressed socially and regionally is difficult to assess. On the other hand, the last quarter of the eighteenth century and the first half of the nineteenth century saw much investigation of the problems of rural Ireland. Comment was biased in various ways, regionally to areas of scenic attraction which were also often the areas of greatest poverty, or because travellers like Arthur Young, with his interest in agrarian improvement, sought out evidence to validate pre-conceived notions.

Many comments concerning improved housing conditions alongside evidence of poverty and archaism between 1800 and 1845 could be quoted. Two will suffice. Having quoted the well-known passage from 'The Irish Hudibras' about the byre-dwelling house type in his Leitrim survey M'Parlan went on:

> . . . but truth also requires to declare, that those hovels are getting fewer by degrees; chimneys, partitions, and separate cow-houses sometimes ornament the little dwelling, and this cow-house, and sometimes a bit of a barn, form the whole extent of the offices.[37]

He also commented on progress in rural housing improvement in Mayo in the same year, 1802.[38] Similar comments, or others stressing the exceptional occurrence of such improvements could be quoted from other county surveys of the same period. In the north, in 1816 Atkinson suggested that in County Antrim:

> When the circumstances of the farmer enable him, and the size of his farm justifies him in doing it, he usually erects a dwelling-house two stories high . . .[39]

Comparable statements can be found in the parish memoirs of the Ordnance Survey for Ulster counties in the 1830s, suggesting a core of building innovation in south Antrim, which probably extended into parts of north Down along the Lagan valley.[40] These comments are all essentially qualitative in nature and the census data on house sizes available from 1841 do little to indicate the scale of building improvements. Nevertheless they identify the existence of large numbers of one-room houses, the numbers of which, however, declined dramatically in the next ten years. For example, class III houses ranged in size from two to four rooms, and would have included older single-storey thatched dwellings of four rooms together with some of the earliest two-storey slated houses with the same number of rooms. These became common in the later nineteenth century in Monaghan and south Down. Even the figures for one-room houses are difficult to assess in some areas. In the west they would have included both byre-dwellings, which might be sizeable structures, harking back to practices of common accommodation of people and cattle separated from each other only by large items of furniture and the tiny cabins of the landless poor.

Detailed statistical surveys of Irish estates by a Dublin surveyor, Maurice Collis, between 1843 and 1848, however, provide some basis to judge the situation.[41] In the later 1830s he was retained by Trinity College, Dublin, to watch over their interests while the Ordnance Survey progressed over the college lands and he was later commissioned to carry out house-by-house statistical surveys of the estates. With this experience he went on to survey in a slightly elaborated form, the Buckingham estates (his data survive only for the Ballyvaughan property in north Clare), the Grocers' Company estate in County Londonderry, and the Marquis of Londonderry's estate in north Down. In an abbreviated form (because they thought his full survey would be too expensive) the estates of the Irish Society in the North-West and North-East Liberties baronies

TABLE 5:1

SIZE, ROOFING AND LIGHTING OF IRISH RURAL HOUSING IN THE 1840s

County	Barony District	Estate	Year	No. of Rural Houses	Thatch*	Storeys* 1	2	3	Sing.* Room	Façade Windows* 0	1	2/3	4+
Armagh	Charlemont	TCD	1843	378	98.4	98.9	1.1	—	14.6	67.3	13.5	15.1	3.7
Armagh	Killylea etc.	TCD	1843	2122	88.2	93.6	6.0	0.3	9.1	26.3	26.3	40.8	6.6
Donegal	Tirhugh Bundoran	TCD	1843	294	99.0	96.3	2.4	1.3	—	13.3	16.3	65.3	5.1
Donegal	Tirhugh Ballintra	TCD	1843	1530	90.2	94.0	5.5	0.5	15.0	23.2	17.2	55.0	4.6
Donegal	Kilmacrenan	TCD	1843	1336	96.8	98.1	1.8	0.1	34.8	46.5	23.6	27.8	2.1
Down	Lr.Ards/Lr.C'reagh N. Down	Londonderry	1848	1863	75.1	95.5	4.3	0.2	23.8	4.3	25.6	55.1	55.1
Down	Lecale	TCD	1843	118	95.8	98.3	1.7	—	18.6	25.4	31.4	37.3	5.9
Fermanagh	Clankelly	TCD	1843	828	97.1	98.1	1.8	0.1	24.5	42.7	21.4	33.5	2.4
Londonderry	Tirkeeran	Grocers	1845	898	90.7	96.5	2.7	0.8	33.4	15.6	27.5	45.4	11.5
Londonderry	NW Liberties	Irish Soc.	1847	1094	81.5	92.8	6.5	0.7	34.7	9.9	28.9	46.3	14.9
Londonderry	NE Liberties	Irish Soc.	1847	334	82.3	91.9	7.8	0.3	13.5	1.8	16.5	62.3	19.4
Clare	Burren	Buckingham	1847	246	98.0	98.0	2.0	—	38.6	53.7	25.6	18.3	2.4
Kerry	Iveragh	TCD	1843	695	88.9	94.7	5.3	—	55.4	83.3	5.2	8.9	2.6
Kerry	Glanarought	TCD	1843	302	96.7	92.4	7.6	—	52.3	71.8	9.6	13.3	5.3
Kerry	Clanmaurice	TCD	1843	270	99.6	99.6	0.4	—	57.4	58.9	18.9	20.0	2.2
Kerry	Iraghticonnor	TCD	1843	2403	98.9	99.4	0.5	0.1	31.1	48.5	20.1	29.0	2.4
Offaly	Clonlisk	TCD	1843	213	85.0	89.2	8.4	2.4	20.7	36.6	16.9	36.2	10.3
Wicklow	Talbotstown Up.	TCD	1843	145	86.2	90.3	9.0	0.7	13.8	22.1	24.8	45.5	7.6

*Percentages of total rural houses.

Statistics calculated from: TCD – surveys of the college estates, 1843 (T.C.D. Mun V 79/1-14); Grocers – Estate of the Most Worshipful Company of Grocers of Londonderry, 1845 (Guildhall Library, London, ms. 11643, also P.R.O.N.I. T 2204/2); Irish Soc. – Irish Society estates survey, enumeration sheets, 1847 (Corporation of London R.O., coll. 440A, also P.R.O.N.I. MIC 9A/Reel 14 (Add)); Buckingham – MS statistical townland summary sheets, dated from internal evidence, 1847, in, Particulars and Conditions of Sale of . . . Fee-Simple Estates . . . for Sale by auction, . . . 1848, endorsed 'Clare Estate' (N.L.I. Maps 14.A.20); Londonderry – Statistical Survey of the Estate of the Most Noble the Marquis of Londonderry situate in the County of Down, 1848 (P.R.O.N.I. T 1536/4). The author is grateful to the various authorities for permission and facilities to consult these documents.

of County Londonderry were also surveyed by Collis. Housing data common to all of his surveys, summarised as estate percentages, are set out in table 5:1; additional information from the more comprehensive later surveys are in table 5:2.

Full discussion of these statistics is beyond the scope of this paper; some general points only can be made. Detailed townland analysis of the Collis material, bracketed by the 1841 and 1851 census housing data, authenticates the former as a reliable source, and shows that in many cases, but not all, house numbers were declining slowly before the great Famine. This makes the very rapid disappearance of the lowest-standard, one-room dwellings after 1845 all the more remarkable. Nevertheless, Collis himself supplies a warning note when, in his north Clare survey in 1847, he clearly identifies six of twenty-four townlands he surveyed for which he claims the 1841 census data are inaccurate; sadly he does not specify the nature of these discrepancies. There is also the problem of the representativeness of the estates which Collis surveyed. Comparison with baronial percentages of one-room housing in 1841 suggests that the material in his surveys in Meath, Westmeath, Laois and Cork must be left out and that his samples in Kildare and Tipperary may be suspect. In addition, because of the fragmented nature of the college lands in Limerick, that county's data are difficult to assess. Although at townland level the Longford and Louth statistics are reliable, the percentages of one-room houses in these counties are grossly anomalous. In Louth the college estate was poor, but in Longford it was one of stark contrasts, the enumeration there producing high percentages of one-room houses (poverty) and of both two-storey and slated houses (suggesting building innovation, and so at least modest prosperity). For the rest, the one-room house percentages are consistent with those derived from the 1841 census, and need no further comment here.

The most striking feature of these data is the predominance everywhere of the one-storey thatched dwelling. Slated houses were present in north Down to a very significant degree, and in the Liberties baronies of County Londonderry; local slate quarries were present in the vicinity of these estates, having been exploited for roofing material in east Down even in the seventeenth century.[42] However, in the Liberties baronies, proximity to relatively prosperous and dynamic centres such as Derry city and Coleraine, was also significant. The Iveragh figure in Kerry is also possibly distorted upwards because of a limited statistical definition of the town of Cahirciveen in Collis's enumeration. The Longford situation has already been noted, and some rural prosperity is

TABLE 5:2

CHIMNEYS AND FLOORING OF IRISH RURAL HOUSING IN THE 1840s

County	Barony District	Estate	Year	No. of Rural Houses	Chimneys				Floors			
					0	Hole	1	2+	Earth	Wood	Flags	Earth & Wood
Down	Lr. Ards/ Lr. C'reagh											
	N. Down	Londonderry	1848	1863	1.7	2.6	44.1	51.2	78.9	8.9	6.9	5.4
Londonderry	Tirkeeran	Grocers	1845	898	0.9	33.0	32.4	33.7	89.4	2.9	2.1	5.6
Londonderry	NW Liberties	Irish Soc.	1847	1094	0.9	22.9	41.8	34.4	79.7	6.1	9.1	5.1
Londonderry	NE Liberties	Irish Soc.	1847	334	0.3	2.1	61.1	36.5	83.2	9.0	3.0	4.8
Clare	Burren	Buckingham	1847	246	—	45.1	49.6	5.3	97.6	2.4	—	—

Percentages of total rural houses.

Sources: as Table 5:1.

probably represented in the percentage of slated houses in the south Donegal college estate, and in those in west Armagh, Offaly and Wicklow.

Essentially the same districts are at issue when the higher percentages of two-storey houses are considered (with the important exception of the Marquis of Londonderry's estate in north Down), and here data referring to façade windows, flooring and chimneys are suggestive of comfort if not prosperity. Other indices in the Collis surveys hint that prosperity need not necessarily be reflected in the building of larger rural houses. Of all the estates Collis surveyed, the north Down one had by far the most literate population; it had the benefit of the 'Ulster custom'; more than a quarter of its occupying families or their forebears had been on their holdings for more than half a century. Value systems, and in particular perceptions of the material aspects of life must be considered in trying to interpret these figures.

Windowless houses as expected were most prevalent in western areas, in the Louth estate already noted as poor and in the small college estate in north-west Armagh, near Charlemont. The north Down and the County Londonderry Liberties estates are outstanding in their low percentages of windowless houses, followed by others already noted as improving in the standard of rural housing. Similar conclusions arise from consideration of the best-lighted houses having four or more façade windows, with two notable variations; the presence of good housing is evident in the Longford figures, and there were remarkably few rural houses in the Fermanagh college estate with more than three façade windows.

The contrast between the fairly prosperous northern estates where Collis gathered data, and the Buckingham property in north Clare is stark; earthen floors, and almost half of the dwellings with only a hole in the roof to allow egress of smoke proclaim the poor living standards of the latter estate. Even in the north, however, there were significant variations. In the north Down and Coleraine areas, almost all houses had at least one chimney, but between a fifth and a third of the dwellings in the west County Londonderry rural properties of the Grocers' Company and the Irish Society had only a hole in the roof. Whether throughout the house, or in rooms other than the kitchen, timber floors were a distinct sign of prosperity. Their insertion demanded sufficient resources to purchase the sawn planks required. They were present in between one in seven and one in fifteen houses in north Down and in the County Londonderry Liberties baronies estates, but clearly there was less prosperity on the Grocers' property, while timber floors were enumerated in only half a dozen houses in the Ballyvaughan estate in north Clare. The prevalence of earthen floors in even the very best estates in the north of Ireland in the 1840s is the most striking fact of all.

In sum, the statistical material on rural housing in the 1840s, such as it is, does not support a view of extensive improvement of rural dwellings in the first half of the nineteenth century.[43] An innovative base for future development was certainly there, and as the Longford data show this may have been at the level of the prosperous farmer. The Irish Society's estates in County Londonderry illustrate the influence of proximity to urban centres for innovation in building and improved living conditions. Circumstances on the Marquis of Londonderry's north Down estate illustrate modest, but not ostentatious rural prosperity. Overall, the well-known east/west dichotomy in nineteenth-century rural Ireland is evident, but superimposed on it is the reality of sudden local changes in domestic circumstances, especially at townland level.

Rural housing 1850-1900

Housing improvements had been introduced, then, in regionally and socially limited contexts, before the middle of the nineteenth century; their dissemination to the generality of rural housing did not take place until after 1840. Census data reveal a massive decline in numbers of one-room houses between 1841 and 1851; yet at the earlier date, two- to four-room houses still represented about half of all rural dwellings in much of Ulster and Leinster, and about one-third in Connacht and Munster. This class III housing in the census, of two to four rooms in size, consisted largely, if not exclusively, of unimproved vernacular buildings.

Larger houses of five to nine rooms represent less than one in ten of all rural dwellings over most of Connacht, and between one in six and one in ten in much of Munster, whereas the proportions were appreciably higher in most Ulster counties and in some Leinster ones, notably Dublin, Kilkenny, Laois, Offaly, Wexford and Wicklow.

During the 1840s most Irish counties experienced considerable growth, of between a quarter and a half, in the numbers of these larger houses with the exception of the western coastal counties. Circumstances differed in the case of the two- to four-room houses. Only thirteen counties experienced an absolute increase in their numbers between 1841 and 1851, and these were dominated by the western coastal counties together with Antrim, Londonderry, west Cork, and Kilkenny. Vernacular houses were obviously still being constructed in significant numbers in these parts of Ireland. At the same time, even in many of the counties where there was a decline in the numbers of these houses, there was still a significant rise of c. 10 per cent in the proportions of total rural houses represented by the diminished absolute numbers. Between 1841 and 1851, only the more prosperous Leinster counties, together with Down in Ulster, experienced rises of less than 10 per cent of all rural dwellings represented by the lower numbers of these houses in 1851 as compared with 1841, and in Dublin the proportion actually declined slightly.

Some of these statistics suggest that improvement was proceeding more rapidly than the Collis surveys suggest. The census classification of housing is based solely on size assessed by mere counting of rooms and this obscures what was happening if the field evidence is examined. The conclusion that may be adduced from the northern evidence is that internal subdivision of existing houses was involved in the changing circumstances suggested in the census figures, and that the addition of upper storeys as a means of enlargement did not become common until the last quarter of the nineteenth century.[44] Neither of these processes in any way interfered with the essentially vernacular character of rural housing, which has persisted since at least the seventeenth century. Evolution continued, and there was no wholesale revolutionary acceptance of new rural house types. Analysis of the growth in floor areas of rural housing would provide a better assessment of real improvements in this period, for what the census data essentially reflect is the spread of ideas of the social desirability of privacy within the home, especially separation of unmarried males and females in the sleeping arrangements.

Other forms of specialisation of internal space-use spread in the same period, for example the desirability of having a parlour, even though in many cases this also accommodated a bed or beds. An innovation based in the provision of parlours at upper and some middle social levels was present at least from the early eighteenth century.[45] Two changes in building materials became widespread after 1840; timber flooring, and later the spread of imported roof slate. This happened towards the end of the century and it was usually associated with the widespread introduction of upper storeys for sleeping.

Based mainly on northern research experience, this paper poses no more than a series of hypotheses as explanations of changes in Irish rural housing over three centuries. Regional variability in the statistical material of the 1840s more than suffices to identify the need for detailed local and regional studies all over Ireland, not alone by those who examine houses for cultural, historical and architectural reasons, but also by social historians.

NOTES

1. Maurice Craig, *The architecture of Ireland from the earliest times to 1880* (London, 1982); idem, *Classic Irish houses of the middle size* (London, 1975); Brian de Breffny and Rosemary ffolliott, *The houses of Ireland* (London, 1975).

2. The background literature on vernacular architecture is not fully referenced here; the relevant literature is in Caoimhín Ó Danachair, *A bibliography of Irish ethnology and folk tradition* (Dublin, 1978), and idem, 'Supplement to a bibliography of Irish ethnology and folklore' in *Béaloideas,* xlviii/xlix (1980-81), pp. 206-27.

3. The most recent discussion of the jamb wall is in Alan Gailey, *Rural houses of the north of Ireland* (Edinburgh, 1984), pp. 164-71.

4. The Raven maps are reproduced in D. A. Chart (ed.), *Londonderry and the London Companies, 1609-1629: the Phillips Manuscripts* (Belfast, 1928).

5. 'A plott for a tenant house at Moneymore', 1615, reproduced in Philip Robinson, ' "English" house built at Moneymore, County Londonderry, c. 1615' in *Post-Medieval Archaeology,* xvii (1983), p. 52.

6. Reproduced in Gailey, *Rural houses of the north of Ireland,* p. 171.

7. William Tighe, *Statistical observations relative to the County of Kilkenny made in the years 1800 and 1801* (Dublin, 1802), p. 413.

8. Gailey, *Rural houses of the north of Ireland,* pp. 151-6.

9. James M'Parlan, *Statistical survey of the County of Mayo* (Dublin, 1802), p. 65.

10. A. T. Lucas, 'Contributions to the history of the Irish house: a possible ancestry of the bed outshot' in *Folk Life,* viii (1970), pp. 81-98.

11. Gailey, *Rural houses of the north of Ireland,* pp. 182-8.

12. The basis for this discussion of early seventeenth-century houses types is Philip Robinson, 'Vernacular housing in Ulster in the seventeenth century' in *Ulster Folklife,* xxv (1979), pp. 1-28.

13. *La boullaye Le Gouz, Tour in Ireland in 1644.* (ed.), T. C. Croker (London, 1837), p. 40.

14. Extent of the lands of Thomas Fitzmaurice, Manor of Insula, County Kerry, 1298 (P.R.O. London, E101/233(6)).

15. Discussion of crucks in a European context is in N. W. Alcock et al., *Cruck construction* (London, 1981).

16. For a different interpretation of these illustrations see Caoimhín Ó Danachair, 'Representations of houses on some 17th century maps' in J. G. Jenkins (ed.), *Studies in folk life* (London, 1969), pp. 92-103.

17. S. P. Ó Riordáin and John Hunt, 'Medieval dwellings at Caherguillamore, County Limerick' in *R.S.A.I. Jn.,* lxxii (1942), pp. 37-63.

18. H. G. Leask and R. A. S. Macaslister, 'Liathmore-Mochoemóg (Leigh), County Tipperary' in *R.I.A. Proc.,* li (1945-8), C, no. 1 (1946), pp. 1-14.

19. N. F. Brannon, 'A small excavation in Tildarg Townland, near Ballyclare, County Antrim' in *U.J.A.,* 3rd ser., xlvii (1984), pp. 163-170.

20. Brian Williams and Philip Robinson, 'The excavation of bronze age cists and a medieval booley house at Glenmakeeran, County Antrim, and a discussion of booleying in north Antrim' in *U.J.A.,* 3rd ser., xlvi (1983), pp. 29-40.

21. The concept of the 'great rebuilding' in English vernacular architecture 1570-1640 is discussed briefly in Ronald Brunskill, *Houses* (London, 1982), pp. 24-5.

22. M. G. L. Baillie, 'Dendrochronology as a tool for the dating of vernacular buildings in the north of Ireland' in *Vernacular Architecture,* vii (1976), pp. 3-10.

23. Studies of these small buildings are Caoimhín Ó Danachair, 'The bóthán scóir' in E. Rynne (ed.), *North Munster studies* (Limerick, 1967), pp. 489-98; Alan Gailey, 'The housing of the rural poor in nineteenth-century Ulster' in *Ulster Folklife,* xxii (1976), pp. 34-57.

24. de Breffney and ffolliott, *The houses of Ireland,* chapter 1.

25. Caoimhín Ó Danachair, 'The combined byre-and-dwelling in Ireland' in *Folk Life,* ii (1964), pp. 58-75.

26. O.S. Memoir, Antrim Parish, 1837 (R.I.A., Box 10, IV, 3, p. 36).

27. Philip Robinson and N. F. Brannon, 'A seventeenth-century house in New Row, Coleraine' in *U.J.A.,* 3rd ser., xliv/xlv (1981-2), pp. 173-8; Philip Robinson, 'Some late survivals of box-framed "Plantation" houses in Coleraine' in *U.J.A.,*3rd ser., xlvi (1983), pp. 129-36.

28. Ian D. Whyte, 'Rural housing in lowland Scotland in the seventeenth century: the evidence of estate papers' in *Scottish Studies,* xix (1975), pp. 55-68.

29. Desmond McCourt, 'Some cruck framed buildings in Donegal and Derry' in *Ulster Folklife,* xi (1965), 39-50.

30. Gailey, *Rural houses of the north of Ireland,* pp. 75-7.

31. For example, issues of the *Belfast News-Letter* in 1739 contain advertisements for imported North European softwoods for building purposes.

32. Philip Robinson and N. F. Brannon, loc. cit., pp. 173-8.

33. Roof timbering systems used in Irish vernacular building are discussed in Gailey, *Rural houses of the north of Ireland,* chapter 5, but systems used outside Ulster are not included.

34. The writer is indebted to his colleague Philip Robinson for much discussion of this matter, arising from his unpublished studies of seventeenth-century Ulster buildings and their roofing systems.

35. Alan Gailey, 'A house from Gloverstown, Lismacloskey, County Antrim', in *Ulster Folklife,* xx (1974), pp. 24-41.

36. A. T. Lucas, 'Contributions to the study of the Irish house: smokehole and chimney' in Alan Gailey and Dáithí Ó hÓgáin (ed.), *Gold under the furze* (Dublin, 1982), pp. 50-66.

37. James M'Parlan, *Statistical survey of the County of Leitrim* (Dublin, 1802), p. 44.

38. James M'Parlan, *Statistical survey of the County of Mayo* (Dublin, 1802), p. 86.

39. A. Atkinson, *Ireland exhibited to England . . .* (London, 1823), pp. 284-5, known to have been written in 1816.

40. Alan Gailey, 'Folklife study and the Ordnance Survey Memoirs' in Gailey and Ó hÓgáin (ed.), *Gold under the furze,* pp. 157-9.

41. This source is described in Alan Gailey, 'Local life in Ulster 1843-1848: the statistical surveys of Maurice Collis' in *Ulster Local Studies,* ix, no. 20 (1985), pp. 120-127.

42. Philip Robinson, 'From thatch to slate: innovation in roof covering materials for traditional houses in Ulster' in *Ulster Folklife,* xxxi (1985), pp. 21-35.

43. For a different view of the progress of housing improvement in early nineteenth-century rural Ireland, see L. M. Cullen, *Economic history of Ireland since 1660* (London, 1972), p. 116.

44. Alan Gailey, 'Some developments and adaptions of traditional house types' in Caoimhín Ó Danachair (ed.), *Folk and farm* (Dublin, 1976), pp. 56-71.

45. Parlours are not mentioned specifically in any of the domestic inventories of an eighteenth-century Quaker community in mid Armagh, but in one case a parlour may be inferred from its contents; see Alan Gailey, 'The Ballyhagan inventories, 1716-1740' in *Folk Life,* xv (1977), pp. 42-6.

Landholding and settlement in the counties of Meath and Cavan in the nineteenth century

T. JONES HUGHES

The divide between Leinster and Ulster is best known as a long-standing administrative boundary. As well as being a county and an interprovincial border it also marks the limits of the pre-Reformation and modern Catholic dioceses of Meath and Kilmore. Even the ardent reformers of the Poor Law Commission of 1835, in their attempt to define tributary territories for towns such as Bailieborough, Oldcastle and Kells, left this ancient line largely undisturbed. In the mid-nineteenth century the Meath-Cavan border was most evident as the northern edge of a market-orientated economy in Leinster as opposed to the peasant world of south Ulster. Our purpose is to examine the nature of this divide with special reference to the rural geography of the two counties in the nineteenth century. The discussion is based on data drawn from large-scale Ordnance Survey maps, the printed books of the Griffith's valuation of rateable property of mid-century and the surviving field evidence. An attempt has been made to present the primary data in map form using baronies and historic or Anglican parishes as plotting units. Our main task entails the description, analysis and tentative interpretation of these distributions. The information employed falls into five main interrelated categories involving the landowner, the tenant farmer, the poor, the names of townlands and the parish framework.

The landowner

In the landowning system which prevailed in nineteenth-century Ireland the basic territorial entity was referred to as the estate and it is possible to rank these estates according to their rateable valuation. The classification adopted here relates only to the land held in each of the two counties. Although County Meath was only 40,000 hectares larger than County Cavan, it contained twice as many estates valued at £100 and over as were found in Cavan. In Meath these estates numbered 270 as compared with 153 for County Cavan. The ownership of land was therefore more fragmented in Meath and for this reason, the estate as a territorial entity, may have had a greater meaning in the lives of Cavan people. The most substantial estates in nineteenth-century Ireland were those valued at over £20,000 and a total of thirty-three of these great estates could be identified in 1876.[1] One-third of these were based on what is now Northern Ireland. The only property of this dimension in our two counties was the Maxwell estate at Farnham alongside the county town of Cavan. There were no more than twelve properties based on Meath whose lands within the county were valued at £5,000 and over (Fig. 6:1). Meath was not therefore a county of great estates. In Meath as elsewhere in Ireland, the great estate as a modern landowning unit was essentially a product of the seventeenth-century confiscations of property. The largest were those of Darnley of Athboy in the barony of Lune, Naper of Loughcrew in the barony of Fore and Headfort of Kells. Their average value was £14,000. Despite its comparative physiographic handicaps Cavan contained the residences of the owners of seven properties which were valued at £5,000 and over (Fig. 6:2) and, in addition to Farnham, the greatest of these were the estates of Saunderson of Castle Saunders and Coote of Cootehill, both in the barony of Tullygarvey on the border with County Monaghan, but with an average valuation of only £7,000. The Tullygarvey group of estates in north-east County Cavan represented the tail-end of Ireland's most complicated web of great landed properties which, in the nineteenth century, extended through County Monaghan and south-east Ulster in the direction of the North Channel. In both Cavan and Meath the numerically dominant category of estates were those valued at less than £1,000. These numbered 168 or over 60 per cent of the total in Meath and 110 or 70 per cent of the total in Cavan. Despite their radically different agrarian

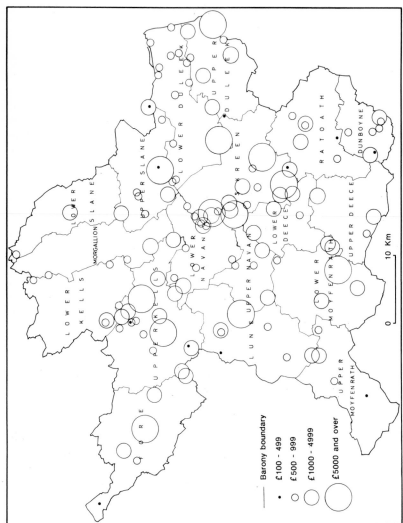

Figure 6:1. The valuation of the estates of resident landowners in County Meath, 1876.

histories, we were therefore surprised to find that in the later nineteenth century, at least, there were no outstanding distinctions to be drawn in the scale of landowning between these two counties lying on either side of Leinster-Ulster inter-provincial divide.

Ireland's historical experiences have frequently been viewed and interpreted in terms of a constant struggle for supremacy between an indigenous population and intruders. The indigenous peoples we shall refer to as Irish or Gaelic and the intruders as English or, where appropriate, New English, to distinguish them from the descendants of an Anglo-Norman population. Furthermore in our attempts to seek explanations of human behaviour patterns we shall refer to the English as colonists and aliens and their culture will be viewed as a colonial culture. In any comparative discussion of conditions prevailing in the provinces of Leinster and Ulster in the nineteenth century this ethnic or national distinction seems to be fundamental, especially as it relates to the ownership and occupation of land. A crude classification of family names enables us to identify and isolate the two main national groups. In County Meath among 130 owners of land identified in this way as many as 84 had New English names, whilst in Cavan 30 out of a total of 47 landowners had English or Scottish names. Among the proprietors of land therefore the colonial presence was as evident in Meath as it was in Cavan. This suggests that the policy of land confiscation and transfer, as this was adopted and implemented from the seventeenth century, had far reaching implications in both counties. What were the circumstances which made possible the ruthless implementation of this policy? It may be important to notice at the same time that in both counties as many as 20 per cent of the owners of land in the closing decades of the nineteenth century appear to have been of Irish stock. Among the owners of land, however, the process of alienation had proceeded over a far longer period in County Meath than in County Cavan. In Meath non-Irish landowners had been shunting for position and status for many centuries, especially in the baronies which were located in the east of the county, where Norman rural colonisation had been most efficient and durable. Distinguished families such as the Plunketts of Dunsany and Killeen in the barony of Skreen, and Preston of Gormanston in the barony of Duleek, had made handsome contributions to the enrichment and diversification of the culture of this pivotal area of pre-urban Gaelic Ireland. The inter-provincial divide, with which we are concerned, denotes the northern limit of the area in eastern Ireland which was most profoundly influenced by the Norman presence. There is little doubt that this limit, in turn, was largely dictated and defined by the major physiographic changes in landforms and land quality which are associated with the Dunany glacial limit, its kame belt and the southern edge of the drumlin collar. Paradoxically, from the seventeenth century, the role of this frontier zone was reversed as it came to mark the limit of the area in south Ulster which was subjected to intensive English and Scottish tenant farmer settlement.

In addition to being classified according to their national origins it has also been found useful to distinguish between owners of land in Ireland in the nineteenth century according to whether they were resident or non-resident. The presence or absence of its owner profoundly influenced the quality of land management locally and absenteeism has been seen as the particular curse of the colonial era. Early modern Ireland must have been exceptional among west European countries in that not only were the owners of land largely aliens, or were of non-Irish stock, but a large pro-portion of them were also absentees. In County Meath in 1876 as many as 150 out of a total of 270 owners of land were non-resident and in Cavan the corresponding figures were 105 and 153. Absenteeism was most prevalent among the owners of the smaller estates. In both counties over three-quarters of the owners of properties valued at less than £500 were non-resident. Absentee ownership and the fragmentation of property therefore went hand-in-hand. The majority of the owners of estates valued at £5,000 and over, were resident. In this group the more notable exceptions were Lansdowne, whose estate at £11,000 was among the most valuable in County Meath, and Annesley of Castlewellan in County Down, whose property in Cavan was valued at £9,000. For both counties one-half of the absentees lived in Dublin or in England. Property links with the ancestral homeland, if they ever existed, were however largely severed by the late nineteenth century. The great Farnham estate, valued at £21,000 in 1876, for instance, was confined to County Cavan. Outstanding among the larger Meath owners who held powerful stakes in the English homeland was Conyngham of Slane. The total value of his estate was no less than £50,000, which included property valued at £17,000 in Kent and a principal residence in Canterbury. Darnley of Athboy, in the barony of Lune, also owned an estate valued at £20,000 in Kent, whilst Headfort of Kells held land in Westmorland valued at £14,000. Three of Meath's most influential landlords were therefore in intimate contact with English, and probably continental lifestyles, and such linkages must have acted as main channels in the transmission and dissemination of outside influences in Ireland in the nineteenth century.

The efficacy of the provincial divide, in terms of land ownership and management, was, however, demonstrated in a more intimate fashion. In the nineteenth century Leinster's agrarian interests rarely extended into Ulster. Whilst thirty-nine or one-quarter of Meath's absentee owners had their residences elsewhere in north Leinster, only three of them lived in the adjacent Ulster counties of Monaghan and Cavan. The Meathman, like the Louthman, had traditionally turned his back on Ulster. At the same time the Ulster of the later nineteenth century was the most self-conscious of the four provinces of Ireland. Commercial and business interests, communications networks, institutions as well as religious denominations were specifically associating themselves by name with the province, and property interests provide important guidelines in the identification and interpretation of regional allegiances and obligations.

In our examination of the wider relevance of the provincial divide separating Meath from Cavan our main concern must be with the whereabouts of resident owners. Despite its ubiquitousness in nineteenth-century Ireland the landed estate has proved to be an elusive territorial entity and it is possible that large landowning units of the kind encountered, for example, in Ulster, may never have existed over the greater part of the Leinster province. The data at our disposal do not enable us to locate and delimit the extent of individual properties. Ireland may have differed from most other west European countries in that the overwhelming majority of the occupiers of land at all social levels were tenants. Their lands were usually in the charge not of their owners but of a cumbersome and fluid web of agents, stewards and middlemen, and it is their interests that are laboriously listed in the valuation returns. In these circumstances an attempt has been made to use what we shall refer to as the estate core, the general area where the landowner resided, as a pertinent guide to the nature and whereabouts of individual properties [Figs. 6:1; 6:2]. Estate cores acted as the local territorial hinges of the landowning system and their leading qualities may be identified and described. When classified according to the valuation or size of their estates they serve to draw attention to similarities and differences in agrarian structures between the areas. In County Cavan estate cores could rarely be traced back beyond the seventeenth century and not one could be identified, for example, which acted as a focal centre for a barony. The rudimentary baronial network in Cavan, as in Ulster generally, was essentially a pre-urban Gaelic creation. In Meath, on the other hand, cores located in such places as Ratoath, Slane, Headfort, Loughcrew,

T. JONES HUGHES

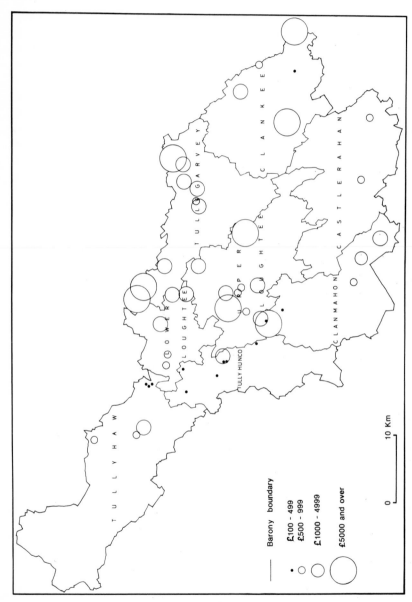

Figure 6:2. The valuation of the estates of resident landowners in County Cavan, 1870.

Athboy, Duleek and Skreen were clearly related to old-established baronial structures, as they acted as the major administrative entities below the county. In Meath estate cores were also frequently associated with the settlement centres of historic parishes. Their principal role in the nineteenth century in both counties, however, were as local bastions of colonial landholding structures.

The distribution of estate cores must not be allowed to convey an impression of stability and continuity in landowning patterns in the post-Famine decades. Between 1850 and 1876, the years with which we are mainly concerned, the ownership of land fluctuated greatly. Few new landlord residences were established during this period of retrenchment. For the uncertain post-Famine years we were more likely to identify abandoned cores as landscape items which we could add to the long list of dead-ends in Irish settlement history. In Kildallan parish in the barony of Tullyhunco in west County Cavan in 1876, the presence of former landlord residences at Drummally, Aghabane and Greenville emphasised the ephemeral qualities of small estates in south Ulster. In Meath the swift turnover of ownership was most apparent in the pastoral or grazier baronies. In this respect the grazier acted as the broker in a colonial assemblage. Pastureland was the most marketable of commodities in a rootless world where the inheritance of property was of little consequence. A familiar example of an abandoned grazier core in 1876 was on the Gibstown estate in Donaghpatrick parish in the barony of Upper Kells. The Gibstown home farm alone had been assessed at £1,300 in 1850. Ironically it was this substantial abandoned core which was selected by government as a base for the daring transfer of one of the earliest Irish-speaking communities to north Leinster from the Atlantic seaboard from 1935, ostensibly to form part of a future Meath Gaeltacht. In Ireland generally by 1876 the distribution of landlord residences was a residual one, after the estate system had long passed its heyday. In Cavan and Meath, as elsewhere in the island, the most persistent survivors were the cores of the largest estates. They, in turn, in the revolutionary early years of the present century were seen as being among the most conspicious and repugnant remnants of colonial culture in the countryside. In Meath, for example, the early eighteenth-century splendid Palladian mansion of the Langford family in Summerhill, in the barony of Moyfenrath, was symbolically burnt in 1922.

In keeping with the general tone of high status settlement elements, landlord residences frequently possessed old-established roots. Their ancient lineages were the more apparent when they were located in pre-

Reformation parish centres and especially where secular estate and parish were co-terminous, as was the case, for instance, among some of the farm villages of the barony of Iverk in south County Kilkenny. Thus the Darnley or Bligh family, when it initially settled in the barony of Lune in west County Meath in the seventeenth century, came to occupy the parish centre farm of Rathmore. Rathmore House was the early modern successor to a medieval tower-house on the same site. The tower-house, in turn, was located alongside what may have been a Norman *motte* or, as the townland name suggests, it may have been a prehistoric *ráth*. The ruins of a fifteenth-century church typically contained monuments and murals to members of the Bligh family as well as their grazier neighbours, whilst the altar was richly adorned with the coats of arms of distinguished Norman families, including the Plunketts, Fitzgeralds, Talbots and Bellews. Traces of what may have been a deserted or aborted village are seen in the vicinity of the church.

In the counties of Meath and Cavan, together, there were as many as 169 surviving landlord residences in 1876 and 48 of these were located in Cavan [Figs. 6.1; 6.2]. In the nineteenth century the landowners remained the principal decision makers locally and the location of their residences was therefore important in the interpretation of the geography of an area. Their distributions served as pointers to regions of better farm management and they indicated the whereabouts of the areas considered the more desirable for residential purposes as these were perceived in the nineteenth century. Within Leinster one-half of the total number of estates valued at £5,000 and over had their core areas located in the four northern counties of Meath, Westmeath, Dublin and Kildare, and twelve of these were in Meath. There were eight cores of estates valued at £5,000 and over located in County Cavan. Cavan therefore, despite its less favourable physiographic potential, contained within it an influential landlord element. In Meath there were 110 resident owners of estates valued at £500 and over. Of these one-quarter resided in the fertile and spacious Boyne and Blackwater valley in the baronies of Skreen and Upper Kells which, like other substantial river basins in the east and south of the island, displays remnants of several climax phases in Ireland's settlement history. This estate core complex was focused on the old towns of Navan and Kells. As elsewhere in Ireland the houses of the gentry were particularly attracted to the hinterlands of trading towns which had prospered during the colonial period. Congregations of estate cores of this type help to identify for us the many areas of exceptional rural and urban wealth and influence that characterised nineteenth-century Ireland. Outstanding among these more affluent pockets were the lower Liffey basin in the counties of Kildare and Dublin, the valley of the River Suir in counties Tipperary and Waterford and the environs of Belfast and Strangford Loughs in County Down. The Navan-Kells complex together accounted for five of the twelve residential cores of estates valued at £5,000 and over and 16 of the 46 valued at between £1,000 and £5,000 in County Meath in 1876. Among this formidable collection of high status residences the most substantial were those of Conyngham of Slane, Gerrard of Boyne Hill, Headfort of Kells, Nicholson of Balrath and Preston of Beallinter.[2] Estates valued at between £3,000 and £5,000 represented in this complex included Boyne of Stackallen, Dillon of Lismullin, Garnett of Williamstown, Rothwell of Rockfield, Russell of Ardsallagh and Tisdall of Charlesfort. Not one Irish name was found among the occupiers of this sumptuous collection of mansions. They were essentially an example from Meath of a privileged group of alien land-owners huddled together on some of the most productive land in the island. Their presence in such numbers helped to sustain Meath's standing as Ireland's premier county during the colonial period.

In Cavan territorial preferences were more precise and more modestly expressed. In this county 15 out of a total of 36 historic parishes had no resident owners in 1876, whilst the baronies of Tullyhunco, Tullyhaw and Castlerahan between them had only six resident landlords whose estates exceeded £500 in value. In Cavan the 35 estates valued at £500 and over represented less than one-third of the Meath total, and half of the core areas of these estates were located in the two northern baronies of Tullygarvey and Upper Loughtee. These two baronies together represented the historic hub of early celtic Breifne, which had retained its territorial pre-eminence. In the nineteenth century this pivotal region embraced not only the core area of the great Farnham estate but also the county town and the pre-Reformation diocesan centre of Kilmore. The clubbing together of landlord residences within easy reach of old-established county towns, and what had become Anglican diocesan centres, was a cardinal feature of the settlement fabric in early modern Ireland. Similar agglomerations were seen in Kilkenny and Clonmel and in Elphin in north County Roscommon, as well as in the vicinity of Monaghan, Enniskillen, Downpatrick and Armagh. In the barony of Loughtee the more opulent landlord residences, in addition to that of Maxwell of Farnham, included Nesbitt of Lismore, Saunderson of Drumkeen, Fay of Moynehall and Stoughton of Bingfield. In Tullygarvey the group focused on the landlord town of Cootehill included Coote of Bellamont, Clements of Ashfield and Rathkenny, Leslie of Cootehill and Townley of Tullyvin. The average valuation of an estate in this Cootehill-Cavan complex was £3,000. No family with an Irish Gaelic name resided in this cluster of mansions. As elsewhere in Ireland estate cores tended to gather in the principal confluence areas of their counties. In modern Cavan, as in Breifne, this was the area where the River Erne and its tributaries merged on Lough Oughter. Here transport linkages with Belfast, along what has been referred to as the 'Clones corridor', met the Enniskillen to Dublin turnpike road and together they represented the county's main axes of movement in the nineteenth century. Access to major markets was becoming an increasingly telling factor in determining the degree of success in the management of estates as the century progressed. In this way the location of estate cores had an indirect bearing on the spread of arterial communications networks in both counties. Landlord towns such as Athboy and Oldcastle in Meath, and Kingscourt and Killashandra in Cavan, became the termini of short-lived railway branch lines, whilst railway stations at places such as Cloverhill and Crossdoney in Cavan, and Bective and Gormanston in Meath themselves became essential components of estate cores.

Estate cores could be ranked not only in terms of land values but also in terms of the value of their settlement centrepieces, namely their mansions and home farms. In the valuation returns mansion and farmstead are assessed together. County Meath possessed as many as 112 great houses and farmsteads which were valued at £30 and over and half of these formed the attractive centrepieces of estate cores. Among the more resplendent were those which were valued at over £100, which included the residences of Conyngham of Slane, Corbally of Corbalton Hall in the parish of Skreen, Headfort of Kells, Naper of Loughcrew and Langford of Summerhill. Only two mansion-farmstead complexes of this standing were found in County Cavan, namely those of Maxwell of Farnham and Humphrey of Ballyhaise, both in the barony of Upper Loughtee. This disparity in rural wealth between the two counties became more apparent when we attempted to classify the home farms of resident landowners according to their valuation. These home farms were unique features among Ireland's colonial agrarian structures, in that they formed the only category of owner-occupied holdings, and Meath contained one of the largest concentrations of such feehold farms in the island at the time. Together they acted as the county's most sturdy and stable agrarian elements in what was otherwise a transient and insecure world of tenant farmers. Out of a total of 121 home farms within the county,

51 were assessed at £300 and over and 23 of the latter were valued at £500 and over. Here therefore in Meath was one of the most opulent collections of farm units in nineteenth-century Ireland. Six of the feehold farms valued at £500 and over were located within the Navan-Kells complex, namely the home farms of Headfort of Kells, Barnwall of Bloomsbery, Garrigan of Drakerath, Nicholson of Balrath, Taaffe of Ardmulchan and Waller of Allenstown. Only the most powerful of estates could generate and sustain landholding units of this standing. In County Cavan there were only four home farms which were valued at over £300. These were the farms of Coote of Bellamont, Maxwell of Farnham, Nesbitt of Lismore Castle and Pratt of Cabra Castle. In Cavan the average valuation of a home farm of an estate assessed at over £1,000 was as low as £160.

The quality of the core area of an estate could also be ascertained in terms of the extent of land held directly from its owner. In Gorey barony in north County Wexford, for example, on compact and carefully maintained estates, it was customary for planter tenants to hold their farms directly from their English owners. In Meath this category of land was surprisingly confined, and was found most typical of the well furbished properties in the western baronies, whose origins, as in County Wexford, could be attributed to the seventeenth-century confiscations. Darnley of Athboy, for instance, held thirty-four townlands directly within the barony of Lune whilst Naper of Loughcrew held thirty-three in Fore. On the more carefully structured cores, townlands held from their owners were sometimes leased to privileged tenants who were, like the owners themselves, of English stock. On the Darnley estate they included Hopkins of Mitchelstown, Askens of Ballyboy, Booker of Gillstown, Walker of Balrath and Allen of the Hill of Ward. It was on estates of this quality that the peak of colonial pride and confidence was attained and this found expression in elegant landscape layouts. In Meath most of these holdings have escaped the wrath of the Land Commission, to survive intact to our time, and to represent some of the largest and best equipped farm units in modern Ireland. Clifton Lodge, the former Irish residence of the Darnley family, for example, is today a well-groomed stud farm. Elsewhere in County Meath, as in Leinster generally, fragmentation of property was intense and when this happened estate cores lost their meaning and purpose. In some Normanised areas of east Leinster the modern landlord estate, as a large and consolidated entity, never emerged. The disintegration was most evident among the grazier baronies where the owners themselves were absentees. In the barony of Ratoath, for example, a total of 130 townlands were held from fifty different lessors. Confused leasing arrangements also prevailed in the tillage coastlands of the barony of Duleek. In Ardcath parish, on the County Dublin border, twenty-two townlands were held from twelve different lessors and most of these were absentees. Similar conditions have been identified elsewhere in Leinster in the old tillage coastlands of counties Louth, Dublin and Wexford. The intensively cultivated coastlands of the barony of Ballaghkeen in east County Wexford, for example, had never known the large, disciplined and highly capitalised modern estate. In these circumstances only the townland framework itself was salvaged as a basis for sorting out increasingly confused landowning and land-working arrangements and, in the absence of the innovative large landowner, older social and economic practices often prevail. It is erroneous to assume, in Leinster at least, that the colonial grip was most efficient and effective in the nineteenth century in the physically better endowed, more productive and more accessible parts of the island.

In Cavan the ratio of townlands held directly from their owners was generally higher than in Meath among the absentee as well as the resident owners of land. In Ulster this was especially characteristic of areas where there was a substantial body of planter tenants as well as planter owners. It was partly for this reason that landlord-tenant relationships were seen to be conducted on a more equitable basis in Ulster than elsewhere in the island. In Templeport parish in the barony of Tullyhaw, for instance, two substantial absentee owners, namely Beresford of Armagh and Annesley of Castlewellan, together held as many as fifty townlands directly in 1850. In the same parish another twenty-six townlands were leased directly from Finlay of Brackley House who was a small resident owner. In the great estate country in the barony of Upper Loughtee, Maxwell of Farnham Castle held thirty-seven townlands directly, in the parishes of Kilmore and Urney, as part of the core area of his property. Similarly in Drumgoon parish in Tullygarvey, forty townlands were held by Coote of Cootehill and on the Young estate in the parish of Bailieborough, in the barony of Clankee, twenty-six townlands were in the hands of their owner. These were the properties in County Cavan with the highest ratios of non-Irish tenants. Throughout Ulster the estate and its core area were more realistic and resilient territorial entities in those regions where there were substantial planter communities.

The most efficient criterion which could be employed in assessing the relative standing of an estate in nineteenth-century Ireland was probably the presence or absence of a village or town at its core. Settlements of this kind marked the climax of landlord enterprise and achievement locally. Away from the planted areas of Ulster it has been shown that only estates which were valued at over £10,000 were capable, in eighteenth- and nineteenth-century Ireland, of initiating and sustaining village and small town life at their cores. In Leinster the creation of new villages and towns was not a primary objective of the early modern colonial process. Landlord inspired villages such as Summerhill in the barony of Moyfenrath were rare in Meath. The majority of Meath's villages and towns had roots which reached back beyond the landlord era and in the nineteenth century their inhabitants were overwhelmingly of Irish stock. Some towns, including Trim, Duleek, Stamullin and Dunshaughlin, in the east and south of the county, never came to be directly involved in estate management. Because they lacked patronage and protection, they suffered severely in the battle for survival in the demanding post-Famine years. Elsewhere in County Meath, especially in the tillage areas of the west and the north, towns such as Oldcastle, Athboy, Kells and Slane, although they possessed pre-landlord roots, came to be deeply embroiled in landlord activity.

As in neighbouring County Monaghan, villages and towns were of late origin in Cavan, and were it not for plantation policy, it is unlikely that either county would have acquired their present range of urban centres, most of which were acting as estate core settlements in the nineteenth century. In Cavan they included Killashandra (on the Hamilton estate), Arvagh (Gosford), Butler's Bridge (Lanesborough), Cootehill (Coote), Bailieborough (Young), Kingscourt (Pratt), Shercock (Ruxton) and Virginia (Headfort). Few counties outside Ulster had this number and variety of modern estate towns. In the mid-nineteenth century they were sturdy settlements, serving a variety of functions, and, unlike most of the Meath towns, they possessed substantial planter communities. Their healthy condition, as compared with settlements of similar standing in a southern county such as Tipperary, was indicated by the absence of vacant dwelling houses and families which could be described as living in poor circumstances in the post-Famine decade. Their presence ensured that the estate and its owner were playing a vigorous role socially as well as economically in the life of County Cavan, and enabled landlord lifestyles and standards to be catapulted more easily into the twentieth century. The powerful landlord presence in urban structures was most evident in Cavan in its county town, which in this sense could be regarded as the principal component of the core area of the Farnham estate. A wide range of institutions, which we associate with Irish urban

development during the colonial era, came to be compacted into Farnham Street, the town's main thoroughfare in the nineteenth century.
These included a county gaol, a town hall, a court house, nonconformist
chapels, a Masonic hall and a large Anglican church. The elegant
residential block in Farnham Street was known as Erskine Terrace. This
consisted of spacious three- and four-storey dwelling houses each valued
at between £25 and £30 in 1850. These town houses accommodated a tiny
professional class of solicitors, bankers and doctors, one of whose duties
was to serve the needs of the Farnham estate. The presence of a substantial
planter population in Cavan towns may account for some of the tensions
that have manifested themselves in this century. The names of the main
thoroughfares in the town of Cavan, for example, have officially been
systematically changed from those that reflected the original colonial
interests and aspirations to those which commemorated the dead patriots
associated with the foundation of the independent state. In this way Farnham Street came to be Roger Casement Street, Church Street is now
Seán McDermott Street and Wesley Street is named after Thomas Ashe.
Yet Farnham Castle is still occupied by the Maxwell family. In Cavan,
if not in Meath, estate core towns remain the finest memorials to an
immensely constructive phase in Ireland's colonial history.

The tenant farmer
    The scale of farming has long been regarded as a useful criterion in the
identification of distinctive social and economic structures in rural areas.
Dramatic contrasts in farming styles characterised the counties on either
side of the Leinster-Ulster inter-provincial divide. Meath possessed some
of the largest and most prosperous congregations of large farms in the
entire island, 1,700 of which were valued at £50 and over. In Meath there
were 540 farms that were valued at £200 and over in 1850. Numerically
by far the most significant farming group in County Cavan, on the other
hand, had holdings valued at between £10 and £20. This group represented
a section of the small farm world of south Ulster, whose presence has
been attributed largely to drumlin swarms in a county where human territorial behaviour patterns are strongly guided by topographic features.
In County Meath farms valued at £50 and over constituted the most
significant elements in the agrarian structure of most townlands. In
Meath the distribution of the largest holdings, assessed at £300 and over
[Fig. 3], should indicate to us the whereabouts of the more influential
elements in rural society in the nineteenth century. As we have seen,
many were the home farms of resident landowners, and in this way there

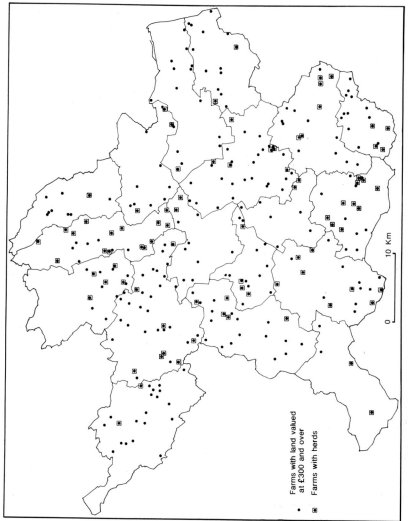

Figure 6:3. Farms with land valued at £300 and over in County Meath, c. 1850.

was an obvious correlation between the whereabouts of strong farmers and the location of estate cores, especially in the tillage areas and where land was assessed at around £1 an acre. This correlation was most evident in the north-western baronies of Fore, Upper Kells and Lune where 40 per cent of the larger farms were valued at £200 and over. In physically less favoured baronies, where land values dropped to ten shillings an acre, such as in Lower Slane, Lower Deece and Upper Moyfenrath, no more than 20 per cent of the larger farms were valued at over £200. In Cavan the distribution of holdings worth £50 and over was much more restricted (Fig. 6:4). One hundred and forty out of a total of 315 were located in the seven adjoining parishes of Kilmore, Drumlane, Annagh and Urney in the barony of Loughtee, Templeport in the barony of Tullyhaw and the parishes of Kildallan and Killashandra in Tullyhunco. Five adjoining parishes in the uplands in the baronies of Loughtee, Clankee and Castlerahan, contained between them only eight holdings that were assessed at £50 and over. These parishes were Lavey, Knockbride, Shercock, Denn and Killintere. In Cavan there were therefore extensive areas from which the strong farmer, as he has been identified for our purposes, was absent.

Judging by their family names, a substantial number of strong farmers in County Meath in the mid nineteenth century were of non-Irish stock. Although the county was not subjected to systematic colonisation and settlement, it offered a good example from Leinster of how far-reaching and devastating in their consequences were the early modern English colonial policies of land confiscation. In Meath the English were most numerous on the most highly valued holdings. Sixty-five per cent of the farms valued at £300 and over were in the hands of families with non-Irish names in 1850, and as many as ten per cent of these names appear to have been of Norman origin. Nineteenth-century County Meath therefore harboured a large non-Irish population, not only among its resident landowners, but also among the tenant occupiers of its largest farms. Were there other west European countries which had experienced traumatic changes of this kind in their landholding structures in the modern period? English names were in the majority on holdings valued at £50 and over in as many as seven out of a total of eighteen baronies. These seven were Navan, Lower Moyfenrath, Lune, Fore, Upper Kells, Lower Slane and Dunboyne. Four of these baronies straddled the Navan-Kells estate core complex. In Lune and Fore thirty out of a total of forty-one farms assessed at £300 and over were in English hands and among these were powerful tenant families such as the Battersbys, Mastersons and Dyas.

In these baronies, and in townlands dominated over by influential planter families, Irish and Gaelic farmers, where they existed, typically occupied physically inferior lands. The highest ratios of Irish strong farmers were found in the south and south-east of the county. In the three adjoining baronies of Deece, Skreen and Ratoath they accounted for a half of the total number of farms valued at £50 and over. In Deece the New English outnumbered the Gaels only in the parish of Kilclone. Irish names were in the majority on holdings assessed at £300 and over in the baronies of Ratoath and Moyfenrath Lower. In the adjoining parishes of Dunshaughlin and Kilbrew, in Ratoath, and Killeen in Skreen, there were twenty-six strong farmers with Irish names as opposed to five with English names. The baronies of Deece, Skreen and Ratoath therefore may have retained an old, influential and stable Irish population throughout the colonial period. They provided examples from north Leinster of families who occupied the highest status attained or retained by Gaels in any part of rural Ireland in the nineteenth century. In an exposed transit area, such as County Meath, they displayed a wide range of personal names. Among the 730 farms of over £50 valuation, which were occupied by families with Irish names in 1850, there were 230 different Gaelic or anglicised transliterations of Gaelic names. The most numerous included Reilly, Lynch, Connell, Flood, Kelly and Murphy, a list which incorporated some of the most widely distributed family names in Ireland in the nineteenth century.[3] Unlike Cavan, Meath possessed few recognisable sept or clan hearths[4] and kin linkages among strong farmers do not appear to have been significant. In Meath's eastern baronies names of Norman origin were encountered among the strong farmers, intermingled with those of Irish graziers. In Culmullin parish in Upper Deece they included Tyrrell, Marmion, Lawless, Dowdall, Rice and Brett. In the tillage parish of Duleek Norman names included Gernon, Teeling, Warren, Fagan, Wogan, Wall and Courtney. These were examples from baronies in the east of County Meath where Gael and Norman had practised large-scale tillage and livestock farming together as neighbours for centuries. They were also the areas from which the Catholic church drew its most influential support in the difficult years of the early nineteenth century.

The Meath-Cavan divide, as we have called it, had important ethnic implications in that it represented the southernmost reach of the area in Ulster which experienced successful early modern Scottish and English colonisation. In the southern counties of Ireland, by the mid nineteenth century, families of planter stock living in the countryside were largely confined to the owners of land. In County Cavan, on the other hand, they represented a substantial portion of the tenant farmer population at all social levels. In Cavan as in Meath the planter tenants were most prominent as occupiers of the largest farms. Two hundred and fifty of the 315 holdings assessed at £50 and over in Cavan in 1850 were in the hands of families with non-Irish names, and within this group 56 of the 66 Irish families occupied holdings that were valued at less than £100. The large farmers in Meath were therefore much more Irish than were their counterparts in Cavan. With the decline in farm values there was always a corresponding reduction in the ratio of planter families. In County Cavan, out of a total of about 4,500 holdings valued at between £10 and £30, only 1,530 appear to have been in planter hands. In this group the planter outnumbered the Irish Gael in only two baronies, namely in Clankee in the south-east of the county, focused on the town of Bailieborough, and in Upper Loughtee which has the town of Cavan as its principal settlement. Among farms valued at £10 and over, the highest ratio of Irish Gaels, 70 per cent of the total, was found in the south-western barony of Clanmahon, adjoining the counties of Longford and Westmeath. The detailed distribution of holdings valued at over £50 should therefore indicate to us some of the territorial preferences of planter tenants in County Cavan (Fig. 6:4). Whilst farmsteads occupied by English or Scottish tenants were most numerous aligned along arterial routeways, in the inter-drumlin bottomlands, their principal territorial anchorages were Anglican parish centres and estate cores, neither of which was strongly developed in Cavan. Planter names were conspicious on larger holdings in the vicinity of the Anglican diocesan centre of Kilmore, Hamilton's estate town of Killashandra and Young's Bailieborough. In the adjoining parishes of Killashandra, Kilmore and Drumlane, only 14 out of a total of 82 farms assessed at over £50 were in Irish Gaelic hands. The heart of Breifne had been inundated with planter families from the early seventeenth century.[5] In the parish of Killashandra the more substantial planter farmers included Arnold, Faris, Wilson, Donaldson, Robinson, Clemenger and Huddleston. In Bailieborough parish there were families named Gibson, McClelland, Chambers, Beck, Maxwell, Peate and Cranston. The cultivation of flax had been an important feature of tillage on small farms occupied by planters in the barony of Clankee, and Bracklin. Lisball and Lisgar were examples of exclusively planter townlands on the Young estate in the parish of Bailieborough in 1850.

Cavan in the nineteenth century provided an important example of a

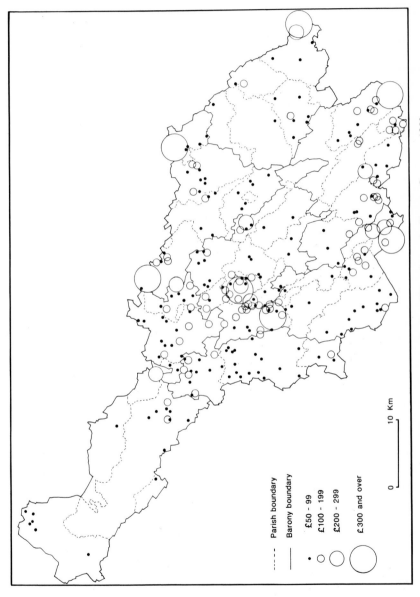

Parish boundary
Barony boundary

£50 - 99
£100 - 199
£200 - 299
£300 and over

0   10 Km

Figure 6·4. Farms with land valued at £50 and over in County Cavan, c. 1850.

county of small subsistence farmers where two ethnic groups, with differing allegiances and historical experiences, intermingled. Meath, on the other hand, provided an example of a county of substantial farmers who participated in two of the major types of marketing economies which prevailed in nineteenth-century rural Ireland. A fluctuating mixed livestock and tillage economy had sporadically evolved in Meath on the lighter loamy or gravelly soils of the coastlands as well as in the Boyne-Blackwater drainage basin, whilst the extensive grazing of cattle and sheep had remained the prerogative of the heavy and poorly drained clays of the southern and south-eastern baronies. We shall confine our attention to examining in greater detail the nature of Meath's pastoral economy as it is depicted in the valuation returns. The main aim was the finishing of livestock for the Dublin and English markets. In the pastoral baronies, old-established grazier dwelling houses stood alone as the centrepieces of their spacious townlands. When the owner or lessor was himself an absentee the land was left in the charge of a herd and herd holdings were identified separately by the valuators. In mid-winter it was the loneliest of countrysides as the empty fields awaited a replenishment of young stock in the spring. The emptiness was made the more apparent by the coarse nature of the enclosure network, where grazing units of twenty hectares were commonplace. These units were bounded by shallow ditches which ran alongside poorly maintained and low earthen banks which were sometimes capped with hawthorn or ash. The hawthorn (*Crataegus monogyna*) yielded a magnificent display of the mayflower when the fields were full of livestock in the early summer. The ditches served as drainage channels in this level land of impervious and stoneless soils. The grazier's rudimentary farmstead was focused on a hay haggard and a foddering yard.

Out of a total of 1,710 holdings assessed at over £50 in County Meath in 1850, one-quarter were in the care of herds. One-half of these herds had non-Irish names, which suggested that in the nineteenth century extensive pastoralism in the county had a strong colonial flavour. Eighty-seven out of a total of 446 herds in Meath were on farms that were valued at £300 and over (Fig. 6:3), but the ratio of large farms that were in the charge of herds fluctuated from barony to barony. Among the tillage farmers of the barony of Duleek only two out of a total of twenty holdings valued at £300 and over were herd holdings. The highest aggregate of grazier farms was in the barony of Upper Deece on the border with County Kildare, where 58 out of a total of 78 holdings valued at £50 and over were grazier holdings, and in this spacious environment ten were valued at £300 and over. In the adjoining baronies of Dunboyne and Ratoath 88 out of a total of 214 farms valued at £50 and over were in grazier hands. In the barony of Ratoath, the parishes of Rathbeggan and Rathregan, astride the Dublin to Enniskillen turnpike road, probably provided the stereotype of grazier landscapes. Parishes of this kind carried the lowest population densities, on land valued at around £1 an acre, in rural Ireland in the nineteenth century. A more confined area devoted to extensive grazing in County Meath emerged in the two northern baronies of Morgallion and Lower Kells. Here herds were in charge of 77 out of a total of 171 holdings valued at £50 and over. In Morgallion 15 out of a total of 22 farms valued at £300 and over were grazier holdings (Fig. 6:3), and such holdings were the dominant elements in the agrarian structures of the parishes of Castletown, Clongill, Drakestown and Kilberry. In Morgallion and Kells the Meath-Cavan divide was seen to correspond closely with the northern limit of extensive pastoralism in eastern Ireland. The overlap into County Cavan was slight, involving only the parish of Kilbride in the barony of Clanmahon and the parishes of Loughan and Mullagh in the barony of Castlerahan. In the parish of Kilbride in County Cavan, 6 out of 10 holdings valued at £50 and over were occupied by herds, and three of these were valued at over £200. Generally in Cavan the herd performed a different role in the farming community. At a time of rapidly declining population, from the mid-nineteenth century, and where the rearing, rather than the finishing of cattle for a market, was the basic role of the small farmer, the herd's main function in the post-Famine years was to take temporary charge of an abandoned holding. In County Cavan, therefore, the distribution of herd holdings provided us with a guide to the local progress of contraction and decay in a subsistence economy.

The poor

A crude attempt has been made to identify and locate the poorer elements in the dispersed rural society in both Meath and Cavan in the mid-nineteenth century. For County Meath the poor have been recognised as those households which were without land or whose land was valued at less than £10 in 1850. In Meath compact communities of smallholders were few and, as elsewhere in Leinster, the majority of the poor in the county were the landless who lived in the most wretched of dwelling houses, usually valued at ten shillings or less each. The total number of householders living in rural areas in Meath in 1850 was around 16,270, of which as many as 11,700 could be designated as being poor according

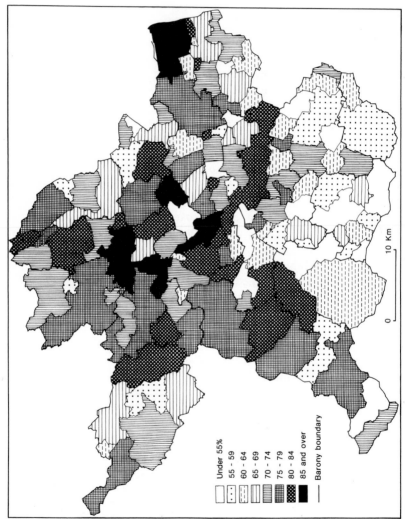

Figure 6:5. The percentage of the total number of households in rural areas in County Meath with land valued at less than £10. c. 1850.

Under 55%
55 - 59
60 - 64
65 - 69
70 - 74
75 - 79
80 - 84
85 and over
Barony boundary

0   10 Km

to our definition. Numerically therefore they represented a substantial proportion of the population in what was, in many other ways, one of Ireland's most affluent counties. The highest aggregates of rural poor were found among the agricultural and casual labourers in the mixed farming areas of the north and west. They were especially numerous in the baronies of Morgallion, Upper Kells, Lune and Lower Navan as well as in Lower Duleek (Fig. 6:5). Rural poverty was therefore most in evidence in the tillage areas, with high population densities, and where there were, as we have seen, large numbers of strong farmers as well as resident landowners.

In Meath it was possible to recognise basic types of congregations of poor people. The most typical and widespread were those scattered communities which had recently emerged along the rims of the unenclosed wetlands of low valuation which were leased from absentee owners. In the townlands of Ardbraccan and Durhamstown in the parish of Ardbraccan in the barony of Navan Lower, for instance, 210 out of a total of 280 householders were either landless or held land which was valued at less than £10. Their dwelling houses were usually aligned along recently erected linear trackways and minor road intersections. Short-lived settlements of this kind acquired no service functions and their names were not recorded on large-scale maps. Their layouts bore little relationship to the townland networks. In the tillage areas of the barony of Duleek, on the other hand, the landless and the occupiers of diminutive holdings were more often huddled together in pre-existing villages such as Bettystown, Donacarney, Mornington and Laytown, in the vicinity of the Boyne estuary, and many of these were inshore fishermen. Old tillage coastlands, with a variety of opportunities of eking a living, have long attracted a rag bag of Ireland's destitute population. Poor villagers were also encountered in the tillage baronies of Upper Kells, Morgallion and Lune. Oristown in the parish of Teltown, Wilkinstown in the parish of Kilberry and the parish centre village of Kildalkey together contained 320 dwelling houses in 1850, 287 of which were occupied by families who were either landless or whose land was worth less than £10. The third type of collections of poor households in County Meath in the nineteenth century was associated with the more desolate fringes of the county's larger and expanding towns, and where landholding and landowning rights were ill-defined and confused. Out of a total of 165 households in the townlands of Balreask Upper and Commons on the south-western outskirts of the town of Navan, 145 could be classed as poor families, and on the commons of the town of Duleek they

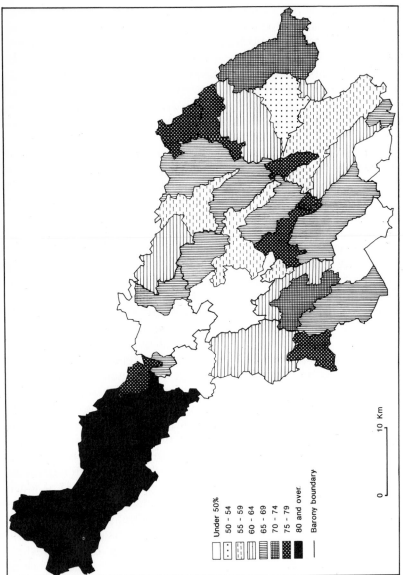

Under 50%
50 - 54
55 - 59
60 - 64
65 - 69
70 - 74
75 - 79
80 and over.

Barony boundary

0   10 Km

Figure 6:6. The percentage of the total number of farm holdings in County Cavan with   land valued at less than £10,
c. 1850.

numbered 55 out of a total of 65 households. Short-lived congregations of poor people were also identified from the valuation reports on what were known as the corporation and manor lands of the town of Trim. The peripheral urban poor were therefore particularly associated with Meath's oldest towns, which possessed rights to common land, and which were not estate core settlements. The lowest tally of poor people in County Meath, less than 65 per cent of the total number of households, was found in the grazier baronies of Deece, Dunboyne, Ratoath and Upper Moyfenrath (Fig. 6:5). In the parishes of Cookstown and Crickstown, on the border with County Dublin, in the barony of Ratoath, only 11 out of a total of 42 households could be designated as being poor. The barony with the lowest aggregate of poor households in 1850 was Upper Deece, on the border with County Kildare, where they numbered 148 out of a total of 267 families. Overall in County Meath therefore the distribution of rural poverty must be understood and inter-preted in terms of the dichotomy between a tillage and a pastoral economy as practised on large holdings.

Unlike Meath the landless population in Cavan was small. In Cavan rural poverty had to be sought among the smallholders or households whose land was valued at less than £10 in 1850 (Fig. 6:6). Nineteenth-century Ireland differed from the countries of Britain in the large extent of the land that was devoted to subsistence agriculture. The peasant farmer had come to epitomise nineteenth-century rural Ireland abroad. County Cavan formed a typical segment of this way of life in south Ulster. There were some 15,770 farmsteads in the county in mid century and 5,470 of these had land which was valued at less than £10. One-third of the farm households in County Cavan in 1850 were therefore poor in the way we have defined it. Outstanding among the baronies showing high aggregates of poor households was Tullyhaw, a long, narrow and remote salient in the north-west, separating the county of Fermanagh from County Leitrim. In Tullyhaw over 80 per cent of the total number of households were poor, and, judging by the surviving field evidence, the history of colonisation and settlement in this barony differed from that in the rest of the county. Tullyhaw belonged to a new west which had emerged in parts of Ulster, Connacht and Munster as a consequence of population pressure on physically marginal land in the seventeenth and eighteenth centuries. In an age of great optimism, efforts had been made to accommodate farming families in linear frameworks of townlands, trackways and fields which were specifically designed for steep and rugged upland slopes. In Tullyhaw these planned arrangements were best developed on the sunnier east and south-east facing slopes of Sliabh Ruisean and Sliabh Cuilceach, where they reached elevations of 300 metres on large absentee estates such as those of Beresford of Armagh and Annesley of Castlewellan. The ruthless marshalling of peoples in this manner appears to have been more doggedly pursued among the barren and lonely uplands of south Ulster than in any other part of the island. Survival under these conditions was aided by the organisation of long-tailed families in co-operative groups, and in the McGoverns and the Dolans, the barony of Tullyhaw possessed examples of some of the most intricate webs of extended family obligations in Ireland in the nineteenth century. For example, land was frequently held in dispersed parcels and not in consolidated farm units. In the post-Famine decade these arrangements may, however, have been among the most obvious consequences of a rapidly declining population in a familial society where inheritance governed the nature of transactions in property. The new west was short-lived and its meticulously planned landscapes are now buried under coniferous forests.

The typical Cavan smallholder of the nineteenth century belonged to an older and a more resilient tradition. The disparate communities that hugged the drumlin belt lived their lives among field, farm and townland layouts that suggested haphazard, unregulated and protracted processes of colonisation and settlement. With its multiplicity of steep and laborious slopes, this was largely a wheelless world, where cultivation was undertaken by means of the spade, and where life was focused on the needs of the dairy cow as a breeding animal as well as a milk producer. A regular cash income was made possible only with the introduction of the co-operative creamery at the turn of the century. Day-by-day movement was reckoned in terms of walking distances and this movement was channelled into tortuous footpaths which linked widely scattered farmsteads with arterial trackways. The web of footpaths in the Cavan hills was significant enough to be depicted cartographically on large-scale Ordnance Survey maps. Holdings with their lands valued at less than £10 accounted for over 70 per cent of the total number of households in an east-west sequence of upland parishes which extended from Tullygarvey to Clanmahon (Fig. 6:6). These parishes with very high aggregates of poor households included Drumgoon in Tullygarvey, Enniskeen in the barony of Clankee, Killinkere in Casterahan, Denn in Loughtee, Ballintemple in Clanmahon and Scrabby in the barony of Tullyhunco. Conspicuous among the areas in County Cavan where the poor numbered less than half the dispersed rural population was the compact area based on

Loughtee and Tullyhunco. This, as we have seen, formed the territorial heart of the former Gaelic entity of Breifne. The parishes concerned were Drumlane, Kilmore, Urney and Kildallan. The rural poor were also in a minority in the parishes of Ballymachugh and Kilbride in the barony of Clanmahon and Munterconnaght in Castlerahan. In many ways, as we have already noted, these parishes had closer affinities with Meath than with Cavan. Otherwise the provincial border served to pinpoint for us the limits of an area to the north where rural poverty was most frequently encountered among subsistence farmers, and an area to the south, with a market-orientated economy, where the poor were most numerous among a landless population.

The names of townlands

In terms of their genesis placenames in Ireland fall into two main groups, namely those that depict physiographic conditions, and those which are of cultural origin and which refer to human activity. In County Meath, out of a total of 1,310 townlands, as many as three-quarters appear to have names that refer to human activity and this must be among the highest ratio of cultural names for any Irish county, other than perhaps County Dublin. Throughout the island cultural name elements are more abundant in the physically more agreeable and accessible areas which have attracted a variety of colonists from outside over long periods of time. The highest ratio of cultural names in Meath, representing over 80 per cent of the total, are found in the central and south-eastern baronies of Deece, Skreen, Navan and Ratoath. The lowest ratio, 55 per cent, occurs in the northern barony of Lower Slane. By far the most numerous cultural element encountered among the townland names in County Meath is the English suffix *town*, which is present in 476 or over one-third of the total of number of townland names, and the majority of these are believed to be of Norman origin. Among the Irish cultural elements the most common are *baile* and *ráth* which, like *town*, refers to units of land or settlement. *Baile* and *ráth* together are found in about one hundred and sixty-five townland names. When we examine the distribution of the suffix *town* in Ireland generally, we find that it is most numerous and widespread in north Leinster, in an area which has been referred to as the *town* zone, and County Meath forms the territorial centrepiece of this zone. It seems that the impact of the Norman presence on rural placenames was greater here than anywhere else in the island. This is in sharp contrast to the dominance of *baile* among the cultural name elements along the coastlands of Wicklow and Wexford. In seventeenth-century English ledger-books the two elements *town* and *baile* are treated as if they were complementary. The placename evidence therefore suggests that the Norman impact prevailed in north Leinster whilst Gaelic influences were the stronger in south-east Leinster north of the Wexford sloblands. In the heart of the *town* zone in Meath the suffix habitually combines with a narrow range of personal names, and this may demonstrate how the Normans used what has come to be known as the townland as the basic territorial entity in the colonisation process. Was this elaborate medieval townland framework in County Meath largely based on pre-existing Gaelic foundations? In the parish of Ratoath we find *town* combining with the following personal names, only two of which may be of Irish origin: Balfe, Brady, Brown, Cheevers, Elgar, Fleming, James, Loughlin, Peacock, Raken and Tankard. The suffix *town* is most frequently encountered in Meath's eastern and south-eastern baronies. It occurs in over half of the total number of names in Skreen, Dunboyne, Navan Lower, Duleek Upper and Ratoath. These may therefore have been the baronies which were most closely settled by Norman colonisers, and in this sense east County Meath may have been among the most alienated parts of rural Ireland in the later medieval period. The lowest ratio of *town* names, less than 30 per cent of the total number of townland names, occurs in the western and northern baronies of Moyfenrath Upper, Lower Kells, Fore, Lune and Morgallion. In Moyfenrath Upper and Lower Kells the ratio is lower than 10 per cent. This seems to confirm our impression of the existence of a long-standing east-west dichotomy in County Meath. Until the seventeenth century the east was more exposed to or responded more readily to outside influences. The surviving Irish name elements in the core area of the *town* zone, if that is what they are, are largely generic elements of physiographic origin, of the kind which are widely distributed throughout the lowlands of central Ireland. In Ardcath parish, in Duleek Upper barony, they include *cloch, cluain, cúil* and *currach* and usually they are found associated with the physically less desirable land within the parish. In north Leinster the *town* zone has an abrupt edge which, in Meath and Cavan, closely follows the provincial border. In this sense the provincial border marks one of the most profound frontiers in Ireland's placename geography.

In Ireland as a whole the range of placename elements of physiographic origin is far richer than that of cultural origin and in Cavan these names reflect the county's wide topographical and botanical diversity. In Cavan, as in Ulster generally, old-established townland names of English origin are rare and our main task in Cavan is to attempt to identify Gaelic or Irish name elements which are particularly associated with the county. They include *druim, corr, cill, doire, achadh, tulach, gort* and *ard,* and together these eight elements account for as many 700 or 45 per cent of the total number of townland names in the county. For the island as a whole this is an unusual concentration of a narrow range of physiographic elements. In County Cavan only 445, or less than 30 per cent of townlands, possess names of cultural origin, and their distribution shows little relationship with those areas most intimately inolved in the seventeenth-century planta- tion schemes. In isolated Breifne the pre-existing Gaelic names survived the colonisation process. Even in the diocesan centre, in Kilmore parish, in the barony of Loughtee, only 16 out of a total of 72 townland names appear to be of cultural origin. Slightly higher aggregates of cultural names occur in the baronies of Clanmahon, Castlerahan and Clankee which share a border with County Meath. Name elements of botanical origin are most prevelant in the inter-drumlin bottom lands. *Doire* and *coill* are both numerous in the Erne basin, especially on lough shores, including Lough Oughter in Tullyhaw and Loughtee. In the county generally, however, the names are overwhelmingly of topographic origin. The dominant themes refer to the presence and variety of hills and hill slopes and among these the more numerous elements are *druim, corr, tulach, mullach* and *ard.* It appears that the drumlin ridges left a deep impression on the minds of the first literate peoples who initially named the territorial units in Cavan which are now known as townlands. *Druim* and *corr* together occur in as many as about 375 or one-quarter of the total number of townland names in the county. No other Irish county is likely to possess such a high ratio of its names incorporating only two physiographic elements. *Druim* is most prolific in a belt of country which extends from Tullygarvey in the east, through Upper Loughtee, to Tullyhunco in the west. In the parish of Kildrumsherdan, in the barony of Tullygarvey, *druim* and *corr* occur in 35 out of a total of 75 townland names and some of the more maturely developed drumlin swarms occur in Tullygarvey and Loughtee. Looked at in a wider perspective the *druim-corr* complex of name elements extends outwards from County Cavan to incorporate most of the neighbouring counties of Monaghan and Fermanagh as well as south County Leitrim in Connacht. Together these areas appear to have formed a part of Ireland which was among the least subjected to outside influences during the medieval period.

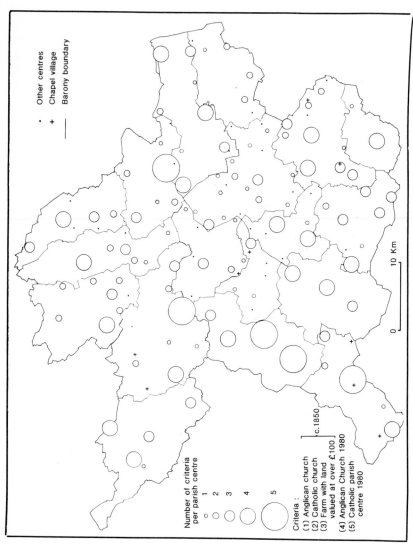

Figure 6:7. The ranking of rural historic parish centres in County Meath.

The parish

In modern Ireland two parochial systems are found operating alongside one another. The Anglican or Church of Ireland system is largely based on a network of pre-Reformation origin, and we shall refer to this as the historic network, as it had lost much of its meaning and function. The modern Catholic parish system, on the other hand, crystallised territorially only from the later eighteenth century and may or may not be closely related to the older arrangements. In common with the other Normanised areas of Leinster, County Meath has inherited a highly fragmented and cumbersome historic parochial network. For the most part these territorial entities were a product of the Norman mind and their settlement centres are among the most enduring of Norman footprints in the landscape. Their enforced abandonment entailed a calamitous break with local secular as well as religious roots. Administrative frameworks, however, once established, are among the more stable of man-made regions and in 1850 there were Anglican churches still in use in forty-eight or one-third of the total number of historic parish centres in County Meath. In the early nineteenth century an ambitious attempt was made, funded by a body known as the Board of First Fruits, to refurbish Anglican churches throughout Ireland and to erect handsome glebe houses which might serve to entice resident clergy. In Meath this renewal of the fabric of the church seems to have been of little consequence, as the mean valuation of Anglican churches in the county in mid century was as low as £8, and six were valued at less than £5. By comparison the average valuation of a Catholic chapel in a rural area in Meath in the early nineteenth century was between £12 and £14. The total number of historic parishes in Meath in 1850 was 132. Sixty-six of these were located in the five eastern baronies of Skreen, Ratoath, Lower Duleek, Upper Deece and Navan. The two baronies of Skreen and Ratoath were themselves shared between no less than thirty-one parishes. By contrast only eighteen parishes were found in the four western baronies of Upper and Lower Moyfenrath, Lune and Fore. As in County Wexford the fragmentation of territorial administrative structures, including parishes, was more evident in the Normanised areas and in County Meath this dichotomy between east and west is also apparent in the nature and content of parish centre settlements.

An attempt has been made to rank historic parish-centre settlements in County Meath according to their function and content (Fig. 6:7). The criteria employed included the presence or absence of parish-centre farms as well as Anglican and Catholic churches both in the mid-nineteenth century and at the present time. A classification of this kind serves to identify degrees of continuity and discontinuity within the two parochial systems in Meath at critical junctures in the history of their development. Sixty out of a total of 132 centres in Meath possessed none of the criteria that were specified. These were the deserted or aborted sites, and they indicated some of the territorial implications in Meath of Ireland's turbulent religious history. Three-quarters of these deserted centres were located in the four eastern baronies of Skreen, Navan, Lower Deece and Lower Slane. They included Martry and Donaghmore in Lower Navan, Killeen and Dowdstown in Skreen, and Scurlockstown in Lower Deece. No abandoned sites were found in the western and northern baronies of Moyfenrath, Lune, Fore and Morgallion. Continuity of territorial structures and their settlement centres was more apparent among the coarser networks prevailing in the less Normanised areas of the county. It follows therefore that the more mature parish centres were found in the western baronies which had experienced English colonisation and settlement from the seventeenth century. Parish centres with four or more of the criteria sought in their ranking included Clonard in Moyfenrath, and Killaconnigan or Ballivor and Kildalkey and Athboy in the barony of Lune. Villages and towns which, in origin, were not related to the parochial system were becoming increasingly significant features of industrial Ulster in the later eighteenth century but they were rare in Leinster away from the greater Dublin area. In the barony of Moyfenrath in Meath, these non-parochial settlements included the landlord induced village of Summerhill as well as Enfield which had emerged in the early nineteenth century at the intersection of arterial road, rail and canal routes.

The dramatic rehabilitation of the Catholic church in County Meath in the eighteenth and nineteenth centuries manifested itself territorially in several ways. One of the most critical indexes that could be employed in identifying degrees of continuity and discontinuity in parish structures in Ireland in the mid-nineteenth century was the presence or absence of modern Catholic churches in historic settlement centres. Of the 86 Catholic churches in the County Meath section of the Meath diocese in 1850 as many as 38 were located in the old centres. In other words over a quarter of the historic parishes in Meath had Catholic churches at their settlement centres in mid century. Modern Catholic communities were therefore emerging within the old territorial frameworks and old mass paths were being given a new lease of life in a diocese where otherwise the old and the new parish networks were rarely co-extensive. Among the few modern Catholic parishes in County Meath which are co-extensive with their historic precursors are Moynalty in the barony of Lower Kells, Drakestown in Morgallion and the parish of Dunboyne. Most of the high-ranking parish centres in the western baronies contained modern Catholic as well as Anglican churches in 1850. In the eastern baronies, where the Anglican church was less significant, Catholic churches alone towered over a great variety of old parish centres. In the barony of Ratoath, for example, there were only Catholic churches in 1850 in the settlement centres of small parishes such as Crickstown, Donaghmore and Rathregan. Modern Catholicism was therefore more deeply entrenched in Meath's eastern baronies.

The vibrant qualities of modern Catholicism in County Meath also found expression in the nineteenth century in the expansion of the rural parish network to incorporate the largely short-lived and poor communities which had emerged in the labour-intensive tillage areas as well as on the county's physically marginal lands. Unlike its Anglican counterpart, the remodelled Catholic church was geared to attempt to capture the allegiance of the majority of the population, irrespective of their social standing. In this way the Catholic church became an immensely powerful cementing force in the countryside and through its effort the Irish nation experienced the rare spiritual pulsations which have spasmodically characterised the history of Christianity in the island. The new rural parishes which emerged from the later eighteenth century included Bohermeen and Dunderry in Lower Navan, Carnaross and Oristown in Upper Kells, Curraha in Ratoath, Enfield in Lower Moyfenrath and Lobinstown in Lower Slane. The apparently fortuitous and casual selection of their names seems to suggest that these new ecclesiastical entities and their settlement centres were selected and created with little reference to any pre-existing Christian territorial linkages. It was within these fresh parochial frameworks that the church further expressed its powerful presence through the simultaneous growth of new forms of parish-centre settlements which have come to be known as chapel villages. Nine chapel villages have been recognised for County Meath (Fig. 6:7). They are Clonard, Ballinabrackey and Longwood in Moyfenrath, Robinstown and Dunderry in the barony of Navan, Carnaross and Ballinlough in Upper Kells and Ashbourne and Batterstown in the barony of Ratoath. Their late emergence underlined the incompatibility of the two cultures, indigenous and colonial, that prevailed in nineteenth-century Ireland.

The secular element employed in the ranking of parish settlements in

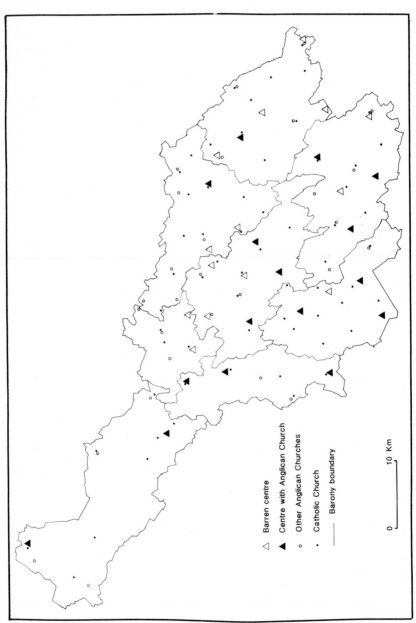

Figure 6:8. Historic parish centres and churches in County Cavan, c. 1850.

△ Barren centre

▲ Centre with Anglican Church

○ Other Anglican Churches

• Catholic Church

—— Barony boundary

0   10 Km

County Meath was the parish-centre farm. This was identified as the holding which was located at the settlement centre, whose land was valued at £100 and over, and on whose land was placed a modern Anglican church, a church ruin or an old-established graveyard in 1850. These were usually the most substantial farms within the parish and they were occasionally referred to as manors as, for example, in the parish of Killyon in the barony of Moyfenrath Upper. The majority of parish-centre farms in Leinster were old and many had come to act as the home farms of the larger estates. The home farms in the settlement centres of the adjoining parishes of Dunsany and Killeen in the barony of Skreen, for example, were located alongside motte sites of the invasion phase of Norman colonisation. Forty-six parish-centre farms were identified in County Meath. They were therefore found in association with no more than one-third of the total number of historic parish centres in the county. Twenty-seven of these farms appear in 1850 to have been occupied by families with non-Irish names and nine of the families with Irish names were acting as caretakers. Moreover 12 of the 19 farms occupied by Irish families were located in the three eastern and central baronies of Skreen, Ratoath and Lower Navan. Nine of the 29 planter farms, on the other hand, were located in the western baronies of Moyfenrath and Kells. Within their confined worlds, historic parish centres therefore acted as tiny alien cells, in a secular as well as an ecclesiastical capacity, in what was generally a hostile environment.

Historic parish frameworks in Ulster, as they had survived, and with their early celtic Christian roots, were of a coarser and simpler structure than those encountered in Normanised Leinster. In Ulster parish networks had little bearing on nineteenth-century patterns of landholding and landownership. Moreover in Ulster fresh forms of ecclesiastical territorial organisation had been introduced with the onset of Protestant nonconformity. Nonconformist communities generated their own territorial entities, usually without reference to any pre-existing parish networks. In County Cavan they focused a great deal of their institutionalised religious activities on landlord or estate core towns such as Killashandra, Cootehill and Bailieborough. In the open countryside, on the other hand, a Presbyterian meeting house at Bellasis in the barony of Castlerahan was obstinately located on the border between the parishes of Killinkere and Lurgan. This meeting house stood for the radically different spatial orders that characterised the robust nonconformist worlds that lay to the north of the Meath-Cavan divide. At Bellasis an open Bible remains as a symbolic alternative to an altar.

In County Meath there were four times as many historic parishes as there were in County Cavan. In Meath only eight parishes exceeded 4,000 hectares in extent and the average size of a parish in the barony of Skreen was only 800 hectares. In Cavan, on the other hand, as in Ulster generally, parishes were large and ill-defined (Fig. 6:4). Twenty-two out of a total of 36 exceeded 4,000 hectares in extent and the largest – Templeport in the barony of Tullyhaw – was 16,000 hectares. In the diocese of Kilmore, which incorporates most of County Cavan, and in common with other dioceses in the north and west of the island which had not known Norman influence, the modern Catholic parishes are closely synchronised with the pre-existing framework. Consequently in Cavan the oldest ecclesiastical entities have retained their meaning to the present day. In Cavan as elsewhere in Ulster, it is the Anglican church which has been the more eager to adapt old territorial structures to accommodate fresh opportunities and obligations. In County Meath, in 1850, 51 Anglican churches served a total of 141 parishes. In Cavan, on the other hand, 39 churches served 34 parishes, but only 17 of these were located in historic parish centre (Fig. 6:8). In Ulster dioceses the presence of large planter tenant-farmer populations, as well as discrete planter communities based on villages and towns, had led to a general reconstruction and extension of the older network. Ten new Anglican or Church of Ireland parishes were created in County Cavan from the seventeenth century, and their location acted as pointers to the areas of more intensive English settlement. The new parishes were Ashfield, Dernakesh, Cloverhill and Killoughter in the barony of Tullygarvey; Quivy, St. Andrews and Derryheen in Loughtee; Ballyjamesduff and Billis in Castlerahan and Arvagh in the barony of Tullyhunco. From the names given to them alone it is clear that many of these parishes were focused on pre-existing estate cores and the residences of their principal lay patrons. To the planter in nineteenth-century County Cavan, therefore, secular estate and ecclesiastical parish were sometimes seen as identical areas and this must have strengthened his feeling of belonging locally.

Despite the synchronisation of the older and the newer parish networks in the diocese of Kilmore, only 5 out of a total of 63 modern Catholic churches in County Cavan in 1850 were located on the old Christian sites. These were in the parishes of Scrabby in the barony of Clanmahon, Castleterra in Upper Loughtee, Killashandra in Tullyhunco, Knockbride in Clankee and Munterconnaught in the barony of Castlerahan. In these circumstances the deserted church site and graveyard was a particularly poignant feature in the landscape of nineteenth-century Cavan (Fig. 6:8). Examples of aborted sites included Drung in the barony of Tullygarvey, Drumgoon in Clankee, and Castleterra, Annagelliff, Denn and Lavey in the barony of Upper Loughtee. Many of these deserted early Christian sites were located alongside attractive but remote inter-drumlin lough shores and the modern churches, both Anglican and Catholic, had to be translated to more accessible locations on arterial routeways. In this way the tiny Poor Law union centre of Bawnboy emerged as the focus for the parish of Templeport in the barony of Tullyhaw. Similarly the centre for the parish of Kilbride in Clanmahon was transferred to the landlord village of Mount Nugent, whilst the landlord town of Virginia became the modern centre for the parish of Lurgan in the barony of Castlerahan. Radical shifts of this kind in nodal points in the settlement system did not take place in County Meath. In the course of the rationalisation process, Anglican churches and their parishes in Cavan came to be more closely tied to and consolidated within estate core villages and towns. Modern Catholic chapels, on the other hand, with their rapidly growing and far-flung congregations, came to be conspicuously lonely items among Cavan's confused topography, and they sometimes conveyed the impression of being thoroughly uprooted institutions. Isolated chapels perched on drumlin summits and slopes were found, for example, at Carrigallen and Clifferna in the parish of Larah in Tullygarvey, at Knockgillagh in the parish of Lavey in Loughtee, and at Coveragh and Killatee in Drumgoon parish in the barony of Clankee. Remote farming communities were in this way, carved out into fresh social neighbourhoods which were tributary areas to chapels. Milltown in the parish of Drumlane in Loughtee and Bellananagh in the parish of Kilmore, in the barony of Clanmahon, were however the only examples from County Cavan of what we have referred to as chapel villages in County Meath. As elsewhere in peasant Ireland Cavan may hitherto have never known village life.

NOTES

1. U. H. Hussey de Burgh, *The landowners of Ireland* (Dublin, 1878).
2. Personal names and placenames are spelt as they occur in the nineteenth-century literature.
3. R. E. Matheson, *Surnames in Ireland* (Dublin, 1909).
4. E. McLysaght, *Irish families* (Dublin, 1972).
5. P. S. Robinson, *The plantation of Ulster* (Dublin, 1984), p. 94.

Pre-famine population in Ulster: Evidence from the parish register of Killyman

WILLIAM MACAFEE

Since the 1950s our knowledge of both the general and regional demographic history of Western Europe has grown considerably, mainly as a result of the greater use of parish registers and the development of the method of family reconstitution. Unfortunately, in Ireland good quality parish registers are rare, particularly for the seventeenth and eighteenth centuries. Furthermore, as Morgan has shown, reconstitution of families is made more difficult because of the fact that Irish parish registers, before the nineteenth century, contain only a minimum of information on individuals, and few registers have a sufficiently long uninterrupted run of good quality entries.[1]

Leaving aside problems associated with the quality of the registers, it could be argued that the major drawback to using them is the fact that before the nineteenth century they are geographically concentrated in Ulster and refer, almost exclusively, to the Church of Ireland population. It was precisely for this latter reason that Connell dismissed them as a significant source. He believed that the Church of Ireland population differed from the remainder in occupation, custom and wealth.[2] Whilst this was probably true in many parts of Ireland it could be argued that it was less true of those areas of Ulster which had experienced a considerable influx of English settlers of all classes during the seventeenth century, for example, the Lagan Valley and mid-Ulster.[3] It is no accident that some of the best surviving pre-nineteenth-century Church of Ireland registers are to be found in this region of Ulster. Outside this area those of reasonable quality tend to be extant only for towns which had significant English settlements, Londonderry and Coleraine for instance. In many ways it is the presence of a substantial urban component in a register which really poses the greatest problem. It could be argued that they exhibit a different socio-economic structure and have, accordingly, a demographic regime at odds with the rest of the rural population. Certainly fertility levels in towns in most of Ireland were lower than in rural areas; Ulster was the exception, the exact opposite being the case.[4] Another problem associated with urban populations is the presence of what might be called a floating population, persons only using the church for one event. This can lead to considerable discrepancies between baptisms and burials.[5]

It would be useful, therefore, to find a parish where a) the density of population was relatively high, b) the Church of Ireland community was completely rural and formed a considerable proportion of the total population, and c) had a well-kept register which spanned, at least, the late eighteenth and early nineteenth centuries. One such parish is Killyman, which is situated to the east of the town of Dungannon on the County Tyrone/Armagh border.[6] It meets the first two criteria completely and goes part of the way towards fulfilling the third.

The region and the quality of the register

Killyman lies within the area of Ulster which, during the eighteenth and early nineteenth centuries, was dominated by the linen industry. Because of this the region was characterised by very small farms and cottier/weaver houses resulting in high densities of population. In Killyman by 1841 there were 582 persons per square mile. According to Lewis in 1837 there were three large bleach greens in the parish and the manufacture of both linen and cotton was carried on extensively.[7] The register gave the occupations of husbands from 1837 onwards and of 317 families identified, 147 were weavers, 132 farmers, 31 in various trades, 15 labourers, 5 professional, 1 servant, and 1 beggar. Since tenants in this region often combined farming and weaving it is very probable that in some of the families where the occupation of the head of household was given as farmer, other members of the family were engaged in the linen trade. Certainly there was ample evidence of this practice in the 1851

Enumerators' Returns for County Antrim.[8] Given the data on occupation, Connell's claim that the Church of Ireland population differed
from the rest of the community in occupation and wealth cannot be sustained in this case. Furthermore since they formed 46 per cent of the total
population in Killyman, it can hardly be said that they were an
insignificant part of society in the area.[9] There were no towns in the
parish so here we are dealing with a population which was entirely rural,
a situation reflected in the fact that there was virtually no floating
population in the register; most of the family names recorded were present
over a long period of time.

Apart from a short period of very poor registration from 1770 to 1775,
the register was well kept, particularly with regard to baptisms, from
1745 through to the Famine. During these years there were six different
rectors: 1745-49 Richard Crump; 1749-75 George Evans; 1775-1817
Charles Caulfield; 1817-24 Thomas Carpendale; 1824-30 William Phelan
and 1830-45 Mortimer O'Sullivan. In the later stages of the register the
entries were made by the clerk of the church. It is more difficult to
establish who, exactly, was responsible for them in the earlier years. Certainly there is a close correlation between changes in handwriting and
changes in rector. Some 6,000 baptisms were recorded during the years
1745-1845, with almost 1,700 burials and just over 1,000 marriages.
Given the number of baptisms the number of burials was much too low
and certainly the number of marriages recorded, particularly during the
earlier years of the register, was also an underestimate.

Burials

The major problem with the Killyman register is the under-registration
of burials. As figure 7:1 shows there is a very wide gap between burials
and baptisms; clearly something is wrong here. Only during the period
1776-87 were there figures which gave any real measure of burials. During these years 145 of the 333 burials recorded were of children. However
in the earlier period 1745-75 only 51 of the 135 recorded burials were of
children, and during the years 1788-1841 there were only 75 child burials
out of a total of 1,159. Clearly the failure to record the burials of many
children was the cause of the under-registration of burials. Further proof
of the absence of child burials is given during the period 1842-50 when
the ages of those buried were recorded. Here we find that of 147 males
buried only 10 were aged twenty or below, and only 3 were ten or below.
The same picture prevailed for the female population where of 152
burials only 15 were twenty or below and only 1 was ten or below.

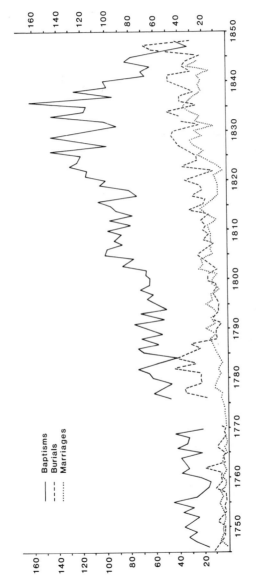

Figure 7:1. Parish of Killyman: burials, baptisms and marriages 1745–1848.

Clearly this cannot be correct. As yet no adequate explanation of why the majority of child burials went unrecorded has been found.

It is possible to get any real indication of the number of burials per annum, particularly those of children, for only a short period, namely 1776-87. Morgan in her analysis of the Blaris register noted a significant decline in the percentage of child burials between the mid-seventeenth and early nineteenth centuries.[10] In Killyman during the years 1776-87, children represented 44 per cent of total burials and in certain years, viz. 1777, 1778, 1782 and 1784 child burials were at least 50 per cent of the total. These kinds of figures contrast with those for Magherafelt in the earlier part of the century where, during the period 1717-36, 75 per cent of burials recorded were of children, a figure which could rise in a single crisis year to 87 per cent.[11] Admittedly the sample of burials is small and only covers twelve years but it does lend further support to the view that mortality, particularly that of children, may have been declining significantly during the second half of the eighteenth century. If this was the case, and given that there had been no appreciable change in celibacy or an influx of outsiders, then some increase in persons marrying might be expected by the 1770s and 1780s.

Number of marriages and baptisms

Table 7:1 shows the number of marriages in each decade from the 1750s Column (a) shows those recorded in the register for each decade, and indicates that there were more than twice as many marriages in the decade 1781-90 than there had been in 1751-60, with the numbers continuing to rise for every decade except 1811-20 and the years 1841-45. Are these figures a true reflection of the actual number of marriages which took place in the parish? This does not seem likely judging by the number of baptisms in relation to the number of marriages, particularly during the years up to 1780. How defective, therefore, is the register in this respect? Furthermore could the number of marriages and baptisms have been inflated by an influx of outsiders into the area? In order to answer these questions two procedures were adopted, the results of which are shown in columns (b) and (c).

It is perhaps best to illustrate the first procedure by way of an example. Take the family of Hugh and Sarah McKeown who had seven children baptised, in 1813, 1814, 1816, two in 1818, 1821, and 1826. Their date of marriage is not known; yet it seems reasonable to assume that they were married within one to two years of their first child. On this basis the McKeown marriage could be assigned to the decade 1811-20. This pro-

TABLE 7:1

PARISH OF KILLYMAN: NUMBER OF MARRIAGES PER DECADE (1751-1845)

Decade	(a) Recorded in Register	(b) Estimate	(c) Sub-Group
1751-1760......................	38	83	40
1761-1770......................	17	108	58
1771-1780......................	44	163	78
1781-1790......................	86	186	82
1791-1800......................	105	178	76
1801-1810......................	137	233	108
1811-1820......................	106	204	101
1821-1830......................	165	290	130
1831-1840......................	228	415	123
1841-1845......................	93	161	56
Total.........................	1,019	2,021	852

For an explanation of columns (a), (b) and (c) see text.
Source– P.R.O.N.I. T 679/383, 384, 386, 387 and 393.

cedure was then adopted for all families. The results of the exercise are shown in column (b) of table 7:1. It must be emphasised that this is a crude measure of the number of marriages in each decade, but it tends to corroborate the view that marriage had increased substantially by 1780. In fact, relative to the previous decade, the estimated number of marriages rose by 30 per cent during the years 1761-70 and 51 per cent during 1771-80.

These increases may have been due to an influx of migrants, so in order to overcome this problem a second procedure was adopted. A sub-group of forty family names which had both marriages and baptisms running from before 1750 was selected from the total population. The results of this analysis are shown in column (c) of table 7:1. It confirms the pattern already noted in column (b) in that, relative to the previous decade, marriages in this group rose by 45 per cent during 1761-70 and by 45 per cent for the years 1771-80. The boom in marriages then began to decline: 1781-90 saw a slower rise of 14 per cent, followed by a 4 per cent decrease during the decade 1791-1800, a reflection, perhaps, of deteriorating conditions within the linen industry. A slight recovery in the linen trade coupled with the economic expansion of the war years were probably responsible for a rise of 31 per cent in marriages during the years 1801-10. This growth was not sustained, however, and the following

decade showing a 12 per cent decrease. Part of this decrease could probably be attributed to the post-war depression but a close inspection of the
figures reveals that depression in the linen industry, at its worst in the
year 1811, was probably also responsible.[12] Then, once again, the
decades 1821-30 and 1831-40 saw a new surge in the number of marriages. The fact that the sub-group showed a decrease during the years
1831-40 suggests that some of the increase at that time might have been
due to an influx of newcomers. At the same time it must not be forgotten
that the sub-group may have been affected more by emigration. The fact
that only the male side of the family was represented in the sample may
have led to some distortion. Both estimated marriages and those
recorded in the register began to decline after 1835.

As figure 7:1 shows the increases in marriages correlate to a reasonable
degree, with the steep rises in the number of baptisms in and around the
same periods. For example, the dramatic increase in marriages in the
1760s and 1770s and again in the early 1800s and the 1820s must have
contributed to the sharp upturn in baptisms at those times. Similarly the
slowing down in the number of marriages in the 1790s and their decrease
during the decade 1811-20 and after 1835 was matched by corresponding
movements in baptisms. However, much of the controversy about marriage
in pre-Famine Ireland concerns not so much the number who married, but
rather the age at which men and women married. The long, relatively
uninterrupted, run of baptisms and marriages from the 1740s made it possible to trace the date of baptism of some of the people, particularly females,
whose marriages were recorded in the register.

Age at first marriage

Before examining the evidence on age at first marriage, we need to explain
how the figures were derived. As mentioned earlier, there were some 1,000
marriage entries in the register and it has been possible to trace both
marriage and baptismal dates for 291 females and 200 males. It has to
be admitted that, because of the inadequacy of the burial register, there
is always the possibility that some of the people identified had in fact
died. Identification was far from easy since it depended, almost
exclusively, on surname and christian name evidence. Addresses and
occupations were only available from the 1830s onwards and were
generally of little use. Tracing christian names like Joshua and Abigail
was relatively easy, but where there was a common name like John or
Mary it nearly proved impossible. The basic rule which was adopted was
that a person would only be included if there was no-one else with the

same christian name, born around the same period, who could conceivably be mistaken for that person. Hence there were many rejections. The ages were calculated, in the first instance, in alphabetical order and then divided up into decades. In other words the author was not aware of any diffferences by decade during the calculation.

In the case of males two sets of figures have been used in order to boost the size of the sample: those where the actual date of the marriage was known from the register (there were 105 of these) and those (a further 95) whose date of marriage was estimated on the basis that their first child was most probably born in the first year of marriage and therefore their date of marriage would be one year earlier. How valid are the results of the second method? The following evidence suggests that it might produce reasonable estimates. First, data from those marriages where actual date was known and the baptism of the first child was usually one year. Secondly, as figure 7:2 shows, when distributions, means, medians, and modes of the two groups are compared they are in fact very similar.

TABLE 7:2

PARISH OF KILLYMAN: MALE AGE AT FIRST MARRIAGE
(1771-1845)

Decade	Sample Size	Mean	S.D.	Median	Mode
1771-1780	17	25.4	2.3	27	27
1781-1790	25	26.4	3.6	26	30
1791-1800	12	25.2	2.7	25	24
1801-1810	38	25.4	3.6	27	27
1811-1820	30	26.1	2.8	26	25/26
1821-1830	30	26.7	4.9	26	27
1831-1840	35	25.4	4.5	24	24
1841-1845	13	26.0	3.8	26	22
1771-1810	92	25.7	3.3	26	27
1811-1845	108	26.1	4.1	26	23

Source: P.R.O.N.I. T.679/383, 384, 386, 387 and 393.

Table 7:2 shows clearly that there was very little change in the male age of marriage from decade to decade; the mean and indeed the median stay round 25/26. As figure 7:3 indicates the distributions of the ages at which men were marrying during the periods 1771-1810 and 1811-45 were very similar. In both periods 18 per cent of men marrying were aged 22 years or below; indeed only 6 per cent were 20 years or below. Evidence from

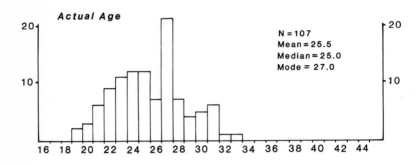

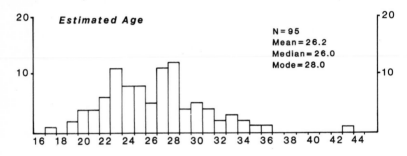

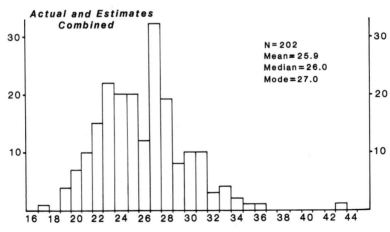

Figure 7:2. Parish of Killyman: male age of marriage.

the nearby parish of Donaghmore and a range of parishes in County Antrim tends to confirm this pattern of marriage ages, at least for the nineteenth century. In Donaghmore a sample of 31 marriages for the period 1800-50 gave a mean of 26.9, a median of 26 and a mode of 25/26; only 13 per cent of men marrying were aged 22 or below and there were only two instances in the sample aged 20 and 19. The indifferent quality of the Donaghmore register during the second half of the eighteenth century coupled with the fact that the parish was divided in 1775 in order to create the new parish of Pomeroy, made it almost impossible to trace many marriages in the 1780s and 1790s.[13] In fact only six could be identified, too small a sample from which to calculate any meaningful

TABLE 7:3

COUNTY ANTRIM: AGE AT FIRST MARRIAGE (1801-1850)

Decade	Sample Size	Mean	S.D.	Median	Mode
Males					
<1801	87	24.0	5.3	23	21
1801-1810	194	26.0	5.9	25	30
1811-1820	468	26.2	5.9	25	26
1821-1830	757	26.1	5.9	25	24
1831-1840	886	26.1	6.2	25	24
1841-1850	972	25.9	5.8	24	21
<1811	281	25.0	5.6	24	
1811-1850	3,083	26.1	5.9	25	
Females					
<1801	148	22.9	5.1	22	20
1801-1810	276	23.9	5.8	23	20
1811-1820	556	24.2	5.9	23	19
1821-1830	840	24.3	5.9	23	19
1831-1840	988	23.7	5.9	22	21
1841-1850	1,079	23.9	5.6	23	21
<1811	424	23.4	5.4	23	
1811-1850	3,463	24.1	5.9	23	

*This includes the parishes of Craigs, Rasharkin, and Dunaghy in mid-Antrim; Tickmacrevan, Carncastle, Larne, Kilwaughter, and Grange of Killyglen in east Antrim; Killead, Ballinderry, Aghalee, and Aghagallon in south Antrim.

Source: Valerie Morgan and William Macafee, 'Irish population in the pre-Famine period: Evidence from County Antrim', *Economic History Review,* Second Series, xxxvii, (1984), pp. 182-196.

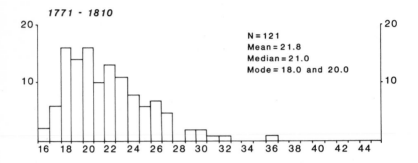

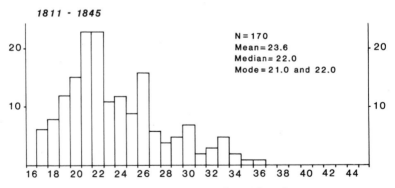

Figure 7:3. Parish of Killyman: male age of marriage.

statistics. The sample for County Antrim, based on an analysis of the 1851 Enumerators' Returns by Morgan and Macafee, is much larger and details relating to age at marriage are shown in table 7:3.[14] Unfortunately it also refers only to the nineteenth century but it does confirm the view that in these parts of Ulster, at least, early marriage for men (if by early we mean 20/21), was not a common feature of the early nineteenth century. Moreover, if the Killyman evidence can be regarded as representative of the linen areas of Ulster, neither does it seem to have been typical of the later years of the eighteenth century. Indeed one of the most significant points to emerge from this research was not so much the fact that the average age at which men married was around 26 (this simply confirms the evidence of the census figures) but rather the fact that the male age at marriage remained relatively unchanged throughout the period 1770-95. This figure of 26 is reasonably close to the mean computed from the 1841 census by Mokyr and Ó Grada[15] and Drake's figure of 25 for 1836.[16] It also lies within the age range of Hajnal's European marriage pattern.[17]

Fertility is not controlled by the age at which men marry, it is much more dependent on the age at which women marry. The research of both Mokyr and Ó Grada, and Morgan and Macafee, mentioned above, produced a mean age at first marriage of 24 for women on the eve of the Famine. Comparison of tables 7:3 and 7:4 for the decade after 1811 indicates that age at first marriage for women in Killyman was very similar to that for County Antrim: the mean for the entire period being 23.6. This contrasts with the earlier period 1771-1810 when the mean age at marriage for women in Killyman was 21.8, a difference of almost two years. Of course the question arises as to whether the difference could have been due to the fact that since the first few decades of the 1771-1810 period were closer to the beginning of the register older persons marrying had been excluded thereby reducing the overall mean. This does not appear to have been the case because the register began in 1745 and the decades which showed the greatest percentage of younger marriages were to be found after 1780, that is, 1791-1800 and 1801-1810. There were some fifty years and more after the beginning of the register, an interval generally agreed to be sufficient to avoid the problem of truncation. Again, because we are dealing with relatively small samples, the differences could be caused by the inclusion or exclusion of even a small number of very low or very high ages. Furthermore since the age at marriage was calculated from the date of baptism, then the true age of marriage was probably slightly higher than the figures shown here. Dates of both baptism and birth are available after 1837 and at that time two-thirds of infants were baptised within two months and 90 per cent had been christened within six months from birth. However, even if the ages were increased by, say 0.5, this difference of 1.8 between the two periods would still remain.

TABLE 7:4

PARISH OF KILLYMAN: FEMALE AGE AT FIRST MARRIAGE (1771-1845)

Decade	Sample Size	Mean	S.D.	Median	Mode
1771-1780	13	22.6	2.9	21	21
1781-1790	28	22.4	4.4	21	19
1791-1800	26	21.3	4.7	20	22
1801-1810	54	21.5	2.7	20	20
1811-1820	26	24.0	4.8	22	21
1821-1830	44	23.0	3.8	22	22
1831-1840	66	23.4	4.0	23	20/22/26
1841-1845	34	24.4	4.9	23	19
1771-1810	121	21.8	3.7	21	18/20
1811-1845	170	23.6	4.3	22	21/22

Source: P.R.O.N.I. T.679/383, 384, 386, 387 and 393.

TABLE 7:5

PARISH OF KILLYMAN: FEMALE MARRIAGES (1771-1845)

Decade	Total Marriages	% Aged 19 & <	% Aged 20 & <	% Aged 23 & <	% Aged 26 & >
1771-1780	13	15	23	62	23
1781-1790	28	39	43	61	21
1791-1800	26	46	50	81	12
1801-1810	54	24	48	78	13
1811-1820	26	15	19	54	31
1821-1830	44	16	23	68	25
1831-1840	66	14	26	56	29
1841-1845	34	18	26	50	38
1771-1810	121	31	45	73	16
1811-1845	170	15	24	58	31

Source: P.R.O.N.I. T.679/383, 384, 486, 387 and 393.

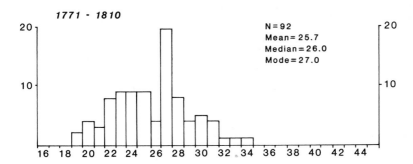

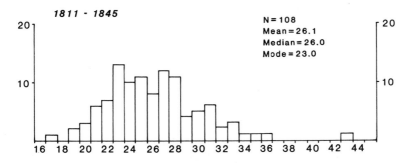

Figure 7:4. Parish of Killyman: Female Age of Marriage.

Essentially the difference can be explained by the percentage of 20-year-olds or below marrying in the decades between 1781 and 1810. During this period they formed some 50 per cent of the total, whereas at other times the figure was nearer to 25 per cent. Conversely the percentage aged 26 or above was as low as 16 per cent for the period 1771-1810, a figure which doubled in the later period. As figure 7:4 and table 7:5 illustrate there was a perceptible shift towards slightly later marriages for females after 1811. In Donaghmore a sample of 44 marriages for the period 1800-50 gave a lower mean of 22.3, a median of 22, and modes of 21 and 23. Any differences between Donaghmore and Killyman could probably be explained by sample size. At the same time it should be noted that 73 per cent of the marriages were aged 23 or below, whereas the comparable figure for Killyman was 58 per cent; however, those aged 19 or below only formed 16 per cent, a similar statistic to Killyman.

Viewed in a European context women in Killyman married relatively early; even in the period 1811-45, 58 per cent of the marriages in the sample took place at age 23 or below. The mean for Killyman during the same

TABLE 7:6

**MEAN AGE AT FIRST MARRIAGE FOR WOMEN
IN SELECTED AREAS OF WESTERN EUROPE (1780-1820)**

England	24.2
France	26.7
Germany	27.5
Belgium	27.9
Scandinavia	29.8

Source: M. W. Flinn, *The European demographic system, 1500-1820,* Harvester Press, Brighton, 1981, pp. 124-127.

period was 22.1, a figure two years younger than women in England and as much as five and almost eight years younger than their counterparts in Germany and Scandinavia (Table 7:6). At the same time there was no evidence of the very early marriage suggested by Connell. There is, however, a suggestion that women may, on average, have been marrying slightly earlier during the period before 1770 and the relatively small size of the sample for the period 1771-80, makes it impossible to assess long term trends in marriage ages throughout this part of the eighteenth century. Certainly the mean ages in the sample for the period 1771-90 suggests that any movement towards slightly earlier marriage after 1790 was from a state of affairs where, by European standards, age at marriage for women was already relatively low. Perhaps the key point to note about female age at marriage was the undoubted shift towards slightly later marriage in the period 1811-45 to an age which is consistent with the census date of 1841. If women in Killyman were marrying earlier than their counterparts in Western Europe than one would expect to find high levels of fertility.

Fertility

The evidence on baptismal intervals suggests that throughout the entire period of the register most women who married in Killyman had a child within their first year of marriage, with subsequent children being born within twenty-four to thirty months of the previous one. It has been possible to calculate the number of baptisms accruing to 334 of the 1,034 marriages recorded in the register between 1745 and 1845. Throughout the entire period up to 1830 there were, on average, 4.7 baptisms per family. Breaking it down into periods we find that before 1770 it was 4.7 (sample size 32); between 1771-90 it was 5.2 (66); 1791-1810, 5.1 (121); and 1811-30, 4.0 (115). The later marriages in the period 1811-30 would have been affected by the fact that the register of baptisms ceases by 1848, that is, the average number of baptisms per marriage for the years 1811-20 was 4.7 (52) whereas in 1821-30 it had dropped to 3.4 (63). Furthermore there is a suspicion that emigration of young couples was having an even more substantial effect. It should be stressed that these means have not been calculated from fully reconstituted families. As a result it has not been possible to establish whether or not families with single baptisms were the result of the death of one of the parents, the family moving on, or the couple simply having no more children. If, for example, the marriages with a single baptism were removed from the periods 1771-90 (8) and 1791-1810 (141), then the average number of baptisms per marriage would have been 5.8 and 5.9 respectively. These sorts of figures are in line with Eversley's results for Irish Quaker women, where he found a completed family size of 6.2 for the period 1750-99 and 5.9 for the period 1800-49.[18]

Strictly speaking, marital fertility can only be measured by relating births to particular marriages. In a closed community, the same result can be calculated by dividing all births by all marriages. However, it is not sufficient to divide the number of births in a decade by the number of marriages contracted in that same decade, because some of the births which took place then are virtually unrelated to those marriages. To overcome this problem the technique of overlapping periods can be used,

TABLE 7:7

PARISH OF KILLYMAN: NUMBER OF BAPTISMS PER MARRIAGE

Period	Marriages (a)	(b)	Baptisms Period		Baptisms per Marriage Period	(a)	(b)
1746-1765	63	200	1751-1770	611	1756-1760	9.7	3.1
1766-1775	55	191	1756-1775	524	1761-1765	9.5	2.7
1765-1775	44	206	1761-1780	687	1766-1770	15.6	3.3
1761-1780	61	271	1766-1785	814	1771-1775	13.3	3.0
1766-1785	79	313	1771-1790	958	1776-1780	12.1	3.1
1771-1790	130	349	1776-1795	1,175	1781-1785	9.0	3.4
1776-1795	176	379	1781-1800	1,227	1786-1790	6.9	3.2
1781-1800	191	364	1786-1805	1,321	1791-1795	6.9	3.6
1786-1805	240	400	1791-1810	1,458	1796-1800	6.1	3.6
1791-1810	242	411	1796-1815	1,589	1801-1805	6.6	3.9
1796-1815	257	411	1801-1820	1,727	1806-1810	6.7	4.2
1801-1820	243	437	1806-1825	1,932	1811-1815	7.9	4.4
1806-1825	219	479	1811-1830	2,106	1816-1820	9.6	4.4
1811-1830	271	494	1816-1855	2,237	1821-1825	8.2	4.5
1816-1835	316	645	1821-1840	2,354	1826-1830	7.4	3.6
1821-1840	393	699	1826-1845	2,111	1831-1835	5.4	3.0

Source: P.R.O.N.I. T.679/383, 384, 386, 387, 389.

for example, the baptisms taking place in 1776-95 are divided by the marriages contracted in the period 1771-90. This tends to produce a ratio which is heavily weighted by the baptisms occurring inside the marriages in existence during the central span of years 1781-90. Table 7:7 shows two sets of figures. This is because, as the ratios for the earlier periods indicate, there was considerable under-registration of marriages. Column (a) used the marriages recorded in the register and column (b) makes use of the estimates of marriages from column (b) of table 1:1. The true measure probably lies somewhere between the two ratios shown by table 7:6. However in interpreting these ratios two points need to be borne in mind. Firstly any increase in the number of baptisms per marriage may be due to the increasing survival of infants immediately after birth. It must be remembered that if a child died before it was baptised then there would be no record of that child in either the baptismal or burial register. Thus, in such circumstances, a decline in infant mortality could give rise to an apparent rise in fertility. Secondly, as mentioned before, part of the decrease in the fertility ratio in the period just before the Famine may have been due to the emigration of young married couples.

Despite these reservations, once again the data is in line with Eversley's conclusion that '. . . some sort of peak of fertility, whatever the age of marriage, occurred some time between 1775 and 1825'.[19] Fertility appears to have reached its highest levels in Killyman during the period 1801-25 a state of affairs which is reasonably consistent with the data on age at first marriage for women. At the same time fertility in the period 1745-70 does not seem to have been unduly low relative to the period 1771-1800. This suggests that even then women were marrying at relatively early ages. Clearly Connell was correct in recognising that high annual rates of growth would have required high levels of fertility. However, the evidence presented here suggests a somewhat different scenario from that postulated by him and is more in line with the findings and postulates of recent research.

Overview

Connell's thesis relied heavily on a very early age at marriage for both men and women. It appears to have required men to have married at around 20 to 21 and many of their brides to have been in their early teens.[20] Furthermore, as it was essentially a Malthusian argument, it required a substantial fall in age at marriage, particularly for men, in order to initiate the original take-off in population. The evidence presented here shows clearly that this was not the case and if Killyman can be regarded as reasonably typical of the linen areas of Ulster then it is not likely to have been so for a substantial part of Ireland's pre-Famine population.

It seems more probable that in Ulster during the first half of the eighteenth century there was, to use Wrigley and Schofield's terminology, a high pressure demographic system characterised by high levels of mortality and fertility. Detailed evidence from Blaris and Magherafelt clearly indicate the former but, admittedly, there is less concrete evidence for the latter. Ó Grada has suggested, on the basis of literary evidence, that perhaps relatively early marriage had been a common feature of Irish life since the seventeenth century.[21] Dickson's analysis of seventeenth-century Cromwellian Transplantation Certificates indicated an average age at marriage of 22 for a sample of women in Counties Dublin and Waterford.[22] Analysis of the Blaris register suggests an average age at marriage for women of 18 to 19 in the late seventeenth and early eighteenth centuries.[23] The fertility data for Killyman show that, relative to the period after 1770, levels of fertility in the years 1745-70 were reasonably high. On this kind of evidence one could speculate that age at marriage for women was not likely to have been much higher then than it was in 1770. If indeed this was the case and child mortality was on the decline then as Clarkson has suggested, '. . . the effects would be cumulative as increasing proportions of children survived to become parents themselves'.[24] A combination of changing age structure and favourable economic conditions may have led to a fall of about one year in the average age at which women married. It has been estimated that such a fall could add approximately a third of a child per family, a figure consistent with the Killyman data on average number of baptisms per family. In short what is being suggested here is that any fall which may have taken place in the female age at marriage during the Napoleonic Wars would have been slight and would have merely fuelled an existing high level of fertility. Such a situation would be consistent with the kinds of growth rates postulated by Dickson, Daultrey and Ó Gráda in their recent re-interpretation of the County Hearth Returns for the eighteenth century.[25] For a combination of the following reasons (worsening economic circumstances, the effects of emigration, an increasing difference in marriage habits between socio-economic groups, increasing celibacy) there was, in Killyman, a perceptible upward movement in the average age at which women married. This was due to the fact that fewer of the marriages contracted in the three decades before the Famine included women of around 19 to 20 and more in their mid to late twenties. This led to the state of affairs portrayed by the official census returns for Ireland as a whole. Even then, as Mokyr and Ó Gráda have shown, marital fertility amongst Irish women still remained high relative to other countries of Western Europe.[26]

In view of the regional differences in annual growth rates revealed by the Dickson, Daultrey and Ó Gráda research, which probably reflected contrasting social and economic circumstances throughout Ireland, and given the fact that the Killyman data refers to one religious group, it would be foolhardy to suggest that the scenario painted here would suffice as an explanation for population growth in Ireland as a whole. Nevertheless it should be remembered that the linen areas of Ulster were amongst the most densely peopled in the island.

NOTES

1. Valerie Morgan, 'The Church of Ireland registers of St. Patrick's Coleraine as a source for the study of a local pre-Famine population' in *Ulster Folklife* xix (1973), pp. 56-67.

2. K. H. Connell, *The population of Ireland, 1750-1845* (Oxford, 1950), p. 29.

3. William Macafee and Valerie Morgan, 'Population in Ulster, 1660-1760' in Peter Roebuck (ed.), *Plantation to partition: Essays in honour of J. L. McCracken* (Belfast, 1981), p. 54.

4. Connell, *Population of Ireland,* pp. 32-6.

5. William Macafee and Valerie Morgan, 'Mortality in Magherafelt, County Derry, the early eighteenth century reappraised' in *I.H.S.,* xxiii (1982-3), p. 51.

6. Church of Ireland register of baptisms, marriages and burials for the parish of Killyman, P.R.O.N.I. T.679/383, 384, 386, 387 and 393.

7. Samuel Lewis, *A topographical dictionary of Ireland* (Dublin, 1837), p. 161.

8. Valerie Morgan and William Macafee, 'Irish population in the pre-Famine period: Evidence from County Antrim' in *Econ. Hist. Rev.,* 2nd ser., xxvii (1984), pp. 182-96.

9. *First report of the commissioners on public instruction (Ireland),* p. 829, H.C. 1835, xxxiii.

10. Valerie Morgan, 'A case study of population change over two centuries: Blaris, Lisburn, 1661-1848' in *Ir. Ec. Soc. Hist.,* iii (1976), pp. 15-16.

11. Macafee and Morgan, 'Mortality in Magherafelt', loc. cit., pp. 55-7.

12. Conrad Gill, *The rise of the Irish linen industry* (Oxford, 1925), pp. 221-6.

13. Church of Ireland register of baptisms, marriages and burials for the parish of Donaghmore, P.R.O.N.I. T.679/19 and T.786.

14. Morgan and Macafee, 'Irish population in the pre-Famine period', loc. cit.

15. Joel Mokyr and Cormac Ó Gráda, 'New developments in Irish population history, 1700-1850', *Econ. Hist. Rev.,* 2nd ser., xxxvii (1984), p. 477.

16. Michael Drake, 'Marriage and population growth in Ireland, 1750-1845', *Econ. Hist. Rev.,* 2nd ser., xvi (1963), p. 303.

17. J. Hajnal 'European marriage patterns in perspective', D. V. Glass and D.E.C. Eversley (ed.), *Population in history* (London, 1965), pp. 101-43.

18. D. E. C. Eversley, 'The demography of the Irish Quakers, 1650-1850', in J. M. Goldstrom and L. A. Clarkson (ed.), *Irish population, economy and society: Essays in honour of the late K. H. Connell* (Oxford, 1981), pp. 75-8.

19. Eversley, 'Demography of the Irish Quakers, loc. cit., p. 74.

20. Connell, *Population of Ireland,* pp. 51-3.

21. Cormac Ó Gráda, 'The population of Ireland, 1700-1900: a survey', *Annales de Demographie Historique* (1979), p. 285.

22. David Dickson, 'A note on the Cromwellian transplantation certificates', unpub. ms, Trinity College Dublin, 1982.

23. Macafee and Morgan, 'Population in Ulster', loc. cit., p. 56.

24. L. A. Clarkson, 'Irish population revisited, 1687-1821', Goldstrom and Clarkson, *Irish population, economy and society,* p. 35.

25. David Dickson, Cormac Ó Gráda and Stuart Daultry, 'Hearth tax, household size and Irish population change, 1672-1821', in *R.I.A. Proc.,* lxxxii (1982), C, no. 6 (1982), pp. 125-81.

26. Mokyr and Ó Gráda, 'New developments in Irish population history', loc. cit., p. 479.

The modernisation of the Irish female

DAVID FITZPATRICK

'Modernisation' should not be treated as a process whereby the mentality of individuals or the culture of social groups is altered according to determinable rules. For historians it is a useful shorthand term for a medley of loosely related processes which happen to have coincided in the recent history of certain 'western' societies. The varieties of human history are more plausibly explained within local rather than universal frameworks. We may admit to the rough coincidence of urban growth, industrial expansion, social deregulation, education and cultural diversification, without inferring that these processes have interacted everywhere according to a general causal model. This distinction applies forcefully to the history of population, the family and the relationship between men and women. Concepts such as 'the demographic transition', the emergence of 'the modern family', or the spread of 'affective individualism', may indeed be useful analytical tools in particular contexts. They should not be construed as inevitable by-products of some process of modernisation through which every society must eventually pass.

This paper is an exercise in particularism, located in what has often been designated as 'modern' Ireland.[1] In common with Britain and most of Europe, Ireland has not escaped urban or industrial growth since the mid-nineteenth century. If growth in these sectors was unusually sluggish until very recent times, the extension of commerce, communications and literacy was spectacular. Yet the trends in demographic and family strategies which coincided with these changes were often at odds with those elsewhere in Europe. In certain respects, Irish family structure became increasingly rigid and 'archaic' in the teeth of economic modernisation. This paradox may be highlighted by considering the functions of females within both the economic and family contexts. Women seeking husbands within Ireland made their choices within an ever more restricted marriage market; while those excluded from an Irish 'match' tended to emigrate rather than find employment at home. The cumulative impact of emigration was to Americanise the mentality of the Irish female whether or not she left Ireland. The contradiction between the growing rigidity of Irish social institutions and the growing cosmopolitanism of their members tended to bring about fragmentation, discontent and depopulation. The Irish female was 'modernised' in the sense that she grew increasingly conscious of making a practical choice between remaining 'Irish' and becoming 'modern'.

During the century and a half after 1800, the dominant family structure in rural Ireland was that of the 'stem family household'. It must be admitted that this assertion would be rejected by many historians of Ireland, and that if true it would render Ireland an exception to the north-western European pattern.[2] Within Ireland there were certainly periods, localities and social or occupation groups within which the 'stem' system was far from universal. The bulk of fixed property was not, in other words, invariably handed over to one newly-married inheritor in the lifetime of at least one parent, with provision being made for simultaneous compensation of non-inheriting siblings and retiring parents. Nevertheless, this type of succession to household control seems to have been unexpectedly widespread. Filial marriage preceding parental retirement may be detected in Connaught as well as Leinster, among small farmers and labourers as well as more prosperous farmers, in the pre-Famine context of preferential partible inheritance as well as the post-Famine context of restraint upon the subdivision of farms.[3] It is likely however that the predominance of the 'stem' system increased during the century after the Famine of the 1840s, as the division of farming land stabilised and as compensation of those not inheriting fixed property became more practicable.[4] Although many newly-married couples at first shared their households with parental families, the period of co-residence was usually and mercifully brief, a fact which explains the predominance of 'nuclear' family households in samples taken from census schedules in Ireland as elsewhere.[5] The convulsion associated with transfer of household control between generations coloured the life prospects of

most Irish females as well as males. But it directly concerned only one
stage of the female life-cycle, and the student of the Irish female in
family context should study her also in childhood, adolescence, adulthood and retirement. At each stage Irish females were faced with different possibilities and restrictions: their choices and responses illustrate
female mentality as it evolved from the cradle towards the grave.

Daughters were largely redundant in nineteenth-century Ireland. As in
most societies, girls were in the minority among infant deaths as well as
births, so tending to create an excess of those least likely to obtain even-
tual employment. Excess male mortality meant that in Cavan, 'boys into
their teens were dressed in petticoats and long frocks in order, or so it
was believed, to mislead the thieving fairies' hoping to make off with
their health or their lives.[6] The economic value of daughters was low,
except in regions where the linen and textiles trades created a demand for
their labour as domestic spinners. As early as 1760, a Sligo observer
remarked upon the beneficient result of child employment for family
solidarity. 'A family now has a better bottom than formerly; residence
is more assured and families become more numerous as increase of
industry keeps them more together'.[7] As the domestic textiles industry
contracted, first in Connaught and the south but later in Ulster also, the
economic contribution of rural daughters was diminished. By 1871, only
a quarter of Ulster girls in their early teens were returned as having
specified occupations, while elsewhere the proportion was about an
eighth. The release of girls from the workforce effectively accelerated
female modernisation by increasing their exposure to rudimentary education. School attendance and literacy were both most common in counties
with few young girls in employment. Moreover these counties also
tended to show high rates of literacy among girls as compared with
boys.[8] Diminishing demand for child labour was however only one of
many factors encouraging literacy, which in general spread far more
rapidly among girls. In 1841, less than a tenth of females aged 15-24
years could read and write English in Mayo, compared with a quarter of
Mayo males (Table 8:3). By the end of the century basic literacy was almost
universal for both sexes, being actually more prevalent among females.[9]
It provides a droll comment on the importance of education in modern
Ireland that those who mattered least profited from it most.

Girls passing beyond school age into adolescence might perform either
of two functions in the decade or so before they attained the age for
emigration or marriage. Depending on the labour requirement and supply
in their own household and in neighbouring households, they might

either take up paid service elsewhere or remain at home as unpaid servants. Farm service in Ireland conformed closely to the model analysed by Hajnal, 'an institution that, so far as is known, was uniquely European and has disappeared'. Hajnal's model stipulates that a 'substantial proportion' of each sex should take up service before marriage, usually on limited-term contracts providing for their board and lodging with a

TABLE 8:1

PERCENTAGE FEMALE ACCORDING TO STATUS WITHIN HOUSEHOLD

	1841	1851	1861	1871	1881	1891	1901	1911
Household heads and their children	49.5	50.7	50.4	50.0	49.9	50.2	50.1	49.2
Servants	54.8	49.2	53.8	59.9	60.9	59.8	60.8	59.6
Visitors, relatives and boarders	57.0	55.1	56.8	57.0	56.2	53.3	53.0	54.3
Inmates of certain institutions[1]	na	56.8[2]	39.8	39.4	40.3	38.9	40.7	37.9
Total population	50.8[2]	51.3[2]	51.1	51.2	51.0	50.7	50.7	50.1

Classification is based upon that used in census reports, 1841-1911.

[1]Institutions include workhouses, gaols, hospitals, sanitary institutions, military barracks and (after 1871) reformatories, industrial schools, orphanages and the R.I.C. depot. Those in alms houses, hotels or in vessels are recorded as 'visitors', while lodgers (not boarders) are counted as separate households.

[2]Military are excluded.

TABLE 8:2

PERCENTAGE DISTRIBUTION OF FEMALES BY HOUSEHOLD STATUS

	1841	1851	1861	1871	1881	1891	1901	1911
Household heads and their children	78.5	78.1	80.7	77.6	78.0	83.5	80.7	77.6
Servants	6.6	6.8	7.2	6.2	5.8	5.4	5.0	4.7
Visitors, relatives and boarders	14.8	10.4	10.8	14.8	14.5	9.3	12.4	15.8
Inmates of certain institutions[1]	na	4.7	1.2	1.4	1.7	1.7	1.9	1.9

See notes to Table 8:1.

[1]Institutions as in Table 8:1.

TABLE 8:3

PERCENTAGE OF THOSE AGED 15-24 ABLE TO READ AND WRITE

	1841	1851	1861	1871	1881	1891	1901	1911
Ireland: females	26.8	34.8	45.9	65.1	78.2	89.7	95.2	97.8
Ireland: males	47.1	48.9	56.5	69.9	77.0	86.4	93.2	96.8
Mayo: females	9.2	14	23.1	41.4	58.5	81.1	92.0	96.9
Mayo: males	24.7	29	37.7	52.1	62.7	79.3	90.1	95.5

See notes to Table 8:1.

master who was not necessarily of higher social rank. In societies such as Berkner's Waldviertel, their 'main function in the peasant household was as a labor substitute for children'.[10] In Ireland the proportion of women employed as servants was rather low by European standards, declining from a peak of 7 per cent in 1861 to 5 per cent by the end of the century (Tables 8:1, 2). From 1871 to 1911 about three-fifths of all Irish servants were female, but in earlier years the sexes were more closely balanced. The proportion of servants in the population was subject to marked regional variation according to the level of prosperity.[11] In a prosperous region of dairy farming, such as Churchtown, County Cork at the turn of the century, almost a sixth of women were employed as servants. Most of these were under 25 years, and nearly half of all Churchtown girls aged 15-24 were in service.[12] Despite the decline of tillage farming and the relatively small scale of holdings in rural Ireland, service remained an important occupation for adolescent girls.

Unpaid service at home or on the family farm was even more important. As in other peasant societies, the productive functions of women extended beyond domestic chores and light outdoor tasks to include many of the most painstaking and back-breaking of pursuits. Particularly in Connaught and the north-west, travellers noted with amazement that the most arduous work was often left to women. In 1834 Inglis remarked that the women of Galway 'appeared to think nothing of whipping up a sack of potatoes, weighing eighteen stone, and trudging away, under the load'. Towards the end of the Famine a Galway driver observed that 'the women are graight slaves in this counthry, yere Arn'r: they carry loads as would do for horses. They do well in *Ameriky*'. Even as late as in 1880, Mayo girls in their late 'teens were seen breaking stones, and (more often) 'carrying weighty baskets of mould or sand on their backs for long distances; in fact doing the work of cattle'.[13] The relatively heavy workload of nineteenth-century Irishwomen may explain the fact that mortality among women of working age was almost as high as male mortality, in marked contrast with contemporary England.[14] By the turn of the century, however, men monopolised spade-work, turf-cutting, byre-cleaning and most other forms of heavy farm labour. Women were now expected to perform complementary functions requiring skill rather than muscle: as a Cork witness remarked rather plaintively in 1938, 'in years gone by the women always milked the cows an' fed pigs an' calves, any man about forty years ago wasn't able to milk, nor wasn't asked to milk . . . Now, it's the men must do all, milking an' feeding, an' that spoils a good part of the day'.[15] The contraction of female participation in farming was hastened by the diffusion of milking-machines and creameries, which not only made the old female skills of hand-milking and butter-churning redundant but also gave prestige to dairying so inviting male involvement. Thus after the Famine the daughters and wives of farmers steadily retreated from the process of production, though their labour remained essential at peak seasons such as saving the hay or lifting the potatoes. Their declining importance was only partly counterbalanced by the greater respectability associated with housekeeping as against rough outdoor labour. In occupation as in education, the growing refinement of the female was a manifestation of diminished utility rather than raised status.

TABLE 8:4

PERCENTAGE PROBABILITY OF NOT SURVIVING FROM AGE 15 TO 55

	1821-41[1]	1864-70	1871-80	1881-90	1891-1900	1901-10
Ireland: females	47.2	29.5	31.8	33.4	33.7	32.1
Ireland: males	47.8	31.6	34.1	34.0	33.9	31.9
Mayo: females[2]	na	22.5	24.9	25.5	26.0	24.2
Mayo: males[2]	na	22.3	27.3	26.2	26.0	24.4

Statistics from 1864 onwards are based upon abridged life tables computed from returns of registered deaths (not adjusted for under-enumeration).

[1]Estimates based upon census age data for 1821 and 1841 (allowing for emigration) are taken from Phelim P. Boyle and Cormac Ó Gráda, 'Estimates of excess mortality during the Great Irish Famine' (typescript 1982), adopting their 'Basis A'.

[2]Death registration in Mayo and other western counties was particularly defective throughout, but most of all in earlier decades.

TABLE 8:5

MEAN AGE AT FIRST MARRIAGE FOR SUCCESSIVE COHORTS, IN YEARS

	Born				
	1821	1831	1841	1851	1861
Ireland: females	26.2	27.3	26.5	26.7	27.5
Ireland: males	30.3	30.2	29.9	30.4	31.0
Mayo: females	24.1	26.7	25.4	25.5	26.3
Mayo: males	29.4	30.3	29.6	30.4	31.1

A version of Hajnal's *Singulate Mean Age at Marriage* has been applied to each cohort from age 15 to 50, using proportions never married at age-groups 15-19, 20-24, 25-29, 30-34, 35-39, 40-44 and 45-49 at successive censuses (boundaries of groups vary in some cases). It is assumed that no marriages occurred before 15 or after 50 (taking proportion single at ages 45-54 as indicating that for the cohort at the end of its marrying period).

TABLE 8:6

PERCENTAGE NEVER MARRIED OF THOSE AGED 45-54 YEARS

	1841[1]	1851	1861	1871	1881	1891	1901	1911
Ireland: females	12.5	12.6	14.3	16.5	17.1	18.5	21.9	24.9
Ireland: males	10.2	12.1	14.7	17.0	17.1	20.0	23.8	27.3
Mayo: females	7.3	7.6	7.9	12.6	7.3	9.1	10.6	15.4
Mayo: males	5.3	6.0	7.1	12.1	7.3	10.6	12.6	18.0

[1]Age-group 46-55 years in 1841.

Female participation in the labour force was greatest in the decade or so following maturity, after which Irish girls were faced with the choices of marrying, emigrating, or remaining unmarried in Ireland. The savings so accumulated and services rendered were crucial in determining a girl's ability to afford either emigration or marriage. In Ireland, as in Britain, Germany, the Netherlands and elsewhere, most girls married several years after entering their phase of peak fecundity. Throughout the nineteenth century marriage postponement (as distinct from marriage avoidance) was unremarkable by European standards. For Irish brides of the mid-nineteenth century, mean age at first marriage was 26 or 27 years, compared with 25 in England, 26 in Norway and German states such as the Palatinate and Bavaria, 27 in the Netherlands and 28 in Belgium. But Ireland deviated from the dominant European pattern in undergoing a fairly consistent increase in marriage age from the early nineteenth century onwards. In most of the countries just mentioned urbanisation was accompanied by a decline in the mean age of brides, continuous in the Belgian case and arrested only after the 1870s in England and the Netherlands.[16] In Ireland, however, female age at marriage increased abruptly by a year or so at the time of the Famine, then declined slightly before rising gradually between the 1860s and the Great War (Table 8:5). Census returns indicate that the proportion of brides under 25 dropped from about three-fifths just before the Famine to less than two-fifths by the first decade of this century. By then minors accounted for only 6 per cent of women marrying. Even in pre-Famine years very early marriage had been far less common than many contemporaries believed, though a third of the recent brides enumerated in Connaught (1841) had been under 21 when married. Women tended to marry slightly earlier in poorer districts, particularly those with extensive domestic textile production. Urban marriages also tended to occur earlier than those in adjacent rural districts. Overall these disparities were quite minor, and no identifiable group of brides in 'modern' Ireland seems to have married either remarkably early or remarkably late.[17] The patterns of marriage postponement suggest a surprisingly stable demographic system, only modestly affected in this respect by the cataclysm of famine and largely insulated from the impact of urbanisation.

The minor increase in marriage age which did occur during and after the Famine was probably caused by the increasing prevalence of the 'match', whereby the bride's family was required to pay a dowry or 'fortune' to that of the groom. Since this payment (unlike the traditional dowry as analysed by Goody) was made over to the father-in-law rather than the husband or the common household purse, it may be treated as a fine for the transfer of a redundant dependent female from one family to another.[18] More fundamentally, the dowry functioned as the principal means of compensating those deprived of control over fixed property under the 'stem' system of succession to land and houses. The dowry made feasible the transfer of control to a chosen successor without provocation of rebellion within the family. Since the 'match' was a monetary transaction conducted in the interests of families rather than individuals, the partners in marriage were restricted to exercising a veto rather than a choice. The form and amount of the bride's fortune varied according to region, period and social class; but some sort of provision was already common before the Famine, as the Poor Inquiry of the 1830s made clear. In Galway there were 'few men so poor in their appearance or in their houses, but that when their daughter comes to be married they can manage to give her a few pounds as a fortune'; though in Cork 'a dresser, a bedstead, or a pig, is not uncommonly a marriage portion' for a labourer. Marriage practices were discussed at 93 public examinations in parishes all over Ireland: reference was made to dowries or arranged marriages in eighteen of these parishes. Similar discussions at baronial level indicated a still higher frequency, usually among the small tenantry rather than the rural proletariat but in some cases also among more 'comfortable' labourers. Very few cases were reported from Ulster, where the earning capacity of women was greatest.[19] The increasing prevalence and value of the dowry after the Famine was in part a reflection of the diminished economic importance of women. It also signified a profound change in the class composition of rural society, as the mass of impoverished labourers, cottiers and squatters gave place to the less vulnerable new régime of small farmers. The coupling of marriage and property redistribution within a family unit, once characteristic of a minority class, became virtually universal in rural Ireland.

Once married, the female became a reproducer rather than a producer. Failure to bear children was generally blamed upon female rather than male incapacity, and cast 'a great shadow' upon a marriage. As a Limerick witness observed in 1951: 'Many's the daughter-in-law who lived with her husband's people and who wasn't inclined to have a family. She often had to suffer bitter reproaches from her people-in-law until such time as she'd prove fruitful'.[20] Indeed childlessness provided grounds for a 'country divorce' in County Clare as late as in the 1930s: husbands could thus send unreproductive wives home to their reluctant families, and ensure the continuity of succession by making over the land to a brother on condition that he find a more satisfactory wife. On occasion the bride's father would withhold part of the dowry until she had survived the birth of her first child, presumably on the assumption that she would be thrown out by her husband, without her fortune, in case of functional failure.[21] Ireland was one of many rural societies in which children were regarded as economic assets rather than liabilities. Despite reduction in home demand for their labour, reproduction continued to serve as a form of social insurance by generating potential emigrants whose remittances would provide parental pensions and the means for further emigration. It was said in County Clare that 'God never created a mouth without creating something to put in it'; while a Donegal novelist pictured a shopkeeper refusing to provide meal on credit to those without children, since 'that kind of people, who have no children to earn for them, never pay debts'.[22] Few Irish parents would have echoed the Earl of Rosebery's remark upon the birth of his eldest son that this was a 'very common event' which 'may cause a good deal of annoyance to me'.[23]

The level of fertility within Irish marriages became remarkable only towards the end of the nineteenth century. In the 1870s, as the Princeton project has revealed, most European countries except France still showed an index of marital fertility exceeding two-thirds of that achieved by a comparable age-distribution of Hutterite mothers (a group celebrated for their unrestrained reproduction). Irish fertility was similar to that in Britain, Belgium or Germany, and substantially below the index for the Netherlands. Thereafter fertility levels in all those countries declined steadily, though in other places such as Austria, Switzerland, the Iberian peninsular and Scandinavia secular decline was somewhat delayed.[24] In Ireland, however, no significant decline in fertility occurred between the pre-Famine period and the Great War. The fertility censuses of 1841 and 1911 indicate a slight augmentation of the number of children ever born to comparable groups of couples, fertility being invariably rather higher in rural than civic districts.[25] Registration data available for the period after 1864 are too unreliable to permit confident interpretation of time trends. Nevertheless it is likely that a minor decline in fertility was occurring in most counties outside the north-west, and that variation between county fertility levels was increasing as less 'backward' counties adopted the European trend.[26] In general the poorest regions continued to produce the largest families, a paradox explained by high emigration rates from the same regions. Yet even in Dublin fertility remained at two-thirds of the Hutterite level just before the Great War, a figure well above those for contemporary Germany, Britain or Belgium and similar to that in the Netherlands.[27] The Irish experience of motherhood became aberrant only because it remained unchanging. For Irish married women, unlike their European counterparts, the burden of child-bearing was not significantly lightened before 1914. A wife's accomplishment was measured according to the number of her successful pregnancies, and the progenitrix of a 'long family' was the object of admiration or envy.

Once a wife had completed her dozen years of child-bearing followed by perhaps a decade of child-rearing, the time of retirement and household succession was approaching. Her role reverted to that of servant to sons as well as husband, her inferior status being symbolised at meals (where she waited on her menfolk before consuming any remaining scraps in seclusion) and in public places (where she walked either with other women or some steps behind her husband). The household 'stem' was ready for further pruning. As Ezra Pound wrote in disgust:

> Go to the adolescent who are smothered in family –
> Oh how hideous it is
> To see three generations of one house gathered together!
> It is like an old tree with shoots,
> And with some branches rotted and falling.[28]

Provision for falling branches of the household stem was an essential ingredient of the process of property transfer. Since the chosen inheritor of a farm or house commonly married and took over control before the death of at least one parent, careful arrangements were necessary for the maintenance of the 'old people'. Apart from supervising allocation of the dowry, the groom's parents often drew up a contract requiring the new householder to provide them with 'liberties' or 'freedoms', such as 'the exclusive enjoyment of the west room of the house with the use of the kitchen fire', or 'the grass of a cow wet and dry and half an acre of "mock", with manure for the same'.[29] Though often placed in the hands of a local 'scholar' rather than a solicitor, these 'writings' were not dissimilar in their formality and extravagance to the Austrian arrangement of *Ausgedinge*.[30]

The Poor Inquiry gives ample evidence that retiring parents of the 1830s both expected and exacted maintenance from their families. Examinations in 106 parishes showed that in almost half these cases children were generally willing to accept their obligations to the 'impotent aged'. In one parish in three some grievance was expressed, while grievance was frequent in a fifth of the parishes. Acceptance was least prevalent in the poorer provinces (Ulster and Connaught). Lack of respect was most likely to emanate from daughters-in-law, while in many Ulster parishes unmarried children were considered more dutiful than married ones. It was in Ulster and Connaught, where the demands of the aged were most difficult to cope with, that explicit agreements were most often drawn up. Parents sometimes took court action if turned out by their children, as in a County Tipperary case where a mother had been evicted by her son without payment of tenant right. The magistrates ordered the son to compensate her as promised or have her back, whereupon 'everybody execrated the son for his treatment of his mother'. In County Mayo, it was 'counted a mark of a very dutiful child that he gives his parent tobacco', which even more than diet was 'the great cause of dissention between the parents and children'.[31] The reduction of poverty after the Famine and provision of public relief after 1838 diminished the tension associated with retirement; and the introduction of the Old Age Pension in 1908 gave aged parents a prestige of which their predecessors had seldom dreamed. But bickering between in-laws remained a theme of Irish folklore: as Peig Sayers remarked of a Blasket Islander in the 1930s, 'her son was married in the house and often the old women and her son's wife used to be in each other's hair-combs'.[32]

For most Irish wives, widowhood was the final stage of their life's cycle. Since grooms tended to be several years older than brides, heavy female mortality did not avert a large excess of widows over widowers. The widows of farmers normally retained control over the farm if their children were unmarried, surrendering control only after the marriage of the chosen inheritor. As a Derry land agent reported in 1844: 'if the father die only, his widow generally holds the farm, and manages it either by her son or sons, or by a servant man'.[33] As suggested by the census returns of female 'farmers', the right of widows to retain nominal and sometimes practical control of land seems to have been recognised more generally after the Famine.[34] A study of five localities in 1901 indicates that the household status of widows aged sixty-five or more was surprisingly secure. Nearly half were heads of households including children or relatives, while a quarter were dependents in such households. A twelfth were servants or inmates, and less than a fifth were living alone. Even in households including married children, widows retained nominal headship in sixteen cases out of thirty-six.[35] Yet the acknowledged rights of a widow were largely limited to her own lifetime. Despite the excess of widowed women over men, their prospects of remarriage were far inferior.[36] For those who remarried when young enough to bear a family, any attempt to transfer property to the latter created severe risk of outrage and retribution from the kinsmen of the deceased husband. Widows might expect lifetime protection, but they could seldom match their menfolk by exercising power beyond the grave.

For a substantial and steadily increasing minority of women in Ireland, adulthood entailed 'celibacy' rather than marriage. As in so many other respects, nineteenth-century Ireland conformed to the European pattern whereby many women as well as men never married. The proportion of fifty-year-old women still unmarried rose from an eighth in 1841 to a quarter by 1911, becoming remarkable only after the Great War (Table 8:6). Non-marriage was a far more important factor than marriage postponement in causing the depopulation of post-Famine Ireland, and also in retarding population growth before the Famine.[37] Widespread failure to find a spouse was the unavoidable consequence of the growing rigidity and diffusion of the match, which required that bride and groom be selected from similar backgrounds enabling the dowry to be an appropriate payment for access to property of a certain value. But the inevitability of spinsterhood did not render it reputable in rural society. As Ó Danachair observes, the 'vinegary old maid' as well as the 'crusty old bachelor' became 'part of the rural comedy and matter for the rural wits and tricksters', subject to indignities on Chalk Sunday or Ash Wednesday.[38] Nor was sexual activity outside marriage condoned, except perhaps in a few isolated communities such as Tory Island. Even before the Famine the occurrence of illegitimacy was evidently less than in contemporary England.[39] Afterwards it declined still further, as did the frequency of associated offences such as rape, indecent assault, infanticide and child desertion. All too often the life of the unmarried Irishwomen, increasingly cut off from male companionship as well as independent employment, was one of humiliation and despair.

TABLE 8:7

PERCENTAGE RATIO OF FEMALES TO MALES AMONG EMIGRANTS FROM IRISH PORTS

	1851-55[1]	1856-65	1866-75	1876-85	1886-95	1896-1905	1906-14
Ireland	100.5	88.8	74.3	93.2	100.4	115.6	90.0
Mayo	100.6	109.0	90.7	120.3	135.5	175.6	131.9

Statistics are based upon the annual returns of emigration from Irish ports as enumerated by the Constabulary (adjusted for non-specification of county of origin and excluding those not native to Ireland). Most emigrants to Britain were evidently missed by the enumerators.
[1]Returns date from 1 May 1851.

TABLE 8:8

PERCENTAGE DEPLETION OF LITERATE AND ILLITERATE COHORTS

	1841-51	1851-61	1861-71	1871-81	1881-91	1891-1901	1901-11
Ireland:							
literate females	41	40	35	33	39	32	30
literate males	43	39	39	33	40	34	31
illiterate females	52	42	46	38	48	33	29
illiterate males	56	56	54	48	56	46	37
Mayo:							
literate females	44	47	47	43	52	49	48
literate males	50	34	42	38	49	47	44
illiterate females	59	51	47	40	59	41	44
illiterate males	64	52	53	51	63	52	45

Notes: Taking those able to read and write, and illiterate, respectively, a proxy for emigration was obtained from the percentage of an age-group (initially, 15-24) which disappeared over the subsequent decade (as indicated by the number aged 25-34 at its end). For the decade 1841-51 the age-groups were those aged 16-25 and 26-35.

The likelihood that a farmer's daughter would find a husband in Ireland receded rapidly after the transfer of household control, typically to one of her brothers. The dowry brought into the household by the 'new woman' was often transformed (possibly undivided) into a dowry for one sister. Since mean family size was about six in the late nineteenth century, this meant that on average two sisters were obliged either to 'travel' or to remain in the brother's household as dependents. The 'writings' associated with the match often made provision for the maintenance, training or emigration of any surplus siblings. Sisters often considered it the duty of their brothers to take wives with fortunes sufficient to maintain them, as in the case of the penniless Kerry woman who asked help from a land agent, explaining that her married brother could not 'support any one after bringing an empty woman to the house'.[40] Settlements upon younger siblings were the subject of an official inquiry in 1870, which treated them as a severe burden upon married farmers: 'frequently the sums which he is thus called upon to pay are so large, and so much beyond his means, that he is hampered and impoverished for years'.[41] The incubus was reflected in statistics of household composition, which show that dependent relatives were a much larger component of Irish households than in those of pre-industrial England.[42] My study of five localities in 1901 suggests that siblings usually accounted for between a third and a half of the resident relatives of household heads, the density being greatest in districts of low emigration.[43] As the new householder's own children multiplied, the simultaneous reduction of living space and labour requirements put further pressure on unmarried relatives to 'travel'. For those who remained single into an Irish old age, the increasing absence of close relatives made them peculiarly vulnerable. In 1901 elderly spinsters were markedly more likely than widows to be servants or boarders, to live alone, or to inhabit workhouses.[44] As the marriage institution became more rigid and restrictive, so the condition of life of those excluded from it deteriorated.

The key to the survival and widespread acceptance of this seemingly oppressive demographic system was emigration. Marriage settlements might provide temporary relief for retiring parents or disappointed siblings, but the chains of emigration made possible by the 'American money' gave relief which was permanent and self-reproducing. As is well known, Irish emigration rates were high by European standards even in the early nineteenth century, unmatched during and for some decades after the Famine, and still considerable until very recent years. Emigration was notably concentrated among those in their early twenties, about to enter the employment and marriage markets. In many periods and places the lifetime probability of emigration exceeded half, so that it may be seen as a practical choice affecting virtually every Irish youth and girl at a certain stage of the life-cycle. In contrast to movement out of most other European countries except Sweden, males and females were almost equally represented. Indeed women formed a slight majority of emigrants just after the Famine and at the turn of the century, the female component becoming most marked in the remote West which was most subject to emigration in general (Table 8:7). The growing female involvement was encouraged by the patterns of overseas demand for unskilled workers, which favoured domestic servants rather than male labourers. But the enthusiastic response to this demand by Irishwomen signified the permeation of rural Ireland with values and aspirations which jarred nastily with the rigid morality imposed upon those who remained behind. Increasingly, Irish girls in particular utilised their access to elementary education in order to prepare for America or Britain. National schools, evening classes and domestic economy courses were mercilessly exploited by country girls desperate to escape Ireland. Whereas literate males remained far less likely to depart than those unable to read and write, female emigration was more intensive among those with basic reading skills before the end of the century (Table 8:8).[45]

For the female remaining in Ireland, her freedom of choice became ever more restricted from the mid-nineteenth century onwards. The demographic changes betokening 'modernisation' elsewhere were either insignificant or reversed in Ireland. David Miller has written that 'the entire process can fairly be called "modernization" because it was an adaptation, albeit an atypical one, to the impact of scientific advance which permitted man's increasing control over his environment'.[46] Yet for the female portion of that controlled environment, modernisation began to have a different meaning: departure. The 'safety-valve' which sustained Ireland's aberrant demographic system eventually became the flood-gate which destroyed it. It is one of the puzzles of history that this alteration took a century to accomplish.

NOTES

1. See, for example, Joseph Spengler, *Population change, modernisation, and welfare* (Englewood Cliffs, N.J., 1974); Edward Shorter, *The making of the modern family* (N.Y., 1975); Lawrence Stone, *The family, sex and marriage in England 1500-1800* (London, 1977). To his credit, Stone rejects the anachronistic notion that 'modernization' gave rise to the 'affective nuclear family' in his conclusion (ch. 13). For Ireland's alleged modernity see Joseph Lee, *The modernisation of Irish society 1848-1918* (Dublin, 1973); L. M. Cullen, *The emergence of modern Ireland 1600-1900* (London, 1981); David W. Miller, 'Presbyterianism and "modernization" in Ulster', *Past and Present*, 80 (1978), pp. 66-90; Charles Townshend, 'Modernization and nationalism: perspectives in recent Irish history', *History*, 66, no. 217 (1981), pp. 233-43; Samuel Clark and James S. Donnelly, Jun. (ed.), *Irish peasants: violence and political unrest 1780-1914* (Manchester, 1983), pp. 8-12.

2. See P. Gibbon and C. Curtin, 'The stem family in Ireland', *Comparative Studies in Society and History*, 20, no. 3 (1978), pp. 429-53; David Fitzpatrick, 'Irish farming families before the first world war', ibid., 25, no. 2 (1983), pp. 339-74; John Hajnal, 'Two kinds of preindustrial household formation system', *Population and Development Review*, 8, no. 3 (1982), pp. 449-94.

3. For the supposed limitation of the stem family system to societies practising impartible inheritance, see Michel Verdon, 'The stem family: towards a general thesis', *Journal of Interdisciplinary History,* 10, no. 1 (1979), pp. 87-105; Walter Goldschmidt and Evalyn Jacobson Kunkel, 'The structure of the peasant family', *American Anthropologist,* 73 (1971), pp. 1058-76; Lutz K. Berkner, 'Inheritance, land tenure and peasant family structure: a German regional comparison', in Jack Goody et al. (ed.), *Family and inheritance* (Cambridge, 1976), pp. 71-95.

4. Kevin O'Neill, 'Agriculture and family structure in pre-famine Ireland' (typescript, 1979); Fitzpatrick (1983), pp. 365-67; Conrad M. Arensberg, 'Irish rural social organization', *Transactions of N.Y. Academy of Sciences* (ser. 2), 4 (1942), pp. 202-7.

5. Fitzpatrick (1983), pp. 363-65.

6. E. Estyn Evans; 'Peasant beliefs in nineteenth-century Ireland', in Daniel J. Casey and Robert E. Rhodes (ed.), *Views of the Irish peasantry 1800-1916* (Connecticut, 1977), p. 43. A Kerry folklore report of 1941 states also that 'if children are dying they are called after their mother's name': Department of Irish Folklore, U.C.D., vol. 782, p. 191.

7. Charles O'Hara, quoted in Brenda Collins, 'Proto-industrialization and pre-famine emigration', *Social History,* 7, no. 2 (1982), p. 134.

8. For each of thirty counties (excluding Antrim and Down) the 1871 census returns were used to compute the following proportions:

(1) girls aged 10-14 with specified occupations, not including the category of farmers' daughters;

(2) girls aged 10-14 able to read and write in English;

(3) the above proportion for boys divided by that for girls;

(4) girls aged 12 attending school during the week up to 17 June 1871;

(5) the above proportion for boys divided by that for girls.

Correlation coefficients (r) were as follows:

(1) and (2), $r = -0.55$	(1) and (5), $r = +0.35$
(1) and (3), $r = +0.57$	(2) and (4), $r = +0.76$
(1) and (4), $r = -0.66$	(3) and (5), $r = +0.20$

9. See table 8:3, and David Fitzpatrick, ' "A share of the honeycomb": education, emigration and Irishwomen', *Continuity and Change,* 1, No. 2, (1986), pp. 217-34.

10. Hajnal (1982), p. 473: Lutz K. Berkner, 'The stem family and the developmental cycle of the peasant household: an eighteenth-century Austrian example', *American Historical Review,* 77, no. 2 (1972), pp. 410-16.

11. See table 8:1, 2 for national proportions and criteria ('servant' here refers to relationship to household head rather than specified occupation, so excluding family members returned as in service). For county variation see Fitzpatrick (1983), p. 349. Richard Breen finds the Hajnal-Berkner model inappropriate for Beaufort, County Kerry, where 'the social gulf between servants and masters was heavily stressed': see 'Farm servanthood in Ireland, 1900-40', *Economic History Review* (ser. 2), 36, no. 1 (1983), pp. 87-102.

12. Fitzpatrick (1983), p. 358. In the Kilmallock of 1890 girls were paid more than boys as servants, a fact ascribed by James S. Donnelly, Jun., to the lower cost of food for females: see *The land and people of nineteenth-century Cork* (London and Boston, 1975), p. 239.

13. Henry D. Inglis, *Ireland in 1834* (London, 1834), vol. 2, p. 24; Sir Francis B. Head, *A fortnight in Ireland* (London, 1852), p. 208; J. A. Fox, *Reports on the condition of the peasantry of the county of Mayo* (Dublin, 1880), p. 17. For similar reports, see also James

Ward, *How to regenerate Ireland; or, facts from the fisheries* (London, 1850), p. 15; [Hugh McCall], *Ireland and her staple manufactures* (Belfast, 3rd ed., 1870), p. 337.

14. See table 8:4. Comparable returns of deaths registered in England and Wales during each quinquennium between 1871 and 1900 give the following probabilities (percentage) that men and women respectively would not survive from 15 to 55:

1871-75,	40.2 and 35.8	1886-90,	36.2 and 31.8
1876-80,	38.8 and 34.3	1891-95,	35.1 and 30.5
1881-85,	37.5 and 33.1	1896-1900,	33.4 and 28.5

Statistics are computed from R.A.M. Case et al. (compilers), *Serial abridged life tables: England and Wales 1841-1960*, pt. 1 (London, 1963).

15. Caoimhín Ó Danachair, 'The family in Irish tradition', *Christus Rex,* 16 (1962), pp. 187-88; Department of Irish Folklore, U.C.D., vol. 58, pp. 411-12. See also John M. Mogey, *Rural life in Northern Ireland* (London, 1947), p. 97; Conrad M. Arensberg and Solon T. Kimball, *Family and community in Ireland* (Cambridge, Mass., 1940), pp. 48-50.

16. See table 8:5. Comparable calculations for England and Wales give the following singulate mean ages at marriage for men and women respectively:

1831 cohort,	26.8 and 25.6	1851 cohort,	26.5 and 25.0
1841 cohort,	26.6 and 25.2	1861 cohort,	26.7 and 25.2

See also J. Hajnal, 'European marriage patterns in perspective', in D. V. Glass and D. E. C. Eversley (ed.), *Population in history* (London, 1965), pp. 101-43; Michael Drake, *Population and society in Norway 1735-1865* (Cambridge, 1969), pp. 77-78 (giving mean age of registered marriages of bachelors and spinsters, not S.M.A.M.); Robert Lee, 'Germany', and Paul Deprez, 'The Low Countries', in W. R. Lee (ed.), *European demography and economic growth* (London, 1979), pp. 179, 271, 273 (giving S.M.A.M. in the case of Belgium at least).

17. In the census reports for 1841, 1851, and 1911, age-breakdowns are given for brides married during the preceding decade and returned as 'wives' at the census. For those married between 1830 and 1840, 29.4 per cent were under 21; whereas 17.8 per cent of those married between 1841 and 1850 were under 20, compared with 7.1 per cent between 1901 and 1910. The Registrar General's returns of marriages involving minors after 1864 suggest a continuous decline in the proportion of brides under 21, and also a smaller proportion than that indicated in the census. Minors accounted for 6.1 per cent of registered brides in 1901-10 compared with 12.8 per cent in 1871-80. All statistics refer to latest marriages, but the census proportions of younger brides are inflated because of heavier pre-censal mortality among older brides. For a local study of class and regional variation in marriage age, see V. Morgan and W. Macafee, 'Irish population in the pre-Famine period: evidence from County Antrim', *Economic History Review* (ser. 2), 37, no. 2 (1984), pp. 182-96. For earlier debate on pre-Famine marriage patterns involving Connell, Drake and others, see for example Joseph Lee, 'Marriage and population in pre-Famine Ireland', *Economic History Review* (ser. 2), 21 (1968), pp. 283-95; and for the post-Famine period, Robert E. Kennedy, *The Irish: emigration, marriage and fertility* (Berkeley, 1973), esp. ch. 7; Jacques Verrière, *La Population de l'Irlande* (Paris, 1979), pp. 450 ff.

18. Jack Goody, *The development of the family and marriage in Europe* (Cambridge, 1983), app. 2; Richard Breen, 'Dowry payments and the Irish case', *Comparative Studies in Society and History,* 26, no. 2 (April 1984), pp. 280-96.

19. *First report from His Majesty's commissioners for inquiring into the condition of the poorer classes in Ireland* [Poor Inquiry], app. F, esp. p. 35; app. A, esp. p. 432; app. D,

passim: in H.C. Papers, 1836 [C. 38], xxxiii; 1835 (369), xxxii, pt. I; 1836 [C. 36], xxxi.

20. Department of Irish Folklore, vol. 1210, p. 283: K. H. Connell, 'Peasant marriage in Ireland: its structure and development since the famine', *Economic History Review* (ser. 2), 14 (1962), pp. 502-23.

21. Arensberg and Kimball (1940) , pp. 137-38; Connell (1962).

22. Department of Irish Folklore, vol. 1043, p. 104 (trans.); Patrick MacGill, *Children of the dead end* (London, 1914), p. 4.

23. David Roberts, 'The paterfamilias of the Victorian governing classes', in Anthony S. Wohl (ed.), *The Victorian family: structure and stresses* (London, 1978), p. 62.

24. Michael S. Teitelboum, *The British fertility decline* (Princeton, 1984), gives comparable fertility indices for most European countries; an appendix giving Irish statistics based upon registered births is misleading as to both the level and temporal trend of fertility within marriage. See also articles in Lee (1979), pp. 143, 221 and 272, giving data for France, Italy and Belgium respectively.

25. Estimates of I_g, the Princeton index of marital fertility, were constructed for each intercensal decade: births during the first eight years of each decade were estimated from the number of censal survivors aged 2-9 years augmented by the probable number of children dying or emigrating (using returns of registered deaths and constabulary returns of emigration from Irish ports, both given by age-group). In this way understatement attributable to under-enumeration of births and of infants was avoided. For Ireland, I_g was .796 in 1871-81, .754 in 1881-91, .752 in 1891-1901 and .743 in 1901-11. Variation between counties rose steadily, the coefficients of variation (percentages for thirty counties excluding Dublin and Antrim) being 4.3, 4.7, 5.6 and 6.3 respectively. Census returns for 1841 and 1911 allow comparison between the number of children born alive to couples marrying in 1830-40 and 1901-11 respectively, controlling for duration of marriage and age at marriage of both spouses.

26. For all counties except Donegal, Galway, Mayo and Sligo, I_g was somewhat higher in 1871-81 than in 1901-11. The index was invariably highest in Kerry and lowest in Dublin.

27. See Teitelbaum (1984).

28. Ezra Pound, 'Commission'.

29. Examples from M. Mc D. Bodkin, *Recollections of an Irish judge* (Dublin, 1914), pp. 357-58. See also Department of Irish Folklore, vol. 1200, p. 402 (Tyrone, 1951).

30. Thomas Held, 'Rural retirement arrangements in seventeenth- to nineteenth-century Austria', *Journal of Family History*, 7, no. 2 (1982), pp. 227-54; articles by Sieder and Mitteraurer and by Schmidtbauer in Richard Wall (ed.), *Family forms in historic Europe* (Cambridge, 1983), pp. 309-78.

31. Poor Inquiry, app. A, loc. cit., esp. pp. 260, 200 (inquiries concerning the 'impotent aged' before promulgation of the Irish Poor Law).

32. Peig Sayers, *An old woman's reflections* (Oxford, 1978 ed.), p. 25.

33. *Her Majesty's commissioners of inquiry into the state of the law and practice in respect to the occupation of land in Ireland, Evidence,* 146/142, H.C. 1845 [C, 606], xix.

34. The percentage ratios of female to male farmers and graziers were as follows, according to the census of occupation: 1841, 4.0; 1851, 5.1; 1861, 6.6; 1871, 8.1; 1881, 15.6; 1891, 19.7; 1901, 21.4; 1911, 16.7.

35. Statistics are drawn from the five local studies of 1901 household census schedules used in Fitzpatrick (1983). See Michael Anderson, *Family structure in nineteenth-century Lancashire* (Cambridge, 1971), Ch. 7 and pp. 140-43, for parallels between exercise of kinship obligations towards old people in rural Ireland and Preston.

36. Widows seldom remarried if beyond their child-bearing period, and if Roman Catholics were generally forbidden to do so, on the grounds that procreation was the primary function of marriage.

37. See table 8:6; Hajnal (1965), p. 102; Kennedy (1973), ch. 7: Ruth B. Dixon, 'Late marriage and non-marriage as demographic responses: are they similar?', *Population Studies,* 32, no. 3 (1978), pp. 460-63; cf. Verrière (1979), p. 448.

38. Caoimhín Ó Danachair, 'Some marriage customs and their regional distribution', *Béaloideas,* 42-44 (1974-76), pp. 170-75.

39. Robin Fox, *The Tory islanders: a people of the Celtic fringe* (Cambridge, 1978), ch. 7; K. H. Connell, 'Illegitimacy before the famine', in *Irish peasant society* (Oxford, 1968), pp. 51-86; S. J. Connolly, 'Illegitimacy and pre-nuptial pregnancy in Ireland before 1864', *Irish Economic and Social History,* 6 (1979), pp. 5-23; Peter Laslett, *Family life and illicit love in earlier generations* (Cambridge, 1977), ch. 3; Edward Shorter et al., 'The decline of non-marital fertility in Europe 1880-1940', *Population Studies,* 25, no. 3 (1971), pp. 375-93; Michael W. Flinn, *The European demographic system 1500-1820* (Brighton, 1981), p. 82.

40. S. M. Hussey, *The reminiscences of an Irish land agent* (London, 1904), p. 143.

41. *Reports from poor law inspectors in Ireland as to the existing relations between landlord and tenant,* H.C. 1870 [C. 31], xiv, esp. p. 31 (Robinson, Leinster).

42. Laslett (1977), pp. 30-31 (English and European comparisons giving degree of kinship); Wall (1983), introduction.

43. Fitzpatrick (1983), p. 362; cf. Breen (1983), pp. 97-98.

44. The population of five localities in 1901 (cf. note 35) included 30 unmarried and 106 widowed women of 65 or more. Nine members of each category were returned as servants or inmates, while 8 spinsters and 19 widows were living alone. Among the 12,834 inmates of Irish workhouses of that age-group, 18.0 per cent were spinsters and 24.7 per cent were widows; whereas in the entire Irish population (1901 census) the corresponding percentages were 9.6 and 27.9.

45. See table 8:8, and article cited in note 9 above.

46. David W. Miller, 'Irish catholicism and the great famine', *Journal of Social History,* 9 (1975), p. 81, referring to marriage postponement.

Index